1. His interest in football began at Junior School when the girls asked soccer questions of the other boys

2. Once owned up to kicking a football through a school window and got the cane – he hadn't done it but the girls were impressed

3. Became a Tottenham supporter through watching a TV serial called 'The Silver Spurs' in the early 60s

4. Was once taken off during a game so he could take an exam in Physics – a subject he'd already dropped

5. Founded Teesside Orient, the first entirely Afro-Asian team in Cleveland

6. On a train in West Germany he once missed his stop by over 100 kilometres because he was caught in a conversation – about football

7. In a college production of 'The Murder in the Red Barn' he was nearly hung for real – which would have prevented his continued interest in football

THE BOOK OF FOOTBALL LISTS

Robert Hutton Moss

A STAR BOOK

published by
the Paperback Division of
W. H. ALLEN & CO. Ltd

A Star Book
Published in 1983
by the Paperback Division of
W. H. Allen & Co. Ltd
A Howard and Wyndham Company
44 Hill Street, London W1X 8LB

Reproduced, printed and bound in Great Britain by
Hazell Watson & Viney Ltd, Aylesbury, Bucks

ISBN 0 352 31427 3

Contents

A. . .	1
Ages	7
Aladdin's Cave	42
Appearances	45
Awards and Honours	50
Alternative Careers	59
Black Power	65
Born and Bred	68
Clubs	98
Soccer Beat	161
In the Family	165
Managers	176
Sad Occasions	178
Second Sight	185
Sexy Side	186
Show Biz	188
Suppliers	189
Supporters and Directors	190
Tongue Twisters	193
Two Timers	195
What's in a Name?	198
. . . Z	233

This book is dedicated to the memory of Paul McClure, who died aged 22. Thanks go to my mother and father whose encouragement and practical help were invaluable in the preparation of this book, numerous football clubs with whom I have had contact, and the *Rothman's Football Year Book*, *International Football Book*, edited by Eric Batty, *Der Kicker, Fussball, Woche, Onze, Guerin Sportivo, Le Foot, World Soccer* and various other sources of inspiration.

Editor's Note

Bob Moss is a certifiable football addict and therefore any opinions, idiosyncrasies or factual errors expressed herein are all his own work. It has not been possible to include all statistics for the end of the 1982/3 football season.

A . . .

THE FIRST 10 PLAYERS ALPHABETICALLY TO HAVE MADE FOOTBALL LEAGUE APPEARANCES SINCE 1945–46

(All Pro. Clubs in brackets)

1. *Jan Einer Aas* (Nottingham Forest 1980–82)
2. *Keith Abbis* (Brighton 1959–60)
3. *Steve Abbley* (Swindon Town 1979–81)
4. *John Abbott* (Crewe Alexandra 1962–64)
5. *Peter Abbott* (Manchester United, Swansea City, Crewe Alexandra and Southend 1970–78)
6. *Ron Abbott* (Q.P.R. 1972–78)
7. *John Abbotts* (Port Vale 1950–51)
8. *Laurie Abrahams* (Charlton Athletic 1977–78)
9. *Brian Abrey* (Chelsea and Colchester United 1956–61)
10. *John Abthorpe* (Notts County 1955–56)

THE FIRST 12 PLAYERS ALPHABETICALLY OF CURRENT LEAGUE STATUS

(Pro. Clubs in brackets)

1. *Jan Einer Aas* (Nottingham Forest)
2. *Michael Adams* (Gillingham)
3. *Tony Adcock* (Colchester)
4. *Nigel Adkins* (Liverpool and Tranmere Rovers)
5. *Reuben Agboola* (Southampton)
6. *Alan Ainscow* (Blackpool, Birmingham City, Everton and Barnsley (Loan))
7. *Carl Airey* (Barnsley)
8. *Mark Aizlewood* (Newport County, Luton Town and Charlton Athletic)

1

9. *Steve Aizlewood*
(Newport County,
Swindon Town and
Portsmouth)

10. *Arthur Albiston*
(Manchester United)
11. *John Aldridge* (Newport County)
12. *Ian Alexander* (Rotherham United)

ENGLAND'S 13 POST-WAR A . . . INTERNATIONALS

(With club they then played for in brackets)

1. *Alan A'Court* (Liverpool) 1958–59 Left Winger
2. *Tony Allen* (Stoke City) 1960 Left Full Back – Left Half
3. *Ronnie Allen* (West Bromwich Albion) 1952–55 Centre Forward
4. *Stan Anderson* (Sunderland) 1962 Wing Half
5. *Viv Anderson* (Nottingham Forest) 1979–82 Right Full Back
6. *John Angus* (Burnley) 1961 Right Full Back
7. *Jimmy Armfield* (Blackpool) 1959–66 Full Back
8. *David Armstrong* (Middlesborough and Southampton 1981–3)
9. *Kenneth Armstrong* (Chelsea) 1955 Right Half
10. *Gordon Astall* (Birmingham City) 1956 Outside Right
11. *Jeff Astle* (West Bromwich) 1969–70 Centre Forward
12. *John Aston* (Manchester United) 1949–51 Full Back
13. *John Atyeo* (Bristol City) 1956–57 Centre Forward

4 A's TO WIN 10 OR MORE ENGLAND CAPS

1. *Viv Anderson*   10 Caps
2. *Charlie Athersmith*
(Aston Villa)   12 Caps
3. *Jimmy Armfield*   43 Caps
4. *John Aston*   17 Caps

THE 5 CURRENT LEAGUE 'A' MANAGERS

(Current clubs in brackets) Manager unless otherwise stated

1. *Colin Addison* (Newport County)
   Hereford United – Player Manager
   Durban City (S.A.)
   Notts County – Assistant Manager
   Newport County
   West Bromwich Albion – Assistant Manager
   Derby County
2. *Malcolm Allison* (Middlesbrough)
   Bath City
   Plymouth Argyle
   Manchester City – Assistant and later Manager
   Crystal Palace
   Galatasaray (Turkey) – Adviser
   Memphis Rogues (U.S.A.)
   Plymouth Argyle – Consultant
   Manchester City – Assistant and then Manager
   Crystal Palace
   Sporting Lisbon
3. *Colin Appleton* (Hull City)
   Barrow – Player Manager
   Scarborough
4. *Len Ashurst* (Cardiff City)
   Hartlepool
   Gillingham
   Sheffield Wednesday
   Newport County
5. *Ron Atkinson* (Manchester United)
   Kettering Town
   Cambridge United
   West Bromwich Albion

THE 8 FORMER LEAGUE 'A' MANAGERS OF THE POST-WAR PERIOD

1. *Jimmy Adamson* – Burnley, Sunderland and Leeds
2. *George Allison* – Arsenal
3. *Peter Anderson* – Millwall
4. *Stan Anderson* – Middlesbrough, Olympiakos, Q.P.R. (Assistant), Doncaster and Bolton
5. *Jimmy Andrews* – Cardiff
6. *Jimmy Armfield* – Bolton and Leeds
7. *Alan Ashman* – Carlisle and West Bromwich Albion
8. *Ron Ashman* – Norwich, Scunthorpe and Grimsby

3

15 CURRENT A . . . INTERNATIONAL PLAYERS

1. *'Alberto' Gomes* (Benfica and Portugal) Left Full Back
2. *Roger Albertsen* (Olympiakos of Greece and Norway) Midfielder
3. *Klaus Allofs* (1. F.C. Köln and West Germany) Striker
4. *Alessandro Altobelli* (Inter Milan and Italy) Central Striker
5. *Manuel Amoros* (F.C. Monaco and France) Full Back/ Midfielder
6. *Carlo Ancellotti* (A.C. Roma and Italy) Midfielder
7. *Sergei Andreyev* (SKA Rostov and Soviet Union) Central Striker
8. *Jose Ramon Alesanco* (Barcelona and Spain) Sweeper
9. *Giancarlo Antognoni* (Fiorentina and Italy) Midfielder
10. *Ibrahmim Aoudon* (Cannes of France and Cameroon) Centre Back
11. *Luis Arconada* (Real Sociedad and Spain) Goalkeeper
12. *Osvaldo Ardiles* (Tottenham Hotspur and Argentina) Midfielder
13. *Frank Arnesen* (F.C. Valencia and Denmark) Midfielder
14. *Gerry Armstrong* (Watford and Northern Ireland) Central Striker
15. *Julio Arzu* (Santander of Spain and Honduras) Goalkeeper

24 FAMOUS A . . . INTERNATIONALS OF THE PAST

(In brackets clubs, country, position and World Cup Final tournaments)

1. *Julio Cesar Abbadie* (Penarol, Genoa and Uruguay; Right Winger 1954 World Cup)
2. *Jovan Acimovic* (Crvena Zvezda or Red Star Belgrade, IFC Saarbrücken and Yugoslavia; Midfielder, 1974 World Cup)
3. *Josef Adamec* (Spartak Trnava and Czechoslovakia; Inside Forward, 1970 World Cup)
4. *'Ademir' da Guia* (Palmeiras, Botafogo and Brazil; Midfield/ Sweeper, 1974 World Cup)
5. *Marques de Meneses Ademir* (Recife, Fluminense, Vasco da Gama and Brazil; Centre Forward, 1950 World Cup)

6. *Florian Albert* (Ferencvaros and Hungary; Centre Forward, 1962 and 1966 World Cups)
7. *Enrico Albertosi* (Cagliari, A.C. Milan and Italy; Goalkeeper, 1966 and 1970 World Cups)
8. *Ivor Allchurch* (Swansea Town, Newcastle United, Cardiff and Wales; Forward, 1958 World Cup)
9. *Norberto Alonso* (River Plate, Olympique Marseille, Velez Sarsfield and Argentina; Midfielder, 1978 World Cup)
10. *Adrian Alston* (Preston North End, St. George of Budapest, Safeway United – both Australia – Luton Town, Cardiff, Tampa Bay Rowdies and Australia; Striker, 1974 World Cup)
11. *José Altafini* (Palmeiras, A.C. Milan, Napoli, Juventus, Chiasso, Mendrisiostar of Switzerland, Brazil and Italy; Centre Forward, 1958 (Brazil) 1962 (Italy) World Cups)
12. *Amaro Amancio* (Deportivo Coruna, Real Madrid and Spain; Midfielder/Winger, 1966 World Cup)
13. *Joao Justino 'Amaral'* (Guarani, Corinthians, Santos and Brazil; Centre Back, 1978 World Cup)
14. *Tavares Da Silva 'Amarildo'* (Botafogo, A.C. Milan, Fiorentina and Brazil; Striker, 1962 World Cup)
15. *Pietro Anastasi* (Varese, Juventus, Ascoli and Italy; Centre Forward, 1974 World Cup)
16. *José Leandro Andrade* (Bella Vista, Nacional, Penarol and Uruguay; Right Half, 1930 World Cup)
17. *Rodriguez Andrade* (Penarol and Uruguay; Left Half, 1950 World Cup)
18. *Toni Antoniadis* (Panathinaikos and Greece; Centre Forward)
19. *Luis Artime* (Independiente, River Plate, Uruguay's Nacional Argentina; Centre Forward, 1966 World Cup)
20. *Kakhi Asatiani* (Ararat Erevan and Soviet Union; Striker/Midfielder, 1970 World Cup)
21. *Juan Manuel Asensi* (Elche, Barcelona, Puebla and Oaxtepec, both Mexican; Midfielder, 1978 World Cup)
22. *Georgi Asparaoukhov* (Levski Sofia and Bulgaria; Centre Forward, 1962 and 1966 World Cups)
23. *José Augusto* (Benfica and Portugal; Inside Forward, 1966 World Cup)
24. *Ruben Ayala* (San Lorenzo de Almagro, Atlético Madrid, Jalisco and Atlante – both Mexican; Striker, 1974 World Cup)

24 IMPORTANT A . . . CLUBS AND THE HONOURS THEY HAVE WON

(LC = League Championships, CW = Cup Wins)

1. F.C. Aarau (Switzerland)	2 LC		
2. Aberdeen; Current Cup Holders	2 LC	and	3 CW
3. Admira Energie-Wacker (Austria)	8 LC	and	5 CW
4. A.D.O. Den Haag (Netherlands)	2 LC		
5. A.E.K. Athens (Greece)	7 LC	and	8 CW
6. A.G.F. Aarhus (Denmark)	4 LC	and	5 CW
7. A.I.K. Stockholm (Sweden)	8 LC	and	3 CW
8. Ajax Amsterdam (Netherlands)	20 LC	and	8 CW
9. Akademisk A.B. (Denmark)	9 LC		
10. Alianza Lima (Peru)	13 LC		
11. Anderlecht (Belgium)	17 LC	and	5 CW
12. Apoel (Cyprus)	12 LC	and	10 CW
13. Ararat Erevan (Russia)	1 LC	and	2 CW
14. Arges Pitesti (Rumania)	2 LC		
15. Aris Bonnevoie (Luxembourg)	3 LC	and	1 CW
16. Aris Salonika (Greece)	3 LC	and	1 CW
17. Arsenal	8 LC	and	5 CW
18. Aston Villa	7 LC	and	7 CW
19. Athlone Town (Eire)	1 LC	and	1 CW
20. Atlético Bilbao (Spain)	6 LC	and	22 CW
21. Atlético Madrid (Spain)	6 LC	and	5 CW
22. Atvidaberg (Sweden)	2 LC	and	2 CW
23. Austria Wien (Austria) Cup Holders	16 LC	and	21 CW
24. AZ '67 Alkmaar (Netherlands) Cup Holders	1 LC	and	3 CW

Ages

'They shall grow not old, as we that are left grow old', watching their exploits on film or video.

Apologies to Binyon

10 PLAYERS WHO MADE THEIR FIRST TEAM DEBUTS IN 1982–83 BEFORE THEIR 17th BIRTHDAYS

1. *Nyrere Kelly* (Bristol City) Substitute v. Sheffield Wednesday, Milk Cup 2nd Round 2nd Leg; 26th October, 1982
2. *Andy Llewellyn* (Bristol City) at Right Back v. Rochdale, Division 4; 4th December, 1982
3. *Neil McDonald* (Newcastle United) in Midfield v. Barnsley, Division 2; 25th September, 1982
4. *Paul Simpson* (Manchester City) as Left Winger v. Coventry City, Division 1; 2nd October, 1982
5. *Perry Suckling* (Coventry City) as Goalkeeper v. Southampton, Division 1; 28th August, 1982
6. *Dave Wintersgill* (Wolverhampton Wanderers) at Left Back v. Blackburn Rovers, Division 2, 28th August, 1982
7. *Chris Moyses* (Lincoln City) at Right Back in the Football League Trophy
8. *Carl Foster* (Shrewsbury Town) Up Front in the Welsh Cup
9. *Gerardo Nardiello* (Shrewsbury Town) as a Substitute in the Welsh Cup
10. *Stuart Hall* (Lincoln City) v. Norwich City in the Football League Trophy

24 CURRENT ESTABLISHED PLAYERS WHO MADE THEIR LEAGUE BOW BEFORE THEIR 17th BIRTHDAY

(In brackets are the clubs the players made their debuts with)

1. *Mark Aizlewood* (Newport County) 1975–76
2. *Steve Aizlewood* (Newport County) 1968–69
   The above are the only brothers to have both made their debuts while 16 or under in the post-war period.
3. *Stephen Bell* (Middlesbrough) Debut v. Southampton, January, 1982
4. *Dave Buchanan* (Leicester City) v. Oldham Athletic, January, 1979
5. *George Burley* (Ipswich Town) Debut 1972–73
6. *Tommy Caton* (Manchester City) v. Tottenham, September, 1979
7. *Jeremy Charles* (Swansea City) Debut 1976–77
8. *Steve Doyle* (Preston North End) v. Tranmere Rovers November, 1974
9. *Kevin Drinkell* (Grimsby Town) Debut 1976–77
10. *Gerry Francis* (Queens Park Rangers) v. Liverpool, 1968
11. *Tony Gale* (Fulham) v. Charlton Athletic, August, 1977
12. *Colin Greenall* (Blackpool) v. Huddersfield Town, August, 1980
13. *Asa Hartford* (West Bromwich Albion) v. Sheffield Wednesday, February, 1967
14. *Robbie James* (Swansea City) Debut 1972–73
15. *Graeme Kirkup* (Exeter City) v. Burnley, March, 1982
16. *Mickey Lewis* (West Bromwich Albion) Debut 1980–81
17. *Neil McNab* (Tottenham Hotspur) Sub. v. Chelsea, April, 1974
18. *Dave Mehmet* (Millwall) Debut 1976–77
19. *Gary Mills* (Nottingham Forest) v. Arsenal, September, 1978
20. *Derek Parkin* (Huddersfield) Debut 1964–65
21. *Paul Rideout* (Swindon Town) v. Hull City, December, 1980
22. *Andy Sussex* (Orient) v. Sheffield Wednesday, November, 1981
23. *Dave Thomas* (Burnley) Debut 1966–67
24. *Neil Webb* (Reading) v. Mansfield Town, February, 1980
25. *Norman Whiteside* (Manchester United) Sub. v. Brighton, April, 1982.

THE 7 PLAYERS BORN BEFORE V.J. DAY (AUGUST 15, 1945) WHO APPEARED IN THE FOOTBALL LEAGUE DURING 1982–83

1. *John Jackson:* Played 4 League Games in Goal for Hereford, the last v. Darlington, on September 11th, 6 days after his 40th birthday. Signed by Brighton in February, as cover for Perry Digweed and Graham Mosley.
2. *Norman Hunter*: Played for Barnsley v. Grimsby, January 1st, 1983, age 39 years 2 months.
3. *Terry Cooper*: The Manager who played Sweeper in Bristol City's youngest ever side reached 39 in July. His intention is not to play in 1983–84.
4. *Peter Noble*: Played regularly in Midfield for 4th Division, Blackpool. He started the season a week after his 38th birthday.
5. *Ron Harris*: Still an important member of Brentford's team. Celebrated his 38th birthday in November, 1982.
6. *Alan Ball*: Regular Southampton Midfield organizer until his 'retirement' to Hong Kong football. Couldn't resist the lure of English football and came back to play an inspiring role for Bobby Gould's 3rd Division 'Hot Shots' Bristol Rovers.
7. *Pat Jennings*: For the first half of the season was kept out of Arsenal and Northern Ireland teams by George Wood and Jim Platt respectively. His brilliance forced him back into Arsenal line-up. He should reach 750 First Division appearances and 100 Northern Ireland Caps before he retires. The baby of the seven, he didn't celebrate his 38th birthday until June. First footballer to play 1,000 Senior games.

13 FORMER LEAGUE PLAYERS WHO MADE THEIR 1ST XI BOWS BEFORE REACHING 17

15 Year Olds.

Roy Parry (Bolton Wanderers). His debut v. Wolves in October 1951, made him the then youngest Division One player at 15 years 207 days.

Jimmy Brown (Aston Villa) 1969–70, Midfielder

Glyn Pardoe (Manchester City) 1961–62, Centre Forward, later moved to Full Back
Frank Sibley (Queens Park Rangers) 1963–64, Midfielder
Jimmy White (Bournemouth) 1957–58, Half Back

16 Year Olds.
John Barton (Preston North End) 1958–59, Goalkeeper
Gerry Bridgwood (Stoke City) 1960–61, Inside Forward
*Trevor Francis** (Birmingham City) 1970–71, Striker
Cec Irwin (Sunderland) 1958–59, Full Back
Denis Law° (Huddersfield Town) 1956–57, Right-sided Striker
Peter Lorimer† (Leeds United) 1962–63, Attacker
Joe Royle (Everton) 1965–66, Centre Forward
Mick Wright (Aston Villa) 1963–64, Full Back

* Francis is still playing of course with Sampdoria of Genoa in Italy and may return to English football.

° Denis Law made his first *two* League appearances against Notts County 24th December 1956, and 26th December 1956.

† Lorimer appeared during 1982–83 with U.C.D. of the League of Ireland.

Life Begins at 40

15 FORMER LEAGUE FOOTBALLERS WHO PLAYED OUTFIELD IN THE 1ST TEAM BEYOND THEIR 39TH BIRTHDAYS

In brackets the club the player last appeared for and the season

Almost 55 players since the war have passed their 39th birthday while playing League Football, and the age that many are playing to today suggests that number could well increase to around 75 or 80 by the close of the century. Super fitness and continued or latently renewed enthusiasm for the game are the reasons behind the longevity of some of the following careers.

For every 'one club' man to reach this age since the war there have been nine who have finished their careers in lower divisions.

1. *John Billingham* (Southport/1954–55) Centre Forward
2. *Billy Bremner*[2] (Doncaster Rovers/1981–82) Midfielder
3. *Jack Brownsword* (Scunthorpe/1964–65) Full Back
4. *Ian Callaghan*[1] (Crewe/1981–82) Midfielder
5. *Bobby Collins*[2] (Oldham/1972–73) Inside Forward
6. *Willy Cunningham*[2] (Southport/1963–64) Full Back
7. *Peter Doherty*[3] (Doncaster/1952–53) Inside Forward
8. *Wally Fielding* (Southport/1958–59) Inside Forward
9. *Frank Hill*[2] (Crewe/1946–47) Wing Half
10. *Matt Middleton* (York City/1949–50) Half Back
11. *Alan Oakes* (Chester/1981–82) Midfielder
12. *John Oakes* (Plymouth/1947–48) Centre Half
13. *Fred Scott* (Nottingham Forest/1956–57) Right Winger
14. *Arthur Turner* (Southport/1947–48) Centre Half
15. *John Warner*[4] (Rochdale/1952–53) Wing Half

Former Internationals

1 England   2 Scotland   3 Northern Ireland   4 Wales

11 POST-WAR GOALKEEPERS WHO WERE AT LEAST WITHIN 12 MONTHS OF 40 WHEN THEY FINISHED PLAYING

1. *Sam Bartram*° (Charlton Athletic/1955–56)
2. *Billy Bly*° (Hull City/1959–60)
3. *Joe Calvert* (Watford/1947–48)
4. *Alex Ferguson* (Swindon Town/1947–48)
   Swindon was his 7th League Club, no other 'keeper with as many clubs has reached close on 40. Ferguson was almost 43½.
5. *Kevin Keelan* (Norwich City/1979–80)
6. *Ted Sagar*°* (Everton/1952–53)
7. *John Smith*° (Sheffield United/1949–50)
8. *George Swindin* (Arsenal/1953–54)
9. *Bert Trautmann*° (Manchester City/1963–64)
10. *George Tweedy*°* (Grimsby Town/1952–53)
11. *Alf Wood* (Coventry City/1956–7)

* England International   ° Served only 1 League Club

3 TEENAGE CAPTAINS

Although there have been several teenage team Captains in the Football League over the years, three of the more recent to be 'Skipper' on the field.
1. *Gary Gillespie*: Falkirk Captain who until his transfer to Coventry City at 17 in March, 1978, was the youngest Captain in professional football worldwide.
2. *Tony Gale*: Fulham Captain at 18 in 1978–79.
3. *Ray Wilkins*: Chelsea Captain from the age of 18 until leaving just short of his 23rd birthday for Manchester United.

4 YOUNGEST FIRST TEAM DEBUTANTS

1. *Cameron Buchanan*: The youngest ever Football League Debutant who played for Wolves in 1942 at 14 years 5 months. Unfortunately because wartime games are not officially recognized his name means nothing to many people. After the war he played in attack for Bournemouth and Norwich, having left Wolves in 1949.
2. *Albert Geldard*: At 15 years 156 days when making his League Debut for Bradford Park Avenue v. Millwall in Division II on 16th September, 1929, Geldard became the youngest recognized League player.
3. *Ronnie Dix*: Reputed to be the youngest ever Division 3 (South) player at 15 years 173 days when he played for his home town club, Bristol Rovers in February, 1928. More importantly the following week 3rd March, 1928, he scored for the 'pirates' against Norwich City becoming the youngest player to score in a Football League match.
4. *Derek Forster*: When pressed into action as Goalkeeper for Sunderland, in place of the injured Jimmy Montgomery, against Leicester City in August, 1964, he became the youngest ever Division I player at 15 years 185 days.

6 CURRENT SCOTTISH LEAGUE PLAYERS WHO MADE THEIR LEAGUE DEBUT BEFORE THEIR 18TH BIRTHDAY

1. *Derek Johnstone* (Rangers) 1969–70. He scored the winning goal against the 'Auld Enemy' Celtic in the 1970 League Cup Final, in only his second 1st XI game. He was then only 16 years 5 months.
2. *Gordon Fraser* (Meadowbank Thistle) Debut at 16 in 1978–79.
3. *John McDonald* (Rangers) Debut at 17 in 1978–79.
4. *Neale Cooper* (Aberdeen) Just beyond his 17th birthday when he first played in 1980–81.
5. *Steve Cowan* (Aberdeen) Debut halfway through his eighteenth year in 1981–82.
6. *Charlie Mitchell* (Aberdeen) made his Debut shortly after his 17th birthday in 1981–82.

6 FORMER SCOTTISH LEAGUE PLAYERS WHO MADE THEIR SCOTTISH CLUB 1ST XI DEBUTS BEFORE THEIR 18TH BIRTHDAYS

1. *Neil McNab*: His League Debut with Morton in 1972–73 makes him at 15 years 8 months the youngest player ever to take part in the Scottish League.
2. *Alex Edwards*: A League bow against Hibernian with Dunfermline Athletic in March, 1962, made him the Scottish League's youngest player for a decade at 16 years 5 days old.
3. *Alan Morton*: for Queen's Park during 1913–14.
4. *Jimmy Robertson*: Cowdenbeath 1961–62.
5. *Eric Carruthers*: Hearts 1971–72.
6. *John McGregor*: Queens Park 1979–80.

4 PLAYERS WHO PASSED 37 YEARS OF AGE WHILE COMPETING IN THE SCOTTISH LEAGUE

1. *Bobby Evans*: Scottish International Centre Back who finished his career with Raith Rovers in 1967–68 beyond his 40th birthday.
2. *Alan Ball*: English Goalkeeper who finished with Queen of the South in 1981–82 at the age of 39.
3. *Andy Rolland*: Defender who retired at 38 in 1981–82. His last games were for Cowdenbeath.
4. *Ronnie Simpson*: Began at 14 during the war (not recognized). Finished at 37 with Celtic.

3 OLDEST COMPETITORS

1. *Neil McBain*– Having won just 3 Scottish Caps during the period 1922–24 while performing as a Wing Half with Manchester United and Everton it must have seemed unlikely that this player would be remembered in footballing history. After squeezing in service with St. Johnstone, Liverpool and Watford after leaving Goodison, he became Manager of New Brighton.
   When he found by some mischance that only nine New Brighton players had managed to be at Victoria Park, Hartlepool on 15th March, 1947, he and an amateur player both took the field, the latter in an outfield position – McBain himself, in Goal.
   He was 51 years 4 months old – an age at which no footballer is ever likely to play at such a high level again.
   He died in 1974.
2. *Sir Stanley Matthews* – This dazzling Winger played his last game for Stoke (a second period at the Club) and in League Football against Fulham on 6th February, 1965. This, his 701st League game was played 5 days after his 50th birthday, making him the oldest First Division player in history. Perhaps the world's most respected ambassador of the game.
3. *Billy Meredith* – The oldest competitor in the F.A. Cup proper when he played for Manchester City against Newcastle United in the semi-final of the 1924–25 season. He was 49 years 8 months. It is likely that had Manchester

City been victorious in the semi-final that the ensuing Cup Final against Aston Villa would have been a greater 'Swan Song' for the 'Welsh Wizard'.

6 Of The Youngest

THE YOUNGEST FULL BACK PAIRING – TROLLOPE AND WOLLEN

The youngest Full Back duo that the Football League has seen is that brought about at the beginning of the 1960–61 season, when Swindon introduced at Right Back local boy Terry Wollen, a couple of weeks past his 17th birthday, to partner fellow Wiltshire lad (Norman) John Trollope, who, some 6 weeks older, was a seasoned player of more than a dozen games.

The partnership continued off and on for almost 3½ years, but it is interesting to note that Terry Wollen finished his career in football at the tender age of 21 having made 84 League appearances.

John Trollope, however, became Swindon Manager, after retiring at 37 years of age having played 770 League and over 80 Cup games, a record number of appearances for one Club.

YOUNGEST 100 LEAGUE APPEARANCES

Robbie James, born 23rd March, 1957, became the youngest player to finish 100 Football League games when he turned out for Swansea City against Torquay United on 14th February, 1976. Within 26 months he had become the youngest to complete *200 appearances* when he appeared against Reading on 24th March, 1978, scoring twice. With 349 League games behind him at the close of 1981–82, he is a possible to beat John Trollope's appearance record.

YOUNGEST PLAYERS TO SCORE
200 GOALS

Jimmy Greaves (Tottenham) 23 years 290 days
Bill 'Dixie' Dean (Everton) 23 years 290 days
Incredibly both Greaves and Dean hit their 200th Goal at
exactly the same age. Perhaps Greaves' 4 months away in Italy
helped Dean catch up, as Greaves was the youngest at 20 years
9 months to bag 100.

YOUNGEST PLAYER TO APPEAR IN
A COMPETITIVE MATCH FOR
A FOOTBALL LEAGUE CLUB

Eamonn Collins: Alan Ball, then Blackpool Player-Manager
introduced Collins as substitute for Blackpool's 1st XI against
Kilmarnock in the Anglo-Scottish Cup-Tie on 9th September,
1980. After taking his place on the field, Collins an Irish
Midfielder became at 14 years and 323 days the youngest First
Team player in the history of the English professional game.
Collins had been signed as a non-contract player in May, 1980,
so didn't have to wait long for a chance of fame. However,
the lad wasn't used in League games and after something of a
wrangle, had his contract with Blackpool cancelled by the
Football League in December, 1981. He was promptly snapped
up by Southampton, presumably acting on the advice of Alan
Ball, as an apprentice. It remains to be seen as to whether
young Collins, not quite 18 yet, can live up to his obvious early
promise. I think he just might.

THE 5 MEMBERS OF THE YOUNGEST
FORWARD LINE

In December, 1965, the Forward Line of

1. Alex Donald 17 years 6 months
2. Paul Bannister 18 years 2 months
3. Roddy Georgeson 17 years 5 months
4. Micky Cullerton 17 years 1 month
5. Paul Ogden 19 years 9 days

turned out for Port Vale against Bradford City in a Division 4
game and became reputedly the Football League's youngest

ever Forward Line with an average age of only 17 years 10 months.
Only Cullerton had a successful League career.

A FURTHER 5 TEENAGE FORWARDS
USED BY PORT VALE
BETWEEN 1965–68

1. *Jim Gough*   3. *Tom McLaren*
2. *John James*   4. *Bill McCartney*
          5. *David McClelland*

(Manager Sir Stanley Matthews was certainly a believer in giving youth a fling.)

3 LATE DEBUTANTS

1. *Andy Cunningham*: When he pulled on the black and white striped shirt of Newcastle United in February, 1929, for the League game at Filbert Street he became the *Oldest First Division Debutant* at the ripe old age of 38 years and 2 days. He had just been signed from Glasgow Rangers in an effort to get the forward line moving a little better. He made 122 League appearances for the 'Magpies', a number of them as Player/Manager.
2. *Tony Book*: A late starter, this fine competitive Full Back joined Manchester City 2 months short of his 32nd birthday, becoming Captain and winning most domestic honours with the club. Owes his latent League career, begun at 28 with Plymouth Argyle, to fortuitously playing under Malcolm Allison at Bath City.
3. *Dave Donaldson*: A Centre Back who served Non-League Clubs for 18 years before getting his League chance in 1977–78 with newly elected Wimbledon. Was 'Player of the Year' in that first season having made his League Debut at 35 years 7 months.

3 YOUNGEST PLAYERS IN F.A.
CUP-TIES

1. *Scott Endersby*: When he turned out as Goalkeeper for Kettering v. Tilbury on 5th December, 1977, in a 1st Round

F.A. Cup-Tie (his Cup Debut v. Tilbury on 26th November, was declared void because of an ineligible player) he became the youngest player in the F.A. Cup proper at 15 years 9 months. He was Tranmere Rovers first choice Goalkeeper in 1982–3.

2. *Alick Jeffrey*: On the 29th January, 1955, Jeffrey entered the record books as the youngest F.A. Cup competitor when he played on his 16th birthday against Aston Villa in a 3rd Round F.A. Cup-Tie. Although Endersby broke his record in 1977, he remains the youngest player with a Football League club to make an F.A. Cup Debut.

3. *Paul Allen*: 17 years and 256 days was the age of West Ham Midfielder Allen when in his debut season he played in the F.A. Cup Final against Arsenal on 10th May, 1980, making him the youngest F.A. Cup finalist in history.

THE 2 OLDEST F.A. CUP COMPETITORS

1. *Billy Meredith*: At 49 years 8 months in the F.A. Cup Semifinal against Newcastle United (see *3 Oldest Competitors*).

2. *John Oakes*: Former Nottingham Forest, Southend and Aldershot Centre Half is the oldest Cup Finalist in the postwar period. When he played for losing Finalists Charlton in 1945–46 his age was 40 years 7 months.

THE 4 YOUNGEST F.A. CUP FINALISTS

1. *Paul Allen* (West Ham – 1980) 17 years 256 days.
2. *Howard Kendall* (Preston North End – 1964) 17 years 346 days.
3. *Cliff Bastin* (Arsenal – 1930) 18 years 2½ months.
4. *Alex Dawson* (Manchester United – 1958) 18 years 2½ months.

THE 5 POST-WAR PLAYERS WHO WERE THE YOUNGEST F.A. CUP WINNERS

Each of these players fleetingly had fame as the youngest postwar F.A. Cup winner.

1. *Jim Bullions* (Derby County, 1946) youngest at 22 years 2 months in the first post-war final.
2. *Ronnie Simpson* (Newcastle United – 1952) took over mantle as youngest post-war F.A. Cup winner, at 21 years 7 months.
3. *Joe Hayes* (Manchester City – 1956) 20 years 3 months.
4. *Johnny Sissons* (West Ham United – 1964) 18 years 7 months. The first post-war teenage Cup winner – the youngest since Bastin.
5. *Paul Allen* (West Ham United – 1980) 17 years 8 months.

THE 23 POST-WAR TEENAGE F.A. CUP FINALISTS

1. *Joe Hayes* (Manchester City – 1955) v. Newcastle
2. *Bobby Charlton* (Manchester United – 1957) v. Aston Villa
3. *Alex Dawson* (Manchester United – 1958) v. Bolton
4. *Graham Cross* (Leicester City – 1963) v. Manchester United
5. *Johnny Sissons* (West Ham United – 1964) v. Preston
6. *Howard Kendall* (Preston North End – 1964) v. West Ham
7. *Graham Pugh*[3] (Sheffield Wednesday – 1966) v. Everton
8. *Sam Ellis*[3] (Sheffield Wednesday – 1966) v. Everton
9. *Wilf Smith*[3] (Sheffield Wednesday – 1966) v. Everton
10. *Jim McCalliog*[3] (Sheffield Wednesday – 1966) v. Everton
11. *Joe Royle* (Everton – 1968) v. West Brom
12. *Tommy Booth* (Manchester City – 1969) v. Leicester
13. *Malcolm Manley*[1] (Leicester City – 1969) v. Manchester City
14. *Peter Shilton* (Leicester City – 1969) v. Manchester City
15. *Ray Kennedy* (Arsenal – 1971) v. Liverpool
16. *Alan Kennedy* (Newcastle United – 1974) v. Liverpool
17. *Mervyn Day* (West Ham United – 1975) v. Fulham
18. *Dave McCreery*[1] (Manchester United – 1976) v. Southampton
19. *Dave McCreery*[1,2] (Manchester United – 1977) v. Liverpool
20. *Arthur Albiston* (Manchester United – 1977) v. Liverpool

1 Teenage Substitute.
2 Second appearance as a teenager in a Cup Final.
3 The only occasion that an F.A. Cup Final has contained more than 2 teenagers.

21. *Paul Allen* (West Ham United – 1980) v. Arsenal
22. *Tommy Caton*[4] (Manchester City – 1981) v. Tottenham
23. *Steve MacKenzie*[4] (Manchester City – 1981) v. Tottenham
24. *Warren Neill* (Queens Park Rangers – 1982) Replay against Tottenham

Of the 23 only Sissons, Booth, Ray Kennedy, Day, McCreery (in 1977) Albiston and Allen appeared on winning sides. Perhaps something worthy of consideration by future Cup Final Managers.

4 Appeared in the Final and its replay.

THE 13 POST-WAR F.A. CUP FINALISTS WHO HAD REACHED 36 YEARS OF AGE

Apart from Oakes at 40½ and Matthews at 38 years 3 months in 1953 all the players were either 36 or 37.

1. *John Oakes* (Charlton Athletic – 1946) v. Derby
2. *Herbert Turner* (Charlton Athletic – 1946) v. Derby
3. *Dally Duncan* (Derby County – 1946) v. Charlton
4. *Don Welsh* (Charlton Athletic – 1947) v. Burnley
5. *Alex Munroe* (Blackpool – 1948) v. Manchester United
6. *Leslie Compton* (Arsenal – 1950) v. Liverpool
7. *Stanley Matthews* (Blackpool – 1951) v. Newcastle
8. *Joe Mercer* (Arsenal – 1952) v. Newcastle
9. *George Swindin* (Arsenal – 1952) v. Newcastle
10. *Stan Hanson* (Bolton Wanderers – 1953) v. Blackpool
11. *Syd Owen* (Luton Town – 1959) v. Nottingham Forest
12. *Danny Blanchflower* (Tottenham Hotspur – 1962) v. Burnley
13. *Jackie Charlton* (Leeds United – 1972) v. Arsenal

THE 4 YOUNGEST F.A. CUP FINAL CAPTAINS

1. *David Nish* (Leicester City – 1969) 21 years 7 months when losing Captain against Manchester City.
2. *Ron Harris* (Chelsea – 1967) 22 years 6 months when he skippered defeated Chelsea against Tottenham.
3. *Bobby Moore* (West Ham United – 1964) Captain at 23 years 1 month of West Ham, victors over Preston.

4. *Raich Carter* (Sunderland – 1937) 23 years 5 months when he captained the 'Roker Men' to victory over Preston.

12 YOUNGEST POST-WAR CUP FINAL SCORERS

1. *Johnny Sissons* (West Ham – 1964) 18 years 7 months
2. *Steve MacKenzie* (Manchester City – 1981 replay) 19 years 5 months
3. *Jim McCalliog* (Sheffield Wednesday – 1966) 19 years 7 months
4. *Eddie Kelly** (Arsenal – 1971) 20 years 3 months
5. *Joe Hayes* (Manchester City – 1956) 20 years 3 months
6. *Charlie George* (Arsenal – 1971) 20 years 6 months
7. *David Ford* (Sheffield Wednesday – 1966) 21 years 2 months
8. *Ronnie Boyce* (West Ham – 1964) 21 years 4 months
9. *Alan Taylor°* (West Ham – 1975) 21 years 5 months
10. *Mike Trebilcock* (Everton – 1966) 21 years 5 months
11. *Ian Hutchinson* (Chelsea – 1970) 21 years 9 months
12. *Jack Dyson* (Manchester City – 1956) 21 years 10 months

* The only substitute to score in an F.A. Cup Final.
° Youngest post-war Cup Final double scorer.

4 YOUNGEST F.A. CUP DOUBLE SCORERS

1. *Harry Hampton* (For Aston Villa v. Newcastle – 1905) 20 years
2. *Alan Taylor* (For West Ham v. Fulham – 1975) 21 years 5 months
3. *Mike Trebilcock* (For Everton v. Sheffield Wednesday – 1966) 21 years 5 months
4. *W. G. (Ginger) Richardson* (For West Brom. v. Birmingham – 1931) 22 years

10 OLDEST POST-WAR F.A. CUP FINAL SCORERS

1. *Herbert Turner* (Charlton Athletic) v. Derby County – 1946 – 36 years 10 months. Turner became the first player in an F.A. Cup Final to score for both sides – Tommy Hutchinson

in 1981 became only the second player to do so.

2. *Danny Blanchflower* (Tottenham Hotspur) v. Burnley – 1962 – 36 years 3 months.
3. *Jackie Charlton* (Leeds United) v. Chelsea – 1970 – 34 years 11 months.
4. *Tommy Hutchison* (Manchester City) v. Tottenham Hotspur – 1981 – 33 years 7 months.
5. *Doug Holden* (Preston North End) v. West Ham United – 1964 – 33 years 7 months.
6. *Peter Doherty* (Derby County) v. Charlton Athletic – 1946 – 32 years 11 months.
7. *Charlie Wayman* (Preston North End) v. West Bromwich Albion – 1954 – 32 years 11 months.
8. *Nat Lofthouse* (Bolton Wanderers) v. Manchester United – 1958 – 32 years 8 months.
9. *Stan Mortenson* (Blackpool) v. Bolton Wanderers – 1953 – 31 years 11 months.
10. *Trevor Brooking* (West Ham United) v. Arsenal – 1980 – 31 years 7 months.

7 YOUNGEST POST-WAR F.A. CUP FINAL TEAMS

Only West Ham were victors

1. *Manchester United* (1957 v. Aston Villa) average age 23 years 1 month. The first finalists to include no players of 30 or over.
2. *West Ham United* (1975 v. Fulham) 24 years. The youngest winners.
3. *Leicester City* (1969 v. Manchester City) 24 years 1 month.
4. *Sheffield Wednesday* (1966 v. Everton) 24 years 2 months.
5. *Manchester United* (1976 v. Southampton) 24 years 3 months.
6. *Everton* (1968 v. West Bromwich Albion) 24 years 4 months.
7. *Chelsea* (1967 v. Tottenham Hotspur) 24 years 4 months.

6 OLDEST POST-WAR F.A. CUP FINAL TEAMS

1. *Arsenal* (1950 v. Liverpool) average age 31 years 2 months. Contained 8 players over 30, yet emerged as winners.
2. *Charlton Athletic* (1946 v. Derby County) 31 years.

3. *Arsenal* (1952 v. Liverpool) 30 years 5 months.
4. *Blackpool* (1948 v. Manchester United) 29 years 2 months.
5. *Charlton Athletic* (1947 v. Burnley) 29 years 1 month.
6. *Preston North End* (1954 v. West Bromwich Albion) 29 years 1 month.

3 YOUNGEST F.A. CUP FINALS (1946–83)

1. *1964 West Ham United v. Preston North End* Average age 24 years 8 months
2. *1967 Tottenham Hotspur v. Chelsea* 24 years 8 months
3. *1969 Manchester City v. Leicester City* 24 years 9 months

3 OLDEST F.A. CUP FINALS (1946–83)

1. *1950 Arsenal v. Liverpool* Average age of 30 years
2. *1946 Derby County v. Charlton Athletic* 29 years 11 months
3. *1947 Charlton Athletic v. Burnley* 28 years 9 months

Of the 37 F.A. Cup Finals (1946–82) 25 winners were the older team. Only on 12 occasions did the younger side win.

THE 12 YOUNGEST LEAGUE CUP FINALISTS

There have been 27 teenage players in the climax of the League Cup since its inception in 1960/61. From 1961–1966 inclusive the Finals were of 2 legs. Amazingly the two youngest Cup Finalists although in different sides were from the same Club.

1. *Ralph Brown** (Aston Villa – 1961, the first Final) 17 years 1 month
2. *Lawson Chatterley* (Aston Villa – 1963) 18 years
3. *John Boyle* (Chelsea – 1965) 18 years 2 months
4. *Chris Woods°* (Nottingham Forest – 1978) 18 years 4 months
5. *Gordon Cowans* (Aston Villa – 1977) 18 years 4½ monhts

* This Derbyshire born Forward never played in a League match for Villa and was transferred 14 months after the Final to Notts. County for whom he played only 18 times before leaving League football.

° The youngest member of a one match League Cup winning team.

6. *Len Cantello* (West Bromwich Albion – 1970) 18 years 6 months
7. *Tom Sweenie* (Leicester City – 1964) 18 years 7 months
8. *Graham Lovett* (West Bromwich Albion – 1966) 18 years 7½ months
9. *John Hollins* (Chelsea – 1965) 18 years 8 months
10. *Alan Baker* (Aston Villa – 1963) 18 years 9 months
11. *Peter Barnes* (Manchester City – 1976) 18 years 9 months
12. *Ian Bowyer* (Manchester City – 1970) 18 years 9 months

THE 7 OLDEST LEAGUE CUP FINALISTS

1. *Jim Langley* (Queens Park Rangers – 1967) 38 years 1 month
2. *Derek Dougan* (Wolves – 1974) 36 years 1 month
3. *Ian Callaghan* (Liverpool – 1978) 35 years 11 months
4. *Ron Ashman* (Norwich City – 1962) 35 years 9 months
5. *Frank Clark* (Nottingham Forest – 1979) 35 years 6 months
6. *George Eastham* (Stoke City – 1972) 35 years 5 months
7. *Stan Milburn* (Rochdale – 1962) 35 years 4 months

Callaghan and Milburn were the only losers.

7 YOUNGEST LEAGUE CUP FINAL SCORERS

1. *Peter Barnes* (Manchester City – 1976) v. Newcastle United. 18 years 9 months.
2. *Harry Burrows* (Aston Villa – 1961) v. Rotherham United. 20 years.
3. *Roger Morgan* (Queens Park Rangers – 1967) v. West Bromwich Albion. 20 years 3 months.
4. *Tony Brown* (West Bromwich Albion – 1966) v. West Ham United. 20 years 4 months.
5. *Ian Rush* (Liverpool – 1982) v. Tottenham Hotspur. 20 years 4½ months.
6. *Ronnie Whelan* (Liverpool – 1982) v. Tottenham Hotspur. 20 years 5 months.
7. *Keith Bebbington* (Stoke City – 1964) v. Leicester City. 20 years 6 months.

Only Bebbington finished on the losing side. Whelan is the youngest of 6 double scorers.

4 OLDEST LEAGUE CUP FINAL SCORERS

1. *George Eastham* (Stoke City – 1972) v. Chelsea. 35 years 5 months.
2. *Dennis Viollet* (Stoke City – 1964) v. Leicester City. 30 years 5½ months.
3. *Chris Nicholl* (Aston Villa – 1977 second replay) v. Everton. 30 years 5 months.
4. *Kenny Dalglish* (Liverpool – 1981 replay) v. West Ham United. 30 years.

6 YOUNGEST LEAGUE CUP FINAL TEAMS

1. *Leeds United* 1968 v. Arsenal. Average age 23 years 4 months.
2. *Chelsea* 1965 v. Leicester City. 23 years 6 months.
3. *West Bromwich Albion* 1967 v. Queens Park Rangers. 24 years 2 months.
4. *Aston Villa* 1963 v. Birmingham City. 24 years 4 months.
5. *West Bromwich Albion* 1966 v. West Ham United. 24 years 4 months.
6. *Arsenal* 1968 v. Leeds United. 24 years 4 months.

3 OLDEST LEAGUE CUP FINAL TEAMS

1. *Rochdale* 1962 v. Norwich City. Average age 28 years 11 months.
2. *Norwich City* 1975 v. Aston Villa. 28 years 8 months.
3. *Nottingham Forest* 1979 v. Southampton. 28 years 4 months.

THE 11 YOUNGEST ENGLAND PLAYERS TO OCCUPY EACH POSITION SINCE 1945

It has to be noted that England selectors have rarely been keen to introduce players at an early age, unlike some other countries where ability has seemed to be the most important and sometimes only consideration. However, each of the 11 here was a little special hence his early introduction.

1. *Alan Hodgkinson* – the youngest Goalkeeper at 20 years 5 months, when he helped England to a 2–1 victory over Scotland at Wembley in April, 1957. A splendidly loyal servant to Sheffield United who made over 600 1st team appearances in his 14 years as a player with the club. He would have won more than 5 Caps but for the unyielding competition from Messrs. Hopkinson, Springett, Waiters and, a little later, Banks.

2. *Bobby Thomson* – Although the first of his eight Caps came when he was only 19 at Left Back in the first floodlit international at Wembley (an 8–3 thrashing of Northern Ireland in November 1963), he occupies this Right Back berth because his appearance there in the 1–1 draw with Portugal in Sao Paulo, Brazil, in June, 1964, made him at 20 years 6 months, the youngest No. 2 that England have used. A handy ball-playing Defender with a penchant for attack, he played over 450 League games in total with Wolves (with whom he was playing when he collected his Caps), Birmingham, Luton, Port Vale and Walsall (Loan) before heading West to firstly Connecticut Bicentennials.

3. *Tony Allen* – 19 years 341 days old when he wore the white of England for the first time in the 1–1 draw against Wales at Ninian Park. It was the first of only 3 Caps for this tall blond Left-sided Defender, a clean kicker of the ball, quick and strong in the tackle. He had been Capped only the previous season for England Youth, and England Under 23's, so in hindsight the jump, perhaps premature, may have affected his long term international career. A fine Club player in 13 seasons with Stoke City, he moved to the centre of Defence towards the end of his stint at the Victoria Ground, before closing the curtain on his career in May, 1971, that final season being spent at Bury.

4. *Ron Flowers* – A calm outstanding Wing Half who was 2 months away from his 21st birthday when he made his England Debut in the 1–0 defeat by the French in Paris, May, 1955. Although winning 49 Caps, had he been playing at a time of inferior Defensive Midfielders (as in the 1970's) then he would probably have gone close to accumulating 100. Hard in the tackle and with a powerful shot, he was an important member of the great Wolves side of the 1950's. He spent two years with Northampton including 11 months as Player/Manager, before closing his

career in 1969 with a two-year spell as Player/Coach at the Bucks head ground, home of Telford United. His last appearance at Wembley was at Right Half in Telford's 1970 team against Macclesfield in the first F.A. Challenge Trophy Final.

5. *Kevin Beattie* – Regarded as the 1970's version of Duncan Edwards (Q.V.). Beattie, a Carlisle born Utility Defender, looked capable at the outset of his international career of emulating Charlton, Moore and Wright by winning over a century of Caps. However, an early brush with authority by failing to turn up to an England camp and later near-crippling injuries to a knee meant that this rugged tamer of Strikers gave only 8 international appearances. The first, in the No. 5 shirt, came against Cyprus on a cool spring night in 1975 when Malcolm MacDonald scored all 5 goals in a 5–0 victory. Beattie was then 4 months into his 22nd year.

He scored one of the best goals by a Defender seen at Wembley when he was instrumental in the build-up to goal, then ran some 50 yards to climb high on the edge of the penalty area and bullet a header past Stewart Kennedy. A 5–1 victory for England over the 'Old Enemy' in May, 1975, is at least a memory for this warhorse to remember over the years.

After 228 League appearances with Ipswich he was forced on doctor's advice to retire. Some five months later, however, he made a come-back with 4th Division Colchester, managed by long time Ipswich Centre Back colleague Allan Hunter. In November, 1982, he was tempted to advance his come-back somewhat by joining Malcolm Allison at 2nd Division Middlesbrough.

6. *Duncan Edwards* – A player who won the praises of all those who saw him, regarded by many (even though playing only 4 seasons of senior football) to be the greatest English footballer in history. When he made his England Debut in the 7–2 slaughtering of Scotland, April, 1955, he became the youngest England player ever at 18 years 6 months. His power, courage, firm tackle, skilled distribution, ability (like Bobby Moore – a future number 6) to read situations and his thunderous shot made him the most complete footballer of his era. When in February, 1958, he died as a result of internal injuries sustained in

the Munich air disaster, he was only 21. He had already played 151 League games for 'Busby's Babes', and 18 times for England.

Upon his death two stained glass windows of Edwards in his Manchester United and England strips were positioned in St. Francis Church, Dudley, Worcestershire, his home town. He was held in such high esteem that supporters and admirers even formed the 'Duncan Edwards Football Club' in Dudley – the only instance known of such an honour.

7. *John Connelly* – A rarity in any age, in that he was a Winger who could play on either flank and was capable of going round the back of or inside the Full Back. He could be woefully inconsistent but was a complete Winger with speed, dribbling ability, an uncanny knack of scoring for a Winger (180 League goals in 571 games) and skill at varying his crosses; he had few equals in his generation. He won 20 Caps during his career at Burnley and Manchester United, winning League Championship medals with both teams. Was 21 years 3 months when he made his England Debut v. Wales in October, 1959, a game at Cardiff resulting in a 1–1 draw.

8. *Jimmy Greaves* – The mercurial Greaves was without doubt England's greatest Goalscorer with an incredible haul of 357 First Division goals in 516 appearances – a goal every 1.4 matches – and on the international front, 44 goals in 57 England appearances between 1959 and 1967. Notched over 100 goals for Chelsea in Reserve and Youth team appearances in 1956–57. From leaving school in Dagenham until his premature retirement in 1971 when he decided that he wasn't enjoying football as he should, he just couldn't stop scoring. He scored on every important debut, with England Youth, England Under 23's, England, Chelsea, A.C. Milan of Italy, Tottenham Hotspur, and West Ham United.

The opportunist supreme who rarely scored with his head or long range shots but who, given a hint of a chance, would take it. In 1962 after an unhappy 4 month spell in Italy he joined Tottenham's League and Cup double side and played an important part in securing the F.A. Cup that season, scoring one of the best ever goals at Wembley in the 3–1 defeat of Burnley. In 1963 he scored in the 5–1

destruction of Atlético Madrid for Spurs to win the
European Cup Winners Cup (the first British Club to win
a European tournament). In 12 of his 14 seasons in England
he was his club's top scorer, on five occasions the First
Division's top scorer. In 1965 he scored a goal of such
brilliance in the 5–1 hammering of Manchester United at
White Hart Lane that many who saw it, including me,
regard it as perhaps the greatest English goal of recent
years.

His Debut for England in May, 1959, against Peru was
something of a disappointment for his country, a 4–1 defeat
in Lima, but Greaves scored the loser's only goal at the
age of 19 years 3 months, marking the beginning of a
brilliant England career.

9. *Mick Jones* – Courageous leader of the attack who won his
first full Cap versus West Germany in May, 1965, aged 20
years 18 days, at the end of his second season with Sheffield
United. Not the most deft or skilful of Centre Forwards but
strong on the ball and a fine 'Target Man'. Won the hearts
of millions when he collected his F.A. Cup Winners Medal
in 1970 with his right arm in a sling. He had hurt himself
in making a determined dash past Arsenal's Bob McNab
to cross for Allan Clarke to score the winning goal. Under
Don Revie, Jones and Allan Clarke forged one of the most
feared striking partnerships in the country during the late
1960's and early 1970's. He won in total just 3 Caps, the
last one in 1970 against the Netherlands.

He retired in 1973 aged only 28, a victim of numerous cuts
and bruises that he'd taken in his stride for the whole of
his 11 year long career.

10. *Johnny Haynes* – When he donned the white shirt of
England for the first time in October, 1954, against
Northern Ireland he became the youngest player to fill the
No. 10 shirt at 19 years 350 days and also one of the
exalted few to have a scoring Debut. Probably the greatest
passer of a ball to be seen in an England shirt. He won 56
Caps between 1954 and 1962, but had it not been for a
serious injury received in a motor accident in Blackpool,
resulting in him not being chosen again for his country, he
would surely have gone on to win close on 100 Caps. Spent
the whole of his career with homely Fulham, but, in 1961,
the lure of lire from Milan, who were keen to sign him,

prompted 'The Cottagers' to make him Britain's first £100 a week footballer.

A player with two good feet, fine close control, great vision, and the ability to split any defence. Rated by Jimmy Greaves as his greatest Inside Forward partner. Also a useful cricketer, golfer, table tennis and tennis player. Upon leaving Fulham in 1970 after more than 650 League and Cup games for the Club he joined Durban City in South Africa, where first his playing then management career blossomed throughout the 1970's.

11. *Alan Hinton* – First Capped in the 1–1 draw with France in October, 1962, three days before his 20th birthday. This outstanding Outside Left won only three Caps but many thousands of admirers for his speed off the mark, a superb consistent standard of crossing and deadly finishing with Wolves, Nottingham Forest and Derby County. Perhaps his greatest personal success was the major role he played as a veteran in the League Championship wins of Derby County in 1971–72 and 1974–75 first under Brian Clough then Dave Mackay. When he retired in 1975 he had scored 116 League goals in 440 matches during his career – a fine tally for a Winger. For the last several years he has managed in the N.A.S.L. with Seattle Sounders to some effect.

Alan Ball is the youngest post-war international not to be included in the above 11 as he was only 19 years 362 days when the then Blackpool youngster took part in the game v. Yugoslavia in May, 1965.

10 ENGLAND PLAYERS TO WIN CAPS AFTER THEIR 35th BIRTHDAY

1. *Stanley Matthews*: His last Cap in May, 1957, came in the 4–1 defeat of Denmark in Copenhagen. The 'Wizard of Dribble' was then 42 years 3 months old.
2. *Les Compton* (Q.V.): Was 38 years 2 months when he turned out against Yugoslavia, in November, 1950.
3. *Tom Finney*: Regarded by the late Bill Shankly as England's greatest ever player, the 'Preston Plumber' was 36½ when he turned out on the Left Wing in the 5–0

demolition of the U.S.S.R. in October, 1958 for the last of his 76 Caps.

4. *Joe Pennington*: The cream of pre-First World War Full Backs he won the last of 25 Caps (he missed only 8 England games between March, 1907 and his retirement from international games) in a thrilling 5–4 win over Scotland at Sheffield in 1920. He was a subtle player of great touch, timing, and positional sense who often went unnoticed through rarely making a mistake.

5. *Ian Callaghan:* A hard working creative Mid-Fielder and great inspiration to Liverpool for 18 years. He was rewarded for a consistently high level of performance during Liverpool's Shankly era with 2 Caps in 1977, 6 months beyond his 35th birthday, against Switzerland and Luxembourg, to add to 2 Caps he won in 1966.

6. *Frank Hudspeth* (Q.V.): was 35½ when he gained his only Cap against Ireland in October, 1925.

7. *Ted Hufton*: West Ham's finest number one with a great reputation for stopping penalties was 35½ when he won his 6th and final Cap against Spain in Madrid at the close of the 1928–29 season. Played in the first Wembley Cup Final in 1923.

8. *Billy Wright*: When he won his 105th Cap (a record at the time) in May, 1959, the 8–1 victory over the U.S.A. was a great send-off; Wright, a fine servant throughout his career to Wolves, was 35 years and 3 months old. Rivals Bobby Moore as England's greatest Captain.

9. *Charlie Wallace*: An exciting Right Winger from Southwick, Sunderland, his main asset with Aston Villa and England was in the outstanding quality and variety of crosses. He was 2 months past his 35th birthday when he played his third and final game for England in the 5–4 victory over Scotland in April, 1920.

10. *Billy Walker*: Between the wars one of the best Inside or Centre Forwards, his 18th Cap and international climax came in the 4–3 defeat of the 'Wunderteam' Austria shortly after his 35th birthday.

THE 6 OLDEST ENGLAND
DEBUTANTS

1. *Leslie Compton* (Arsenal) Although Capped during wartime, Leslie, the elder of the footballing and cricketing Comptons, won his first official 'Cap' against Wales in November, 1950, at the ripe old age of 38 years 2 months. Won only one more Cap, v. Yugoslavia in the same month, sandwiched at No. 5 between fellow double sportsman Willie Watson (Q.V.) and Jimmy Dickinson of Portsmouth.

2. *Frank Hudspeth* (Newcasle United) A powerful Geordie Left-Back who had gone the rounds of Tyneside non-League Clubs before joining the 'Magpies' in 1910, serving them for 19 years. Made his only England appearance v. Ireland in October, 1925, a 0–0 draw aged 35 years 6 months. Partnered Aston Villa's Tommy Smart in perhaps the most awesome twinning in England's history.

3. *Jackie Bestall* (Grimsby Town – earlier Rotherham United) More than halfway through his 35th year this diminutive schemer with exceptional close control won a long overdue Cap (his only one) in a 2–1 victory over Northern Ireland at Goodison Park, in February, 1935.

4. *Jack Howe* (Derby County – also Hartlepools United 1934–36 and Huddersfield, 1949–51) Sturdily built, Hartlepool born Left Full Back who gained the first of 3 full England honours at the age of 34 years 7 months in one of England's best ever selections: Swift, Scott, Howe, Wright, Franklin, Cockburn, Matthews, Mortenson, Lawton, Mannion and Finney – they thrashed Italy 4–0 in May, 1948.

5. *John Davison* (Sheffield Wednesday) Another North Easterner who is believed at around 5'8" to be the shortest ever England custodian. A well-built, courageous goalminder whose remarkable agility belied his lack of inches. He was 34 when chosen for his only international appearance v. Wales in 1922.

6. *Arthur Chadwick* (Southampton) One of the earliest footballing nomads, his career spanning 25 years and 8 Non-League Clubs, 5 of whom were to join the Football League by the 1920's. A sturdy stopper whose skill quotient may not have been too high, nevertheless his determined no-nonsense play won him 2 Caps a month after his 34th birthday in 1900.

8 PLAYERS WHO WERE THE YOUNGEST FINALISTS IN WORLD CUPS FROM 1954–82

1. *1954 – Horst Eckel* (1.F.C. Kaiserslautern and West Germany) Right Half of 20 years 5 months in Germany's 3–2 victory over Hungary.
2. *1958 – Pelé* (Santos and Brazil and New York Cosmos) The brilliant Inside Forward who at 17 years 7 months became the youngest ever World Cup finalist. He was to score 2 brilliant goals in helping Brazil to a 5–2 victory over the Swedes.
   The rest of his career is legend.
3. *1962 – Amarildo* (Botafogo, A.C. Milan and Brazil and Fiorentina) A replacement for Pelé, injured in only Brazil's second game, he took his chance graciously, scoring twice in the 2–1 defeat of Spain (losing to Gento and his team mates would have meant elimination) and again in the Final, a 3–1 victory over Czechoslovakia. A 23 year old striker who did well in the surrounds of Italian League Football during the 1960's.
4. *1966 – Franz Beckenbauer* (SC 1906 München, Bayern München and West Germany and New York Cosmos and Hamburger SV) Like fellow German Eckel before him, his first World Cup Final was his 14th full appearance for his country. He was 20 years 10 months old when he played in midfield against England. There were already signs that he would be a great player, but that he would become the greatest defensive footballer, virtually create the 'Libero' position for himself and act as one of soccer's greatest ambassadors were not thought of. In winning 103 Caps for his country he became one of an exclusive set of players.
5. *1970 – Clodoaldo* (Santos and Brazil) One of the great mysteries of modern day football is why Clodoaldo, who looked to be as outstanding a prospect as Beckenbauer had been in the previous World Cup, never fulfilled his promise to go on to become an 'All-Time Great.' At just 20 years of age this handsome, swashbuckling Midfielder with speed, poise, tackling ability and vision, forming with Gerson the 'Engine Room' of the team, was an integral part of the most complete international side since the Brazil of 1958. From the time in 1974 that he failed to merit a place in the

Brazil World Cup squad, due to lack of fitness, his desire to recapture the great form of 1970 seemed to disappear. The later stages of his career were spent moving around South America.

6. *1974 – Rainer Bonhof* (SuS Emmerich, Borussia Moenchengladbach, F.C. Valencia, 1.F.C. Köln and West Germany) A very brief glimpse of international soccer was afforded him before reaching the pinnacle of success, a World Cup Final triumph. In only his 8th game and at 22 years 2 months this Gladbacher Midfield player was a World Champion. The power and drive that he added to an already outstanding side seemed to be the final piece in the jigsaw. In the Final against Holland his strong run down the left-hand of the Dutch penalty area beating Krol and Haan and the finely judged pass led to Gerd Müller hitting the World Cup winning goal. Bonhof has gone on to win 53 Caps for his country, but somehow never become the outstanding player that he should have been. For some time he was one of German soccer's heart throbs.

7. *1978 – Ernie Brandts* (PSV Eindhoven and Holland) Just a month younger than Argentina's Alberto Tarantini, Brandts a Central Defender of some quality and 22 years 5 months old made the world sit back and take notice when he scored one of the 1978 World Cup's best goals in the 2–1 defeat of Italy. From his introduction to the team earlier in the year Brandts had looked comfortable but many expected him to come unstuck amongst the greats of the world scene. Nothing could have been further from the truth, for Brandts went on to play a major role in taking the Dutch to their second successive Final (albeit a losing one).

8. *1982 – Giuseppe Bergomi* (Inter Milan and Italy) This teenage Full Back, or Centre Back, became the youngest winner since Pelé and the least experienced possessor of a World Cup Medal of all time. In only his fourth appearance he gave a sterling display as an extra Defender, in the absence of the suspended Antognoni, to help Italy take the World Cup for the third time against an injury-weakened West Germany. A player of whom we will hear a great deal more.

OLDEST PLAYER IN EACH OF THE
LAST 8 WORLD CUP
FINALS (1954–82)

1. *1954 – Anton 'Toni' Turek* (Fortuna Düsseldorf and West Germany) He was 35 years 5 months old when he performed heroics in goal for West Germany against red hot favourites Hungary, helping his country to a memorable 3–2 victory. He was to play only one more international match, his 20th Cap v. France in October, 1954, before retiring.

2. *1958 – Gunnar Gren* (IFK Gothenburg – A.C. Milan – Fiorentina – Genoa and Sweden) The 'Professor' as he was known was only 4 months short of his 38th birthday when he played in the marvellous 1958 Final against Brazil. Sweden who were the best ever international side emanating from Scandinavia included Gren, the great Nils Liedholm, Kurt Hamrin and 'Nacka' Skoglund (all of whom had already or were later to provide great moments in Italian League Football) but were totally outplayed by what many people regard as the greatest international side of all time – Brazil 1958.

3. *1962 – Nilton Santos* (Botafogo and Brazil) was 36 when he took part in the 1962 World Cup Final which ended in a 3–1 win for Brazil over Czechoslovakia. Had first represented his country in 1949, continuing to do so off and on until 1966, having accumulated 82 Caps. A sturdy classy Left Full Back, who always seemed to have time to clear or more often play the ball constructively to a team mate, he scored several goals through having a strong left foot shot, and would advance whenever possible (like Full Back partner Djalma Santos) into attacking positions.

4. *1966 – Ray Wilson* (Huddersfield, Everton and England) Wilson was 31 years 7 months old when he performed to his usual standard of excellence in English football's greatest hour – England's World Cup Final victory over West Germany. Although his inexplicable error in the game was capitalized upon by Helmut Haller to put the Germans 1–0 up he was regarded throughout most of the 1960's as the best Left Back in the world. Very rarely beaten by an orthodox Winger, his accuracy of pass, swashbuckling play down the left flank (he had begun as a Winger) and great character and warm heart helped make him England's

regular No. 3 for 8 years from 1960–68. He won 63 Caps, a record for an English Full Back.

5. *1970 – Felix* (Fluminense and Brazil) Had it not been for his outspoken criticism of Brazil's manager, Mario Zagalo, he may well have played a part in his country's advance to the semi-finals stages in the 1974 World Cup in West Germany. Nevertheless he was at 32 the oldest participant in the 1970 World Cup Final in Mexico City, helping Brazil to a well-fought 4–1 triumph over Italy. A solid rather than spectacular Goalkeeper he was like many South American custodians, Quiroga of Peru springs to mind, prone to leave his line a little too early and rush out of his area as evidenced by his dash out at Boninsegna in the 1970 World Cup Final. While not perhaps on a par with the legendary Gylmar, he was still a worthy enough last line of defence to play for Champions of the World.

6. *1974 and 1978 – Jan Jongbloed* (F.C. Amsterdam, Roda JC Kerkrade and Holland) The first person to be the oldest participant in a World Cup Final on two separate occasions, 33 years and 9 months old in 1974 against West Germany, and (naturally) 4 years older in Holland's defeat by Argentina. Arguably the best Dutch Goalkeeper during the period of their emergence as a world footballing force, he was, however, never really first choice for very long. Indeed his appearance in the 1978 finals was only because of PSV Eindhoven's Jan Van Beveren's decision not to go to Argentina on political and moral grounds.
In the event Jongbloed turned in creditable performances throughout both competitions.

7. *1982 – Dino Zoff* (Udinese, Mantua, Napoli, Juventus and Italy) The oldest player to take part in the 1982 World Cup, and the oldest winner of a Winners Medal when 4 months beyond his 40th birthday, he performed resolutely throughout the Finals to help Italy to their first World Cup success since 1938. The early part of Zoff's career was spent with modest First Division Clubs Udinese and Mantua but by the time he joined Napoli in 1967 his acrobatic goalkeeping came to the public's and more importantly to the Italian international selectors' notice. First selected for Italy against Bulgaria in the Nations Cup during 1968, he had to wait until after the 1970 World Cup (in which tournament he was reserve to Cagliari's Enrique Albertosi)

to become the regular first choice for his country. Shortly
after leaving school his talent was spurned by both
Internazionalle of Milan and Juventus who were to invest
around £400,000 in him in 1972, some months after his 30th
birthday. In the 10 years since arriving in Turin Zoff has
missed fewer than 10 League games and by the close of the
1982–83 season he should have broken the record of most
First Division appearances (566 held for over 30 years by
Centre Forward Silvio Piola). Just three months before
going to Spain, where he was to skipper Italy to success, he
passed Albertosi's figure of 532 'Serie A' games. Zoff, by
the beginning of 1983 had won 109 Caps, Captain in more
than a third of those games, and looked capable of breaking
almost every record available to him – most Italian First
Division appearances (achieved); most Caps of any player
in football (shouldn't take long); longest period for keeping
an International goal intact, some 1143 minutes and 13
Internationals had passed before Emmanuel Sanon of Haiti
scored against him in the 1974 World Cup (achieved); to
have appeared in the final stages of the European
Championship or World Cup tournaments on a record 7
occasions (achieved). He has won most domestic honours,
to date 6/7 League Winners Medals, an Italian F.A. Cup
and an F.A. Cup Winners Medal.

For all his attributes as a Goalkeeper, safe handling,
command of his penalty area, bravery, alertness (some
would say otherwise after conceding long range shots against
Holland and Argentina in the 1978 World Cup) and general
knowledge of goalkeeping, it has been suggested that he
and Albertosi have through their consistency (they are the
only two Goalkeepers to be Capped more than a few times
by Italy in a generation) blighted the careers of a string of
fine Goalkeepers. It can, however, hardly be Zoff's fault if
for a dozen years he has had no equal.

It is interesting to note that in the last 8 World Cup Finals
Goalkeepers have been the oldest player on 5 occasions; and
also in 1966 the second oldest, Tilkowski, was his side's Senior
player.

THE 5 YOUNGEST WORLD CUP FINAL
SCORERS 1950–82

1. *Pelé* (Brazil v. Sweden 1958) 17 years 7 months
2. *Agne Simonsson* (Sweden v. Brazil 1958) 21 years
3. *Wolfgang Weber* (West Germany v. England) 22 years
4. *Martin Peters* (England v. West Germany) 22 years 7 months
5. *Paul Breitner* (West Germany v. Holland) 22 years 9 months

THE 5 OLDEST WORLD CUP FINAL
SCORERS 1950–82

1. *Nils Liedholm** (Sweden v. Brazil 1958) 35 years 9 months
2. *Josef Masopust* (Czechoslovakia v. Brazil) 31 years 5 months
3. *Paul Breitner* (West Germany v. Italy) 30 years 10 months
4. *Zito* (Brazil v. Czechoslovakia) 29 years 10 months
5. *Pelé* (Brazil v. Italy) 29 years 8 months

Note that both Pelé and Breitner, having scored in two Finals each, have been both amongst the youngest and the oldest scorers.

* The second oldest Captain after Zoff of a World Cup Final team.

3 YOUNGEST EUROPEAN
FOOTBALLERS OF THE YEAR

1. *1968 George Best* (Manchester United and Northern Ireland) 22 years 7 months
2. 1975 *Oleg Blokhin* (Dynamo Kiev and Soviet Union) 23 years 1 month
3. 1965 *Eusebio* (Benfica and Portugal) 23 years 11 months

3 OLDEST EUROPEAN
FOOTBALLERS OF THE YEAR

1. 1956 *Stanley Matthews* (Blackpool and England) 41 years 11 months
2. 1963 *Lev Yashin* (Moscow Dynamo and Soviet Union) 34 years 2 months
3. 1959 *Alfredo Di Stefano* (Real Madrid and Spain) 33 years 5 months

77 TEENAGE INTERNATIONALS

15 Years Old

1. *G. Dorval* (Brazil) – The youngest Full International of all time when he played against Argentina in 1957. Unfortunately, the rest of his career was something of an anti-climax, never living up to the early promise.

16 Years Old

2. *Raimond Braine* (Beerschot and Belgium)
3. *Wlodzimierz Lubanski* (Gornik Zabrze and Poland)
4. *Diego Maradona* (Argentinos Juniors and Argentina)
5. *Alberto Spencer* (Penarol and Equador)

17 Years Old

6. *Florian Albert* (Ferencvaros and Hungary)
7. *George Best* (Manchester United and Northern Ireland)
8. *Jimmy Holmes* (Coventry City and Eire)
9. *Norman Kernoghan* (Belfast Celtic and Northern Ireland)
10. *Sammy McIlroy* (Manchester United and Northern Ireland)
11. *Mitar Mrkela* (O.F.K. Belgrade and Yugoslavia)
12. *Jimmy Nicholson* (Manchester United and Northern Ireland)
13. *Edson Arantes do Nascimento – 'Pelé'* (Santos and Brazil)
14. *Paul Van Himst* (Anderlecht and Belgium)
15. *Norman Whiteside* (Manchester United and Northern Ireland)

18 Years Old

16. *Ferenc Bene* (Ujpest Dozsa and Hungary)
17. *Guiseppe Bergomi* (Inter Milan and Italy)
18. *Liam Brady* (Arsenal and Eire)
19. *John Charles* (Leeds United and Wales)
20. *Teofilo Cubillas* (Alianza Lima and Peru)
21. *Eduardo – 'Edu'* (Santos and Brazil)
22. *Alex Elder* (Burnley and Northern Ireland)
23. *da Silva Ferreira – 'Eusebio'* (Benfica and Portugal)
24. *Johnny Giles* (Manchester United and Eire)
25. *Andrzej Iwan* (Wisla Krakow and Poland)
26. *Pat Jennings* (Watford and Northern Ireland)
27. *Dennis Law* (Huddersfield Town and Scotland)

28. *Michael Laudrup* (Brondbyoerne and Denmark)
29. *Bobby Lenarduzzi* (Reading and Canada)
30. *Graham Moore* (Cardiff City and Wales)
31. *Karl Odermatt* (F.C. Basel and Switzerland)
32. *David O'Leary* (Arsenal and Eire)
33. *Ferenc Puskas* (Honved and Hungary)
34. *Gianni Rivera* (A.C. Milan and Italy)
35. *Gary Sprake* (Leeds United and Wales)
36. *Hugo Sotil* (C.D. Municipal and Peru)
37. *Fritz Walter* (1.F.C. Kaiserslautern and West Germany)
38. *Patricio Yanez* (San Luis de Quillota and Chile)

19 Years Old

39. *José Altafini* (Palmeiras and Brazil)
40. *Georghi Asparoukhov* (Levski Sofia and Bulgaria)
41. *Gary Aubert* (Winnipeg Fort Rouge and Canada)
42. *Patrick Battiston* (Metz and France)
43. *Bruno Bellone* (F.C. Monaco and France)
44. *Giampiero Boniperti* (Juventus and Italy)
45. *Daniel Bravo* (Nice and France)
46. *Paul Breitner* (Bayern München and West Germany)
47. *Dan Corneliusson* (I.F.K. Gothenburg and Sweden)
48. *Tavares De Santana – 'Clodoaldo'* (Santos and Brazil)
49. *Johan Cruyff* (Ajax Amsterdam and Holland)
50. *Ramon Diaz* (River Plate and Argentina)
51. *Jean-Marc Ferreri* (Auxerre and France)
52. *Elias Figueroa* (Colo Colo and Chile)
53. *Brian Flynn* (Burnley and Wales)
54. *Helmut Haller* (BC Augsburg and West Germany)
55. *Ronnie Hellstroem* (Hammarby and Sweden)
56. *René Houseman* (Huracan and Argentina)
57. *Jair Ventura Filho – 'Jairzinho'* (Botafogo and Brazil)
58. *Kurt Jara* (Innsbruck and Austria)
59. *Wim Kieft* (Ajax Amsterdam and Netherlands)
60. *Oscar Mas* (River Plate and Argentina)
61. *Severino Minelli* (Servette and Switzerland)
62. *Johan Neeskens* (Ajax Amsterdam and Holland)
63. *Juan Oblitas* (Sporting Cristal and Peru)
64. *Ruben Paz* (Penarol and Uruguay)
65. *Toni Polster* (F.K. Austria and Austria)
66. *Frank Rijkaard* (Ajax Amsterdam and Holland)
67. *Sergei Rodionov* (Spartak Moscow and Soviet Union)

68. *Winton Rufer* (National Mutual Miramar and New Zealand)
69. *Pedro Rocha* (Penarol and Uruguay)
70. *Bernd Schuster* (1.F.C. Köln and West Germany)
71. *Uwe Seeler* (Hamburger S.V. and West Germany)
72. *Allan Simonsen* (Veijle B.K. and Denmark)
73. *Piotr Skrowbowski* (Wisla Krakow and Poland)
74. *Miguel Tendillo* (Valencia and Spain)
75. *Eduardo Goncalves Andrade – 'Tostao'* (Cruzeiro and Brazil)
76. *Willie Van Der Kuylen* (PSV Eindhoven and Netherlands)
77. *Wladyslaw Zmuda* (Gwardia Warsaw and Poland)

16 VETERAN INTERNATIONALS AGED 35 OR OVER

In brackets is the player's club at the end of his International career

1. *Ivor Allchurch* (Swansea Town and Wales)
2. *Danny Blanchflower* (Tottenham and Northern Ireland)
3. *Fernando Bulnes* (Marathon and Honduras)
4. *Ron Burgess* (Tottenham and Wales)
5. *Hector Chumpitaz* (Sporting Cristal and Peru)
6. *Alfredo Di Stefano* (Real Madrid and Spain)
7. *Lazlo Fazekas* (Royal Antwerp and Hungary)
8. *Elias Figueroa* (Colo Colo and Chile)
9. *Pat Jennings* (Arsenal and Northern Ireland)
10. *Richard Kress* (Eintracht Frankfurt and West Germany)
11. *Angel Labruna* (River Plate and Argentina)
12. *Nils Liedholm* (A.C. Milan and Sweden)
13. *Ferenc Puskas* (Real Madrid and Spain)
14. *Toni Turek* (Fortuna Düsseldorf and West Germany)
15. *Wilfried Van Moer* (Beveren and Belgium)
16. *Fritz Walter* (1.F.C. Kaiserslautern and West Germany)

Aladdin's Cave

11 PLAYERS WHO CHANGED POSITIONS AND ADVANCED THEIR FORTUNES

1. *Trevor Brooking* – Centre Forward to Midfielder
2. *Terry Cooper* – Winger to Left Back
3. *Paul Hegarty* – Forward to Centre Back
4. *Emlyn Hughes* – Midfielder to Defender
5. *Geoff Hurst* – Wing Half to Centre Forward
6. *Malcolm MacDonald* – Full Back to Centre Forward
7. *Derek Parlane* – Right Half to Striker
8. *Leighton Phillips* – Midfielder to Sweeper
9. *Bruce Rioch* – Striker to Midfielder
10. *Bryan Robson* – Left Back to Midfielder
11. *Ladislao Mazurkiewicz* – Right Back to Goalkeeper, the Uruguayan of Polish and Spanish extraction who became one of the world's top custodians

77 WORLD STARS WHO WERE AT THE TOP OF THEIR FORM IN THE 1970's

Goalkeeper
Ray Clemence (England)
Ubaldo Fillol (Argentina)
Pat Jennings (N. Ireland)
Sepp Maier (West Germany)
Christian Piot (Belgium)
Peter Shilton (England)
Ivor Viktor (Czechoslovakia)

Right Back
Carlos Alberto (Brazil)
Manni Kaltz (West Germany)
Danny McGrain (Scotland)
Phil Neal (England)
Roberto Perfumo (Argentina)
Jan Pivarnik (Czechoslovakia)
Berti Vogts (West Germany)

Centre Back

Allan Hunter (N. Ireland)
Josip Katalinski (Yugoslavia)
Roy McFarland (England)
Anton Ondrus (Czechoslovakia)

Bruno Pezzey (Austria)
Georg Schwarzenbeck (West Germany)
Wladyslaw Zmuda (Poland)

Sweeper

Franz Beckenbauer (West Germany)
Horst Blankenburg (Holland)
Hector Chumpitaz (Peru)

Elias Figueroa (Chile)
José Pirri (Spain)
Colin Todd (England)
Marius Tresor (France)

Left Back

Ivan Buljan (Yugoslavia)
Terry Cooper (England)
Everaldo (Brazil)
Ruud Krol (Holland)

Francisco Marinho (Brazil)
Dragoslav Stepanovic (Yugoslavia)
Alberto Tarantini (Argentina)

Right Midfield

Rainer Bonhof (West Germany)
Kazimierz Deyna (Poland)
Uli Hoeness (West Germany)
Wlodzimierz Lubanski (Poland)

Marian Masny (Czechoslovakia)
Johan Neeskens (Holland)
Paul Van Himst (Belgium)

Centre Midfield

Paul Breitner (West Germany)
Clodoaldo (Brazil)
Johan Cruyff (Holland)

Jean-Marc Guillou (France)
Aarie Haan (Holland)
Branko Oblak (Yugoslavia)
Wilfried Van Moer (Belgium)

Left Midfield

Teofilo Cubillas (Peru)
Günter Netzer (West Germany)
Tibor Nyilasi (Hungary)

Martin Peters (England)
Roberto Rivelinho (Brazil)
Ivica Surjak (Yugoslavia)
Wim Van Hanagem (Holland)

Right Sided Strikers

Kenny Dalglish (Scotland)
Jürgen Grabowski (West Germany)
Jairzinho (Brazil)
Grzegorz Lato (Poland)

Francis Lee (England)
Fernando Morena (Uruguay)
Dominique Rocheteau (France)

Central Strikers
Georgio Chinaglia (Italy/ USA)

Francesco Graziani (Italy)

Martin Chivers (England)

Henning Jensen (Denmark)

Klaus Fischer (West Germany)

Hans Krankl (Austria)

Gerd Müller (West Germany)

Left Sided Strikers
George Best (N. Ireland)

Dragen Dzajic (Yugoslavia)

Roberto Bettega (Italy)

Mario Kempes (Argentina)

Oleg Blokhin (Soviet Union)

Rob Rensenbrink (Holland)

Allan Simonsen (Denmark)

In compiling any list of this description, in what is virtually a selection of the greatest players of the 1970's, the choice is purely arbitrary.

In some cases one might argue players are not listed in their best or normal position e.g. Ivan Buljan, Marius Tresor (more usually a Stopper throughout the 1970's) and Johan Cruyff whose free role in a Holland shirt was more of a deep lying Centre Forward à la Di Stefano. Is there a case for arguing that Best should have been excluded, as his most outstanding displays were during the late 1960's or that Clemence, Shilton, and Fillol had improved further with their maturing years by the 1980's? Perhaps.

6 FOOTBALLERS WHO SOUGHT THE RICHES OF BOGOTA

During 1949 and 1950 scores of good players from around the world joined the exodus to Columbia where a 'rebel' Football League paying good money had started up. The League wasn't the success that had been expected and many, like Neil Franklin, returned home, disillusioned and upset when their International careers were brought to a premature close.

1. *Alfredo Di Stefano* (Argentina)
2. *Neil Franklin* (Stoke and England)
3. *Charlie Mitten* (Manchester United)
4. *George Mountford* (Stoke City)
5. *Adolfo Pedernera*
6. *Nestor Rossi*

International Appearances

130 FOOTBALLERS, PAST AND PRESENT, WHO HAVE WON MORE THAN 50 INTERNATIONAL CAPS

Caps are as at 31st December, 1982. (70+ as in the case of Antognoni, or 58+ for Blokhin, means that total is still increasing.)

		Caps	
1.	*Jovan Acimovic*	56	Yugoslavia
2.	*Florian Albert*	74	Hungary
3.	*Ivor Allchurch*	67	Wales
4.	*Giancarlo Antognoni*	70+	Italy
5.	*Ossie Ardiles*	56	Argentina
6.	*Sadok Attouga*	109	Tunisia
7.	*Laszlo Balint*	74	Hungary
8.	*Josef Barmos*	53	Czechoslavakia
9.	*Vladimir Beara*	60	Yugoslavia
10.	*Franz Beckenbauer*	103	West Germany
11.	*Orvar Bergmark*	94	Sweden
12.	*Billy Bingham*	56	Northern Ireland
13.	*Danny Blanchflower*	56	Northern Ireland
14.	*Oleg Blokhin*	58+	Soviet Union
15.	*Rainer Bonhof*	53	West Germany
16.	*Zbigniew Boniek*	58+	Poland
17.	*René Botteron*	59+	Switzerland
18.	*Jozef Bozsik*	100	Hungary
19.	*Bernd Bransch*	72	East Germany
20.	*Fernando Bulnes*	54	Honduras
21.	*Toninho Cerezo*	64+	Brazil
22.	*Hector Chumpitaz*	127	Peru
23.	*Mario Coluna*	73	Portugal
24.	*Jürgen Croy*	93	East Germany
25.	*Teofilo Cubillas*	58	Peru
26.	*Kaz Deyna*	102	Poland

27.	'Didi'	73	Brazil
28.	Bernard Dietz	53	West Germany
29.	Dragen Djazic	60+	Yugoslavia
30.	Peter Ducke	68	East Germany
31.	Herbert Erhardt	50	West Germany
32.	Giacinto Facchetti	97	Italy
33.	Laszlo Fazekas	89+	Hungary
34.	Brian Flynn	54+	Wales
35.	Claudio Gentile	65+	Italy
36.	Johnny Giles	60	Eire
37.	Don Givens	56	Eire
38.	Francesco Graziani	62+	Italy
39.	Gyula Grosics	89	Hungary
40.	Gylmar	100	Brazil
41.	Bryan Hamilton	50	Northern Ireland
42.	Gerhard Hanappi	93	Austria
43.	Ronnie Hellström	76	Sweden
44.	Nandor Hidegkuti	68	Hungary
45.	Horst Höttges	66	West Germany
46.	Allan Hunter	53	Northern Ireland
47.	Valentin Ivanov	59	Soviet Union
48.	Jairzinho	85	Brazil
49.	Leighton James	53+	Wales
50.	Paul Janes	71	West Germany
51.	Kurt Jara	56	Austria
52.	Pat Jennings	95+	Northern Ireland
53.	Cliff Jones	59	Wales
54.	Jef Jurion	64	Belgium
55.	Manni Kaltz	69+	West Germany
56.	Sandor Kocsis	68	Hungary
57.	Ivan Kolev	76	Bulgaria
58.	Friedl Koncilia	68+	Austria
59.	Hans Krankl	65+	Austria
60.	Ruud Krol	75+	Holland
61.	Grezegorz Lato	103	Poland
62.	Ernst Lehner	65	West Germany
63.	Wlodek Lubanski	73	Poland
64.	John Mahoney	50	Wales
65.	Mick Martin	50+	Eire
66.	Sepp Maier	95	West Germany
67.	Roger Marché	62	France
68.	Marian Masny	74	Czechoslovakia

69.	Jimmy McIlroy	55	Northern Ireland
70.	Sammy McIlroy	64+	Northern Ireland
71.	Jef Mermans	56	Belgium
72.	Severino Minelli	79	Switzerland
73.	Rajko Mitic	59	Yugoslavia
74.	Gerd Müller	62	West Germany
75.	Paddy Mulligan	51	Eire
76.	Walter Nausch	70	Austria
77.	Zdenek Nehoda	88	Czechoslovakia
78.	Terry Neill	59	Northern Ireland
79.	Sammy Nelson	52+	Northern Ireland
80.	Igor Netto	56	Soviet Union
81.	Jimmy Nicholl	50+	Northern Ireland
82.	Bjorn Nordqvist	115	Sweden
83.	Tibor Nyilasi	52+	Hungary
84.	Ernst Ocwirk	62	Austria
85.	Martin O'Neill	51+	Northern Ireland
86.	'Oscar'	50+	Brazil
87.	Wolfgang Overath	81	West Germany
88.	Antonin Panenka	60	Czechoslovakia
89.	Daniel Passarella	64*	Argentina
90.	Pelé	93*	Brazil
91.	Dimitar Penev	86	Bulgaria
92.	Leighton Phillips	58	Wales
93.	Frantisek Planicka	74	Czechoslovakia
94.	Herbert Prohaska	65+	Austria
95.	Ferenc Puskas	84	Hungary
		+4	Spain
96.	Roberto Rivelinho	108	Brazil
97.	Pedro Rocha	68	Uruguay
98.	Karl-Heinz Rummenigge	61+	West Germany
99.	Karoly Sandor	75	Hungary
100.	Leonel Sanchez	104	Chile
101.	Djalma Santos	100	Brazil
102.	Nilton Santos	82	Brazil
103.	Hector Scarone	64	Uruguay
104.	Willi Schulz	66	West Germany
105.	Gaetano Scirea	57+	Italy

* FIFA recognized Pelé's total as 110 but 17 of the games were against clubs or regional sides.

106.	*Uwe Seeler*	72	West Germany
107.	*Ferenc Sipos*	77	Hungary
108.	*Ivica Surjak*	54	Yugoslavia
109.	*Thorbjorn Svenssen*	105	Norway
110.	*Andrzej Szarmach*	61	Poland
111.	*Marco Tardelli*	65+	Italy
112.	*Rod Thomas*	50	Wales
113.	*Tichy*	71	Hungary
114.	*Jozsef Toth*	50+	Hungary
115.	*Marius Tresor*	64+	France
116.	*Brian Turner*	85+	New Zealand
117.	*Willie Van Der Kerkhoff*	53	Holland
118.	*René Van Der Kerkhoff*	53	Holland
119.	*Puck Van Heel*	64	Holland
120.	*Paul Van Himst*	81	Belgium
121.	*Berti Vogts*	96	West Germany
122.	*Valeri Voronin*	55	Soviet Union
123.	*Fritz Walter*	61	West Germany
124.	*Wolfgang Weber*	53	West Germany
125.	*Lev Yashin*	74	Soviet Union
126.	*Terry Yorath*	59	Wales
127.	*Branco Zebec*	65	Yugoslavia
128.	*'Zico'*	77+	Brazil
129.	*Wladyslaw Zmuda*	80	Poland
130.	*Dino Zoff*	109+	Italy

Remarkably two of Europe's greatest ever footballers, Northern Ireland's George Best and Holland's Johan Cruyff, only played for their countries 37 and 48 times respectively.

THE 15 ENGLAND PLAYERS TO WIN MORE THAN 50 CAPS

		Caps			Caps
1.	Bobby Moore	108	8.	Kevin Keegan	63
2.	Bobby Charlton	106	9.	Ray Wilson	63
3.	Billy Wright	105	10.	Emlyn Hughes	62
4.	Tom Finney	76	11.	Ray Clemence*	60
5.	Gordon Banks	73	12.	Jimmy Greaves	57
6.	Alan Ball	72	13.	Johnny Haynes	56
7.	Martin Peters	67	14.	Stanley Matthews	54
			15.	Ray Wilkins*	53

* Still adding to the total, which is correct at 31.12.82.

THE 12 MOST CAPPED SCOTLAND INTERNATIONALS

1.	Kenny Dalglish*	89	7.	Alan Rough	51
2.	Danny McGrain	63	8.	Asa Hartford	50
3.	Denis Law	55	9.	Bobby Evans	48
4.	Billy Bremner	54	10.	John Greig	44
5.	George Young	53	11.	Archie Gemmill	43
6.	Joe Jordan	52	12.	Eric Caldow	40

8 NOMADS OF THE FOOTBALL LEAGUE

1. *Tommy Anderson* – Scottish Schoolboy International Inside Forward who spent 10 years at Watford, Bournemouth, Q.P.R., Torquay, Stockport, Doncaster, Wrexham, Barrow, Watford for a second time and Orient, before retiring aged 33.

2. *Albert Broadbent* – Prolific Outside Left with Notts County, Sheffield Wednesday, Rotherham, Doncaster, Lincoln, Doncaster again, Bradford P.A., Hartlepool and Rotherham for a second visit.

3. *Tony Coleman* – Exciting, skilled Outside Left whose only honours were a Cup Winners' Medal and a League Champions Medal. He served between 1960–75 Stoke, Tranmere, Preston, Bangor (Wales), Doncaster, Manchester City, Sheffield Wednesday, Blackpool, Durban City (S.A.), Southport and Stockport.

4. *Bobby Gould* – Goal scoring Striker chiefly in the top two

divisions, with Coventry, Arsenal, Wolves, W.B.A., Bristol City, West Ham, Wolves again, Bristol Rovers, and Hereford before going into management.

5. *Bob Hatton* – The only 'wanderer' still around. Has scored consistently for Wolves, Bolton, Northampton, Carlisle, Birmingham, Blackpool, Luton, Sheffield United and currently Cardiff, one of the few League players of today to have hit over 200 goals.

6. *Bobby Kellard* – Talented Inside Forward who paints as well as he played. He began with his home town club, Southend, in 1959 and went on to Crystal Palace, Ipswich, Portsmouth, Bristol City, Leicester, Crystal Palace once more, Portsmouth, Hereford on loan and Torquay, retiring when only 32.

7. *Frank Large* – Bustling Centre Forward from Leeds who over a 15 year span gave service to Halifax, Q.P.R., Northampton, Swindon, Carlisle, Oldham, Northampton again, Leicester, Fulham, Northampton – yet again – and Chesterfield.

8. *Laurie Sheffield* – Swansea born Centre Forward whose scoring record was most impressive. He shone for Bristol Rovers, Newport, Doncaster, Norwich, Rotherham, Oldham, Luton (earning his club promotion), Doncaster and Peterborough.

Awards and Honours

EUROPEAN PLAYER OF THE YEAR

This poll has been organised since the outset of the award by the leading soccer magazine '*France Football*'.
Around 200 Football newspapers, radio and television journalists take part in the voting.

1956	*Stanley Matthews*	Blackpool and England
1957	*Alfredo Di Stefano*	Real Madrid and Spain
1958	*Raymond Kopa*	Real Madrid and France
1959	*Afredo Di Stefano*	Real Madrid and Spain

1960	*Luis Suarez*	Barcelona and Spain
1961	*Omar Sivori*	Juventus and Italy
1962	*Josef Masopust*	Dukla Prague and Czechoslavakia
1963	*Lev Yashin*	Moscow Dynamo and Soviet Union
1964	*Denis Law*	Manchester United and Scotland
1965	*Eusebio*	Benefica and Portugal
1966	*Bobby Charlton*	Manchester United and England
1967	*Florian Albert*	Ferencvaros and Hungary
1968	*George Best*	Manchester United and Northern Ireland
1969	*Gianni Rivera*	A.C. Milan and Italy
1970	*Gerd Müller*	Bayern München and West Germany
1971	*Johan Cruyff*	Ajax Amsterdam and Holland
1972	*Franz Beckenbauer*	Bayern München and West Germany
1973	*Johan Cruyff*	Barcelona and Holland
1974	*Johan Cruyff*	Barcelona and Holland
1975	*Oleg Blokhin*	Dynamo Kiev and Soviet Union
1976	*Franz Beckenbauer*	Bayern München and West Germany
1977	*Allan Simonsen*	Borussia Mönchengladbach and Denmark
1978	*Kevin Keegan*	Hamburger S.V. and England
1979	*Kevin Keegan*	Hamburger S.V. and England
1980	*Karl-Heinz Rummenigge*	Bayern München and West Germany
1981	*Karl-Heinz Rummenigge*	Bayern München and West Germany
1982	*Paolo Rossi*	Juventus and Italy

THE 12 SOUTH AMERICAN PLAYERS OF THE YEAR

Around 136 journalists from U.S.A., Canada, Central and South America are asked by Argentinian weekly paper *El Grafico* each year to name in order of preference their 5 outstanding players from the Americas over the previous 12 months.

1.	*1971 Tostao*	– Cruzeiro and Brazil
2.	*1972 Teofilo Cubillas*	– Alianza Lima and Peru
3.	*1973 Pelé*	– Santos and Brazil
4.	*1974 Elias Figueroa*	– Internacional of Porto Alegre and Chile
5.	*1975 Elias Figueroa*	– Internacional of Porto Alegre and Chile
6.	*1976 Elias Figueroa*	– Internacional of Porto Alegre and Chile
7.	*1977 "Zico"*	– Flamengo and Brazil
8.	*1978 Mario Kempes*	– FC Valencia and Argentina
9.	*1979 Diego Maradona*	– Argentinos Juniors and Argentina
10.	*1980 Diego Maradona*	– Argentinos Juniors and Argentina
11.	*1981 Diego Maradona*	– Boca Juniors and Argentina
12.	*1982 "Zico"*	– Flamengo and Brazil

A different poll which ran in the 1950's and 1960's chose Pelé as South American player in 1960, 1964 and 1965.

13 AFRICAN PLAYERS OF THE YEAR

The Golden Trophy award run by *France Football*

1. *1970 Salif Keita*, Striker of Saint Etienne and Mali.
2. *1971 Ibrahim Sunday*, Striker of Ghana.
3. *1972 Cherif Souleymane,* of Guinea.
4. *1973 'Bwanga' Tschimen*, Centre Back of Tout-Puissant Mazembe. His elder brother, Goalkeeper *Kazadi Nwamba* of Zaire, won the Silver football.
5. *1974 Paul Moukila* of the Congo.
6. *1975 Ahmed Faras* of Morocco.
7. *1976 Roger Milla* (pronounced Millar), Striker from Tonnerrg Yaounde and Cameroon.
8. *1977 Tarak Dhiab* Midfielder of Es Tunis and Tunisia.
9. *1978. Abdul Razak*, Striker from Ghana.
10. *1979 Thomas N'Kono*, Goalkeeper, Canon and Cameroon.

11. *1980 Jean Manga-Onguene*, Centre Forward, Canon Yaounde and Cameroon.
12. *1981 Lakhdar Belloumi*, Midfielder, Mascara and Algeria.
13. *1982 Thomas N'Kono*, Goalkeeper, Espanol and Cameroon.

THE 15 GOLDEN BOOT AWARD WINNERS PLUS THE SILVER AND BRONZE RUNNERS UP

The Golden Boot is awarded each year to Europe's highest goal scorer in the League only

1. *1968*
   Eusebio   – Benfica, 42 goals, Gold
   Antal Dunai   – Ujpest Dozsa, Silver
   Bobby Lennox   – Celtic, Bronze
2. *1969*
   Petar Jekov   – Cska Sofia, 36 goals, Gold
   Georges Sideris   – Olympiakos, Silver
   Helmut Kögleberger – FK Austria, Bronze
3. *1970*
   Gerd Müller   – Bayern München, 38 goals, Gold
   Jan Devillet   – Spora Luxembourg, shared Silver
   Petar Jekov   – Cska Sofia, shared Silver
4. *1971*
   Josip Skoblar   – Olympique Marseille, 44 goals, Gold
   Salif Keita   – St. Etienne, Silver
   Georges Dedes   – Panionios, Bronze
5. *1972*
   Gerd Müller   – Bayern München, 40 goals, Gold
   Antonis Antoniadis – Panathinaikos, Silver
   Joe Harper   – Aberdeen, shared Bronze
   Francis Lee   – Manchester City, shared Bronze
   Slobodan Santrac   – OFK Belgrade, shared Bronze
6. *1973*
   Eusebio   – Benfica, 40 goals, Gold
   Gerd Müller   – Bayern München, Silver
   Petar Jekov   – Cska Sofia, Bronze
7. *1974*
   Hector Yazalde   – Sporting Lisbon, 46 goals, Gold
   Hans Krankl   – Rapid Vienna, Silver

Carlos Bianchi	– Reims, shared Bronze
Jupp Heynckes	– Borussia Mönchengladbach, shared Bronze
Gerd Müller	– Bayern München, shared Bronze

8. 1975

Dudu Georgescu	– Dinamo Bucharest, 33 goals, Gold
Hector Yazalde	– Sporting Lisbon, shared Silver
Ruud Geels	– Ajax, shared Silver
Delio Onnis	– Monaco, shared Silver

9. 1976

Sotiris Kaiafas	– Omonia Nicosia, 39 goals, Gold
Carlos Bianchi	– Reims, Silver
Peter Risi	– FC Zurich, Bronze

10. 1977

Dudu Georgescu	– Dinamo Bucharest, 47 goals, Gold
Bela Varadi	– Vasas, Silver
Ruud Geels	– Ajax, shared Bronze
Dieter Müller	– 1.F.C. Köln, shared Bronze

11. 1978

Hans Krankl	– Rapid Vienna, 41 goals, Gold
Carlos Bianchi	– Paris, St. Germain, Silver
Ruud Geels	– Ajax, Bronze

12. 1979

Kees Kist	– AZ '67 Alkmaar, 34 goals, Gold
Laszlo Fekete	– Upjest Dozsa, shared Silver
Thomas Mavros	– AEK Athens, shared Silver

13. 1980

Erwin Vandenberg	– Lierse SK, 39 goals, Gold
Laszlo Fazekas	– Upjest Dozsa, Silver
Walter Schachner	– Austria Vienna, Bronze

14. 1981

Georgi Slavkov	– Trakia Plovdiv, 31 goals, Gold
Tibor Nyilasi	– Ferencvaros, Silver
Karl-Heinz Rummenigge	– Bayern München, Bronze

15. 1982

Wim Kieft	– Ajax, 32 goals, Gold
Kees Kist	– AZ '67, shared Silver
Delio Onnis	– Tours, shared Silver

Unlike the European Footballer of the Year this competition does not disqualify non-Europeans from winning. Yazalde, Bianchi and Onnis are all Argentinians.

THE 33 RECIPIENTS OF THE FOOTBALL WRITERS ASSOCIATION 'FOOTBALLER OF THE YEAR' AWARD

1. *Stanley Matthews* (Blackpool) 1947–48 and (Stoke) 1962–63
2. *Johnny Carey* (Manchester United) 1948–49
3. *Joe Mercer* (Arsenal) 1949–50
4. *Harry Johnston* (Blackpool) 1950–51
5. *Billy Wright* (Wolves) 1951–52
6. *Nat Lofthouse* (Bolton) 1952–53
7. *Tom Finney* (Preston) 1953–54 and 1956–57
8. *Don Revie* (Manchester City) 1954–55
9. *Bert Trautmann* (Manchester City) 1955–56
10. *Danny Blanchflower* (Tottenham) 1957–58 and 1960–61
11. *Syd Owen* (Luton) 1958–59
12. *Bill Slater* (Wolves) 1959–60
13. *Jimmy Adamson* (Burnley) 1961–62
14. *Bobby Moore* (West Ham) 1963–64
15. *Bobby Collins* (Leeds) 1964–65
16. *Bobby Charlton* (Manchester United) 1965–66
17. *Jackie Charlton* (Leeds United) 1966–67
18. *George Best* (Manchester United) 1967–68
19. *Dave Mackay* (Derby County) 1968–69
20. *Tony Book* (Manchester City) 1968–69 (Shared)
21. *Billy Bremner* (Leeds United) 1969–70
22. *Frank McLintock* (Arsenal) 1970–71
23. *Gordon Banks* (Stoke City) 1971–72
24. *Pat Jennings* (Tottenham) 1972–73
25. *Ian Callaghan* (Liverpool) 1973–74
26. *Alan Mullery* (Fulham) 1974–75
27. *Kevin Keegan* (Liverpool) 1975–76
28. *Emlyn Hughes* (Liverpool) 1976–77
29. *Kenny Burns* (Nottingham Forest) 1977–78
30. *Kenny Dalglish* (Liverpool) 1978–79
31. *Terry McDermott* (Liverpool) 1979–80
32. *Frans Thijssen* (Ipswich) 1980–81
33. *Steve Perryman* (Tottenham) 1981–82

THE 16 PLAYERS HONOURED WITH SELECTION FOR THE REST OF THE WORLD AGAINST ENGLAND IN OCTOBER, 1963

To mark the centenary of the F.A.

1. *Lev Yashin* – Soviet Union
2. *Djalma Santos* – Brazil
3. *Karl-Heinz Schnellinger* – West Germany
4. *Svatopluk Pluskal* – Czechoslovakia
5. *Jan Popluhar* – Czechoslovakia
6. *Josef Masopust* – Czechoslovakia
7. *Raymond Kopa* – France
8. *Denis Law* – Scotland
9. *Alfredo Di Stefano* – Spain
10. *Eusebio* – Portugal
11. *Francisco Gento* – Spain
12. *Soskic* – Yugoslavia
13. *Eyzaguirre* – Chile
14. *Jim Baxter* – Scotland
15. *Uwe Seeler* – West Germany
16. *Ferenc Puskas* – Spain

THE 11 PLAYERS FOR ENGLAND IN THE SAME CENTENARY MATCH

1. *Gordon Banks* – Leicester
2. *Jimmy Armfield* – Blackpool
3. *Ray Wilson* – Huddersfield
4. *Gordon Milne* – Liverpool
5. *Maurice Norman* – Tottenham
6. *Bobby Moore* – West Ham
7. *Terry Paine* – Southampton
8. *Jimmy Greaves* – Tottenham
9. *Bobby Smith* – Tottenham
10. *George Eastham* – Arsenal
11. *Bobby Charlton* – Manchester United

THE 12 WEST GERMAN PLAYERS OF THE YEAR

1. *Uwe Seeler* – Hamburger S.V. 1960, 1964 and 1970
2. *Max Morlock* – 1. FC. Nürnberg 1961
3. *Karl-Heinz Schnellinger* – 1 F.C Köln 1962
4. *Hans Schafer* – 1. FC. Köln 1963
5. *Hans Tilkowski* – Borussia Dortmund 1965

6. *Franz Beckenbauer* – Bayern München 1966, 1968, 1974 and 1976
7. *Gerd Müller* – Bayern München 1967 and 1969
8. *Hans-Hubert Vogts* – Borussia Mönchengladbach 1971 and 1979
9. *Gunter Netzer* – Borussia Mönchengladbach 1972 and 1973
10. *Sepp Maier* – Bayern München 1975, 1977 and 1978
11. *Karl-Heinz Rummenigge* – Bayern München 1980 and 1981
12. *Karl-Heinz Förster* – VfB Stuttgart 1982

THE 6 KNIGHTS OF FOOTBALL

1. *Sir Stanley Rous** 1949
2. *Sir Stanley Matthews* 1965
3. *Sir Alf Ramsey* 1967
4. *Sir Matt Busby* 1968
5. *Sir Walter Winterbottom* 1978
6. *Sir Denis Fellows** 1978

* While receiving his knighthood for services to football, he is an administrator as opposed to a footballer.

THE 5 AWARDED THE FREEDOM OF THE CITY

1. *Franz Beckenbauer* – Munich
2. *Paolo Rossi* – Turin
3. *Jackie Milburn* – Newcastle
4. *Matt Busby* – Manchester
5. *Tom Finney* – Preston

40 FOOTBALLERS OR MANAGERS WHO HAVE RECEIVED AWARDS IN THE NEW YEAR OR BIRTHDAY HONOURS LIST SINCE 1946

1. *Ivor Allchurch*
2. *Alan Ball*
3. *Gordon Banks*
4. *Billy Bingham* as N.I. manager
5. *Billy Bremner*
6. *Trevor Brooking*
7. *Ian Callaghan*
8. *Bobby Charlton*
9. *Jackie Charlton* as manager
10. *Ray Clemence*
11. *Denis Compton*
12. *Jimmy Dickinson*
13. *Derek Dougan*
14. *George Eastham*

15. *Tom Finney*
16. *Ron Greenwood* as England manager
17. *Arfon Griffiths*
18. *Emlyn Hughes*
19. *Geoff Hurst*
20. *Pat Jennings*
21. *Bernard Joy*
22. *Kevin Keegan*
23. *Kevin Keelan*
24. *Danny McGrain*
25. *Frank McLintock*
26. *Joe Mercer* as manager
27. *Bobby Moore*
28. *Alan Mullery*
29. *Martin O'Neill*
30. *Terry Paine*
31. *Bob Paisley* as manager
32. *Martin Peters*
33. *Don Revie* as manager
34. *Bill Shankly* as manager
35. *Jock Stein* as manager
36. *John Toshack* as manager
37. *John Trollope*
38. *Tom Whittaker* as manager
39. *Walter Winterbottom* as manager
40. *Billy Wright*

THE 20 FOOTBALL CELEBRITIES WHO HAVE RECEIVED EAMONN'S RED BOOK AND HEARD HIS WORDS, 'TONIGHT . . . THIS IS YOUR LIFE'

Since Thames Television began to produce the programme in 1968

1. *Bobby Charlton*   26th November, 1969
2. *Joe Mercer*   25th March, 1970
3. *Bobby Moore*   6th January, 1971
4. *Sir Matt Busby*   12th May, 1971
5. *George Best*   17th November, 1971
6. *Gordon Banks*   8th March, 1972
7. *Bill Shankly*   10th January, 1973
8. *Jackie Charlton*   2nd May, 1973
9. *Derek Dougan*   16th January, 1974
10. *Don Revie*   24th April, 1974
11. *Denis Law*   19th February, 1975
12. *Alan Mullery*   24th March, 1976
13. *Bob Paisley*   28th December, 1977
14. *Kevin Keegan*   14th February, 1979
15. *Emlyn Hughes*   27th February, 1980
16. *Lawrie McMenemy*   29th October, 1980

17. *Ian Botham**	4th November, 1981	
18. *John Toshack*	17th February, 1982	
19. *Jackie Milburn*	9th December, 1982	
20. *Kenny Dalglish*	16th February, 1983	

* Obviously he was the subject of the programme for his cricketing achievements, but nonetheless he had played League Soccer.

Thanks go to Melanie Schofield and Thames Television for help in preparing the above list.

Alternative Careers

50 FOOTBALLERS' PREVIOUS JOBS

1. *Steve Archibald*	Clyde, Aberdeen, Tottenham and Scotland	Motor Mechanic
2. *Gerry Armstrong*	Bangor, Tottenham, Watford and Northern Ireland	Local Government Worker
3. *Jim Arnold*	Blackburn and Everton	Local Government Officer
4. *Rainer Bonhof*	1. FC. Köln, Valencia, Borussia Mönchengladbach, Hertha Berlin and West Germany	Mechanic
5. *Roger Brown*	Bournemouth, Norwich and Fulham	Production Engineer
6. *Micky Burns*	Blackpool, Newcastle, Cardiff and Middlesbrough	Teacher
7. *Willie Carlin*	8 clubs inc. Carlisle, Sheffield United and Leicester	Apprentice Electrician
8. *Keith Cassells*	Watford, Oxford, Southampton and Brentford	Postman
9. *Sandy Clark*	Aidrie, Wt Ham	Officer Manager in Finance Company
10. *Davie Cooper*	Clydebank, Rangers and Scotland	Printer

11. *Bob Crompton*	Blackburn Trinity, Blackburn Rovers and England	Plumber
12. *Sammy Crooks*	Derby County and England	Miner
13. *Terry Curran*	6 clubs inc. Nottingham Forest, Derby and the Sheffield clubs	Paint Sprayer
14. *Peter Daniel*	Hull, Wolves and England Under 21.	Painter and Decorator
15. *Gordon Davies*	Fulham and Wales	P.E. Teacher
16. *Alan Devonshire*	West Ham and England	Storeman/Fork Lift Truck Operator
17. *Kerry Dixon*	Tottenham and Reading	Tool Maker
18. *Justin Fashanu*	Norwich, Nottingham Forest, Notts County and England Under 21	Steel Erector
19. *Tom Finney*	Preston and England	Plumber
20. *Tony Galvin*	Tottenham and Eire	Student Teacher
21. *Rodney Green*	8 clubs inc. the Bradford clubs, Grimsby and Watford	Insurance Worker
22. *John Gregory*	Northampton, Aston Villa, Brighton and Queens Park Rangers	Laboratory Technician
23. *Ashley Grimes*	Manchester United and Eire	Perfume Rep.
24. *Billy Hamilton*	Queens Park Rangers, Burnley and Northern Ireland	Student Teacher
25. *Paul Hegarty*	Hamilton, Dundee United and Scotland.	Insurance Officer
26. *Paul Hince*	Manchester City, Charlton, Bury and Crewe	Journalist
27. *Colin Irwin*	Liverpool and Swansea	Apprentice Electrician
28. *Mick Lambert*	Ipswich and Peterborough	Member of Lord's ground staff
29. *Paul Mariner*	Plymouth, Ipswich and England	Fitter
30. *Ally McCoist*	St. Johnstone and Sunderland	Civil Servant
31. *Ian McCulloch*	Kilmarnock, Notts County and Scotland Under 21	Central Heating Engineer
32. *Gordon McQueen*	St. Mirren, Leeds, Manchester United and Scotland	Chrysler Worker

60

33.	*Kevin Moran*	Manchester United and Eire	Accountant
34.	*Arnold Mühren*	Ajax, Twente Enschede, Ipswich, Manchester United and Holland	Office Worker in family furniture business
35.	*Iain Munro*	Hibernian, Rangers, St. Mirren, Sunderland and Scotland	P.E. Teacher
36.	*Neil Orr*	Morton, West Ham and Scotland Under 21	Green Keeper and Safety Officer
37.	*Phil Parkes*	Walsall, Queens Park Rangers, West Ham and England	Carpenter
38.	*Stuart Pearson*	Hull, Manchester United, West Ham and England	Yorkshire Electricity Board Worker
39.	*Cyrille Regis*	West Brom. and England	Apprentice Electrician
40.	*Graham Roberts*	Southampton, Portsmouth and Tottenham	Fitter's Mate
41.	*Wynton Rufer*	New Zealand	Trainee Shipping Manager
42.	*Rolf Russmann*	Schalke 04, F.C. Bruges, B. Dortmund and West Germany	Bank Clerk
43.	*Peter Shaw*	Charlton and Gillingham	Computer Programmer
44.	*Alan Spence*	Sunderland, Darlington, Southport, Oldham and Chester	Teacher
45.	*Brian Stein*	Luton and England	N.H.S. clerk
46.	*Kenny Swain*	Chelsea, Aston Villa and Nottingham Forest	P.E. Teacher
47.	*Billy Thomson*	Partick Thistle, St. Mirren and Scotland	Apprentice Motor Mechanic
48.	*Toine van Mierlo*	PSV Eindhoven, Willem II Tilburg, Birmingham and Holland	Teacher
49.	*Peter Weir*	St. Mirren, Aberdeen and Scotland	Assistant Green Keeper
50.	*George Wood*	East Stirling, Blackpool, Everton, Arsenal and Scotland	Apprentice Stonemason

8 FOOTBALLERS WITH ANOTHER CAREER – SIMULTANEOUSLY

1. *Andrew Amos*	Old Carthusians, Hitchin, Corinthians and England	Minister in S.E. London
2. *Wally Ardron*	Rotherham United and Nottingham Forest	Railway Worker
3. *John Brockbank*	No professional clubs – Capped while at Trinity College, Cambridge	Professional Actor
4. *Colin Grainger*	6 clubs inc. Sheffield United, Sunderland, Leeds and England	Semi-professional Singer
5. *Ken Hegan*	Corinthians and England	Army Officer – rose to Lt. Col.
6. *Lance Robson*	Newcastle, Darlington and Hartlepool	Dental Surgeon
7. *Andy Stratford*	Northampton Town	Plumber
8. *George Wilson*	Corinthians, Casuals, Southampton and England	Student Physician and Surgeon

36 FOOTBALLERS 'SECOND CAREERS'

1. *R. D. Anderson*	Old Etonians and England	Orange Planter in Florida
2. *C. T. Ashton*	Corinthians and England	Chartered Accountant – Later on the Stock Exchange
3. *Jeff Astle*	Notts County, West Brom. and England	Owns Industrial Cleaning Business
4. *Jimmy Armfield*	Blackpool and England	Journalist
5. *Johnny Atyeo*	Bristol City and England	Teacher
6. *Norman Bailey*	Clapham Rovers, Corinthians, Wanderers and England	Solicitor
7. *John Bain*	Oxford University	Master of Marlborough College and Barrister
8. *Danny Blanchflower*	Glentoran, Barnsley, Aston Villa, Tottenham and Northern Ireland	Journalist

9. *Warren Bradley*	Manchester United, Bury and England	Schoolteacher – Headmaster of Manchester Comprehensive from early 1970's.
10. *Ivor Broadis*	Carlisle, P/M Sunderland, Manchester City, Newcastle Queen of the South, England	Journalist
11. *Johnny Brooks*	Reading, Tottenham, Chelsea, Brentford, C. Palace and England	Exchange broker's messenger
12. *Willie Carlin*	8 clubs inc. Halifax, Derby and Notts County	Owns newsagents and bakery
13. *Bobby Charlton*	Manchester United, Preston and England	Travel Agent
14. *A. G. Doggart*	Corinthians, Darlington and England	Chartered Accountant
15. *Jimmy Dugdale*	W.B.A., Aston Villa, Q.P.R., and England	Moseley Rugby Club Steward
16. *Micky Dulin*	Tottenham	Waltham Forest Recreation Officer
17. *Mal Finlayson*	Millwall and Wolves	R. & F. Stockholders Ltd. (his own business)
18. *Ron Flowers*	Wolves, Northampton and England	Owns a sports outfitting business
19. *Harry Goodhart*	Old Etonians and England	Edinburgh University Professor
20. *Arfon Griffiths*	Wrexham (Twice), Arsenal and Wales	Own newsagents business
21. *Mick Jones*	Sheffield United, Leeds and England	Sportswear Rep.
22. *Francis Lee*	Bolton, Manchester City, Derby and England	Owns paper mill business
23. *Paul Madeley*	Leeds United and England	Runs his own building business
24. *David Payne*	Crystal Palace and Orient	Metropolitan Police
25. *Jimmy Pearce*	Tottenham Hotspur	Distribution Manager for clothing company
26. *Laurie Scott*	Bradford City, Arsenal, C. Palace and England	Sales Rep. for GK Group (Tools)
27. *Jim Standen*	5 clubs inc. Luton and West Ham	Product Consultant for 'Le Sport'

28. *Ian Storey-Moore*	Nottingham Forest, Manchester United and England	Bookmaker
29. *Peter Thompson*	Preston, Liverpool, Bolton and England	Owns and runs caravan site
30. *Frank Upton*	5 clubs inc. Derby, Chelsea and Notts County	Soccer Coach for Repton Public School
31. *Dave Walsh*	W.B.A. Aston Villa, Walsall and Eire	Sports Outfitter
32. *Herbert Whitfield*	Old Etonians and England	He became a Director of Barclays Bank
33. *Bert Williams*	Walsall, Wolves and England	Sports Outfitter and Factory Owner
34. *Maxwell Woosnam*	Chelsea, Corinthians, Manchester City and England	Personnel Manager, I.C.I.
35. *Neil Young*	Manchester City, Preston, Rochdale	Sports Shop Owner

14 UNIVERSITY EDUCATED PLAYERS OF RECENT YEARS

Player	*Degree*	*University*
1. *Osvaldo Ardiles*	Law	Cordoba (Argentina)
2. *Gary Bailey*	B.Sc in Physics	Witts (S. Africa)
3. *Steve Coppell*	Econ.	Liverpool
4. *Tony Galvin*	Russian	Hull
5. *Alan Gowling*	Econ.	Manchester
6. *Brian Hall*	Science	Liverpool
7. *Steve Heighway*	Econ.	Warwick
8. *John Lacy*	Econ.	London
9. *Tony Mitchell*	B.Sc.	Exeter
10. *Phil Neale*	Russian	Leeds
11. *Paul Power*	Law	Manchester
12. *Keith Sanderson* (ex. Q.P.R.)	B.A.	Cambridge
13. *Bill Slater*	B.A.	Leeds
14. *Gordon Taylor*	Econ.	Manchester

8 T.V. PERSONALITIES FROM THE SOCCER FIELD

1. *Derek Dougan*
2. *Jimmy Greaves*
3. *Jimmy Hill*
4. *David Icke*

5. *Ian St. John*
6. *Denis Law*
7. *Bob Wilson*
8. *Billy Wright*

7 INTERNATIONAL FOOTBALLERS WHO ENTERED POLITICS

1. *Jozef Bozsik* Member of the House of Deputies 1960's and 1970's in Hungary.
2. *Sir William Bromley-Davenport* Macclesfield M.P. 1886–1906.
3. *William Kenyon-Slaney* M.P. for Newport for 22 years until his death in 1908.
4. *The Hon. Alfred Lyttelton* M.P. for Leamington (1895–1906) and St Georges, Hanover Square (1906–13).
5. *John F. Rawlinson* M.P. for Cambridge 1906–26.
6. *Toninho Cerezo* Social Democrat Councillor for the state of Minas Gerais in Belo Horizonte. Elected in early 1983.
7. *Wilson Piazza* Member of the Brazilian Parliament since the late 1970's.

Black Power

Considering that only 25 years ago there were rarely more than one or two black players in the Football League at any one time, and as little as 10 years ago, fewer than 10 First Division 'Coloureds', the sudden emergence of a flock of black England Internationals in the late 70's and early 80's is amazing. The increasingly important role that blacks will play on the international scene proves just how welcome their development has been.

ENGLAND INTERNATIONALS

1. *Laurie Cunningham* – W.B.A., Real Madrid and England
2. *Chris Whyte* – Arsenal and England Under 21
3. *Paul Davis* – Arsenal and England Under 21
4. *Mark Walters* – Aston Villa and England Youth and Under 21
5. *Danny Thomas* – Coventry and England Under 21
6. *Garry Thompson* – Coventry and England Under 21
7. *David Barnes* – Coventry, Ipswich and England Youth
8. *Ricky Hill* – Luton and England
9. *Remi Moses* – W.B.A., Manchester United and England Under 21
10. *Viv Anderson* – Nottingham Forest and England
11. *Justin Fashanu* – Norwich, Nottingham Forest, Notts County and England Under 21
12. *Danny Wallace* – Southampton and England Youth
13. *Mark Chamberlain* – Port Vale, Stoke City and England
14. *Garth Crooks* – Stoke, Tottenham and England Under 21
15. *Luther Blissett* – Watford and England
16. *John Barnes* – Watford and England Under 21
17. *Cyrille Regis* – W.B.A and England
18. *Bobby Barnes* – West Ham and England Youth
19. *Vince Hilaire* – Crystal Palace and England Under 21
20. *Terry Connor* – Leeds and England Youth and Under 21
21. *Bob Hazell* – Wolves, Q.P.R. and England Under 21
22. *Ian Benjamin* – Sheffield United, W.B.A. and England Youth

11 CURRENT LEAGUE PLAYERS
FROM NON-LEAGUE CIRCLES

	First League Club	Non-League side
1. *John Barnes*	– Watford	Parks football
2. *Paul Canoville*	– Chelsea	Hillingdon Borough
3. *Tony Cunningham*	– Lincoln (now Barnsley)	Stourbridge
4. *Errington Kelly*	– Bristol Rovers	Ledbury Town
5. *Trevor Lee*	– Millwall (now Bournemouth)	Epsom and Ewell
6. *Alan Paris*	– Watford	Slough

7. *Cyrille Regis*	– W.B.A.	Hayes
8. *Brian Stein*	– Luton	Edgware
9. *Phil Walker*	– Millwall (now Charlton)	Epsom and Ewell
10. *Keith Walwyn*	– Chesterfield (now York)	Winterton
11. *Eric Young*	– Brighton	Slough

12 PAIRS OF BLOOD BROTHERS

1. *Chris Ampofo*	West Ham	*Greg*	West Ham
2. *Tristan Benjamin*	Notts County	*Ian*	Peterborough
3. *David Bennett*	Cardiff City	*Gary*	Cardiff City
4. *Neville Chamberlain*	Stoke	*Mark*	Stoke
5. *John Charles**	West Ham	*Clive°*	West Ham and Cardiff
6. *Justin Fashanu*	Notts County	*John*	Norwich
7. *Vince Hilaire*	Crystal Palace	*John°*	Millwall
8. *Chris Hughton*	Tottenham	*Henry*	Crystal Palace
9. *Tony La Ronde°*	West Ham	*Everald*	West Ham
10. *Garry Thompson*	W.B.A.	*Keith*	Coventry
11. *Valmore Thomas°*	Coventry and Hereford	*Danny*	Coventry
12. *Brian Stein*	Luton	*Eddie*	Barnet (A.P.L.)

* Now retired.   ° No longer in League Football.

5 GERMAN/DUTCH – INTERNATIONALS.

1. *Rigobert Gruber* – Werder Bremen and West Germany 'B'
2. *Ruud Gulitt* – Feyenoord and Holland
3. *'Jimmy' Hartwig* – Hamburger S.V. and West Germany
4. *Erwin Kostedde* – Ex Standard Liege, Werder Bremen and West Germany
5. *Frank Rijkaard* – Ajax and Holland

Born and Bred

29 COUNTY OR CITY TEAMS
Selected from Players born in that County/City

Unlike the Yorkshire county cricket team, football clubs have never restricted themselves to signing players from their own immediate areas. However, had it ever been the case that transfers were not allowed and clubs could only use footballers from their own county, then some of the game's leading clubs would not have ruled the roost, and there may have been closer competition.

The following imaginary teams have been selected from the English Football League in the post-war period.

ABERDEEN

1. *Adam Blacklaw* Burnley, Blackburn, Blackpool and Scotland
2. *Andy Beattie* Preston and Scotland
3. *Bobby McDonald* Aston Villa, Coventry and Manchester City
4. *John Fitzpatrick* Manchester United
5. *Ron Yeats* Dundee United, Liverpool, Tranmere and Scotland
6. *Martin Buchan* Aberdeen, Manchester United and Scotland
7. *Graham Leggat* Aberdeen, Fulham, Birmingham City, Rotherham and Scotland
8. *Lou Macari* Celtic, Manchester United and Scotland
9. *Alex Dawson* Manchester United, Preston, Bury and Brighton
10. *Denis Law* Huddersfield, Manchester City, Torino, Manchester United and Scotland
11. *Dally Duncan* Aberdeen, Hull, Derby County, Luton and Scotland

Reserves

Ian Black Aberdeen, Southampton, Fulham and Scotland
Doug Fraser Aberdeen, West Bromwich Albion, Nottingham
Forest, Walsall, and Scotland
John Sjoberg Leicester City and Rotherham
Ian Wilson Aberdeen, Elgin City and Leicester City
Ian Moir Aberdeen, Manchester United, Blackpool, Chester,
Wrexham and Shrewsbury

BELFAST

1. *Ronnie Briggs* Manchester United, Swansea City, Bristol
Rovers and Northern Ireland
2. *Pat Rice* Arsenal, Watford and Northern Ireland
3. *Mal Donaghy* Larne, Luton and Northern Ireland
4. *Danny Blanchflower* Glentoran, Barnsley, Aston Villa,
Tottenham and Northern Ireland
5. *Jackie Blanchflower* Manchester United and Northern
Ireland
6. *Terry Neill* Arsenal, Hull and Northern Ireland
7. *Billy Bingham* Glentoran, Sunderland, Luton, Everton,.
Port Vale and Northern Ireland
8. *Gerry Armstrong* Bangor, Tottenham, Watford and
Northern Ireland
9. *Derek Dougan* Portsmouth, Blackburn, Aston Villa,
Peterborough, Leicester City, Wolves and Northern Ireland
10. *Sammy McIlroy* Manchester United, Stoke and Northern
Ireland
11. *George Best* Manchester United, Stockport County,
Fulham and Northern Ireland

Reserves

Hugh Kelly Belfast Celtic, Fulham, Southampton, Exeter City
and Northern Ireland
Sammy Nelson Arsenal, Brighton and Northern Ireland
Jack Vernon Belfast Celtic, West Bromwich Albion and
Northern Ireland
Jimmy Nicholson Manchester United, Huddersfield, Bury and
Northern Ireland
Bobby Campbell Aston Villa, Halifax, Huddersfield, Sheffield
United, Bradford City and Northern Ireland.

BRISTOL

1. *Nicky Johns* Millwall, Sheffield United and Charlton
2. *Harry Bamford* Bristol Rovers
3. *Jack Bailey* Bristol City
4. *Larry Lloyd* Bristol Rovers, Liverpool, Coventry City, Nottingham Forest, Wigan and England
5. *Gary Collier* Bristol City and Coventry City
6. *Gary Mabbutt* Bristol Rovers, Tottenham Hotspur and England
7. *Dave Burnside* West Bromwich Albion, Southampton, Crystal Palace, Wolves, Plymouth, Bristol City and Colchester
8. *Johnny Atyeo* Portsmouth, Bristol City and England
9. *Alf Biggs* Bristol Rovers, Preston, Walsall, and Swansea City
10. *Geoff Bradford* Bristol Rovers and England
11. *Roy Bentley* Bristol City, Newcastle, Chelsea, Fulham, Queens Park Rangers and England

Reserves

Dick Sheppard West Bromwich Albion, Bristol Rovers and Torquay
Phil Taylor Liverpool and England
Kevin Mabbutt Bristol City and Crystal Palace
Arthur Milton Arsenal, Bristol City and England
Ronnie Dix Tottenham and Reading

CARDIFF AND NEWPORT

1. *Graham Vearncombe* Cardiff City and Wales
2. *Peter Rodrigues* Cardiff City, Leicester, Sheffield Wednesday, Southampton and Wales
3. *Neil Slatter* Bristol Rovers
4. *Terry Yorath* Leeds United, Coventry City and Wales
5. *Derek Sullivan* Cardiff City, Exeter City, Newport County and Wales
6. *Peter Nicholas* Crystal Palace, Arsenal and Wales
7. *Gil Reece* Cardiff City, Newport County, Sheffield United, Swansea City and Wales
8. *John Mahoney* Crewe Alexander, Stoke City, Middlesbrough, Swansea City and Wales

9. *John Toshack* Cardiff City, Liverpool, Swansea City and Wales
10. *David Williams* Bristol Rovers
11. *Roy Clarke* Cardiff City, Manchester City, Stockport County and Wales

Reserves

Len Weare Newport County
Ron Stitfall Cardiff City and Wales
Colin Baker Cardiff City and Wales
Nigel Vaughan Newport County
Keith Pring Newport County, Rotherham, Notts County, Southport and Wales
Stan Richards Cardiff City, Swansea City and Wales
Mark Aizlewood Newport County, Luton, Charlton and Wales

CLEVELAND

1. *Johnny Bollands* Oldham, Sunderland and Bolton Wanderers
2. *Jack Howe* (QV) Derby County, Huddersfield and England
3. *George Hardwick* Middlesbrough, Oldham and England
4. *Peter Murphy* Coventry City, Tottenham and Birmingham
5. *Willie Maddren* Middlesbrough
6. *Mick McNeil* Middlesbrough, Ipswich and England
7. *Brian Clough* Middlesbrough, Sunderland and England
8. *Wilf Mannion* Middlesbrough, Hull City and England
9. *Micky Fenton* Middlesbrough and England
10. *Don Revie* Leicester, Hull City, Manchester City, Sunderland, Leeds United and England
11. *Colin Dobson* Sheffield Wednesday, Huddersfield, Brighton, Bristol Rovers and England

Reserves

Bob Wesson Coventry City, Walsall and Doncaster
Stan Rickaby Middlesbrough, West Bromwich Albion and England
Andy Linighan Hartlepool
Dennis Thwaites Birmingham City
Alan Peacock Middlesbrough, Leeds United, Plymouth and England

71

CUMBRIA

1. *John Burridge* Workington, Blackpool, Aston Villa, Southend, Crystal Palace and Queens Park Rangers
2. *Gary Stevens* Everton
3. *Emlyn Hughes* Blackpool, Liverpool, Wolves, Rotherham and England
4. *Keith Eddy* Barrow, Watford and Sheffield United
5. *Ron Suart* Blackpool and Blackburn
6. *Kevin Beattie* Ipswich, Colchester, Middlesbrough and England
7. *David Geddis* Ipswich, Luton and Aston Villa
8. *Jackie Sewell* Notts County, Sheffield Wednesday, Aston Villa, Hull City and England
9. *Davy Dunmore* York City, Tottenham, West Ham, and Orient
10. *Charlie Woods* Newcastle, Bournemouth, Crystal Palace, Ipswich, Watford, Colchester and Blackburn
11. *Peter Thompson* Preston, Liverpool, Bolton Wanderers and England

Reserves

John Simpson Lincoln City and Gillingham
Geoff Twentyman Carlisle and Liverpool
Ron Simpson Huddersfield, Sheffield United and Carlisle
Glen Skivington Derby County
Vic Metcalfe Huddersfield, Hull City and England

DERBYSHIRE

1. *Bob Wilson* Arsenal and Scotland
2. *Eddie Shimwell* Sheffield United, Blackpool, Oldham and England
3. *Ray Wilson* Huddersfield, Everton, Oldham, Bradford City and England
4. *Jack Parry* Derby County
5. *Ray Young* Derby County
6. *Russell Osman* Ipswich and England
7. *Peter Ward* Brighton, Nottingham Forest and England
8. *Ray Parry* Bolton Wanderers, Blackpool, Bury and England
9. *Ian Hutchinson* Chelsea

10. *Jimmy Hagan* Sheffield United and England
11. *John Tudor* Coventry City, Sheffield United, Newcastle and Stoke City

Reserves

Alan Stevenson Chesterfield and Burnley
Geoff Thomas Nottingham Forest
Steve Powell Derby County
Geoff Barrowcliffe Derby County
Tony Hateley Notts County, Chelsea, Liverpool, Coventry City, Aston Villa, Birmingham City and Oldham

DEVON, CORNWALL, SOMERSET AND AVON

1. *Kim Book* Bournemouth, Northampton, Mansfield and Doncaster
2. *Pat Jones* Plymouth
3. *Colin Gibson* Aston Villa
4. *Bert Head* Torquay and Bury
5. *Norman Piper* Plymouth and Portsmouth
6. *Maurice Setters* Exeter City, West Bromwich Albion, Manchester United, Stoke City, Coventry City and Charlton
7. *Mike Trebilcock* Plymouth, Everton, Portsmouth and Torquay
8. *Colin Addison* York City, Nottingham Forest, Arsenal, Sheffield United and Hereford
9. *Trevor Francis* Birmingham City, Nottingham Forest and England
10. *Don Rogers* Swindon, Crystal Palace, Queens Park Rangers
11. *Cliff Bastin* Arsenal and England

Reserves

Larry Taylor Bristol Rovers
Alan Skirton Arsenal, Blackpool, Bristol City and Torquay
Tony Book Plymouth Argyle and Manchester City

DUBLIN

1. *Alan Kelly* Drumcondra, Preston and Eire
2. *Joe Kinnear* Tottenham, Brighton and Eire
3. *Johnny Carey* Manchester United and Northern Ireland and Eire

4. *Johnny Giles* Manchester United, Leeds United, West Bromwich Albion and Eire
  5. *Con Martin* Glentoran, Leeds United, Aston Villa and Northern Ireland and Eire
  6. *Kevin Moran* Manchester United and Eire
  7. *Ray Treacy* West Bromwich Albion, Charlton, Swindon, Preston, Oldham and Eire
  8. *Bill Whelan* Manchester United and Eire
  9. *Frank Stapleton* Arsenal, Manchester United and Eire
10. *Liam Brady* Arsenal, Juventus, Sampdoria and Eire
11. *Tom Eglington* Shamrock Rovers, Everton, Tranmere, Northern Ireland and Eire

Reserves

Jim O'Neill Everton, Stoke, Darlington, Port Vale and Eire
Tony Dunne Manchester United, Bolton Wanderers and Eire
Mick McGrath Home Farm, Blackburn, Bradford P.A. and Eire
Peter Farrell Shamrock Rovers, Everton, Tranmere, Northern Ireland and Eire
Ron Whelan Home Farm, Liverpool and Eire
Eamon Dunphy Manchester United, York City, Millwall, Charlton, Shamrock Rovers, Reading and Eire
Steve Heighway Liverpool and Eire

DUNDEE

  1. *Bill Brown* Tottenham, Northampton and Scotland
  2. *Ewan Fenton* Blackpool and Wrexham
  3. *Ian Phillip* Dundee, Crystal Palace and Dundee United
  4. *Alex Forbes* Sheffield United, Arsenal, Orient, Fulham and Scotland
  5. *Frank Munro* Wolves and Scotland
  6. *Jimmy Gabriel* Everton, Southampton, Bournemouth, Brentford and Scotland
  7. *Peter Lorimer* Leeds United, York City and Scotland
  8. *Ian Britton* Chelsea and Dundee
  9. *Alex Bruce* Preston and Newcastle
10. *Jackie Mudie* Blackpool, Stoke City, Port Vale and Scotland
11. *Jim McEwan* Aston Villa and Walsall

Alex 'Sandy' Davie Dundee, Luton and Southampton
Tom McAnearney Dundee, Sheffield Wednesday,
Peterborough and Aldershot
Jim McAnearney Sheffield Wednesday, Plymouth, Watford and
Bradford City

DURHAM

1. *Jeff Wealands* Wolves, Darlington, Hull City and
Birmingham City
2. *John Robson* Derby County and Aston Villa
3. *Tom Garrett* Blackpool, Millwall and England
4. *Bobby Robson* Fulham, West Bromwich Albion and
England
5. *Bill Dodgin* Fulham, Arsenal and Millwall
6. *Colin Todd* Sunderland, Derby County, Everton,
Birmingham, Nottingham Forest and England
7. *Alan Suddick* Newcastle, Blackpool, Stoke City and Bury
8. *Colin Bell* Bury, Manchester City and England
9. *Sammy Crooks* Derby County and England
10. *Gordon Cowans* Aston Villa and England
11. *Bryan Robson* Newcastle, West Ham, Sunderland, Carlisle
and Chelsea

Reserves

George Tweedy Grimsby and England
Bobby Cowell Newcastle
Laurie Brown Darlington, Northampton, Arsenal, Tottenham,
Norwich City and Bradford P.A.
Stan Anderson Sunderland, Newcastle, Middlesbrough and
England
Jimmy Adamson Burnley
Charlie Wayman Newcastle, Southampton, Preston,
Middlesbrough and Darlington
Billy Gray Orient, Chelsea, Burnley, Nottingham Forest,
Millwall and England 'B'

EDINBURGH

1. *Tommy Younger* Liverpool, Stoke City, Leeds United and
Scotland

2. *Charlie Aitken* Aston Villa
3. *Arthur Albiston* Manchester United and Scotland
4. *Graham Souness* Tottenham, Middlesbrough, Liverpool and Scotland
5. *Billy Baxter* Ipswich, Hull City, Watford and Northampton
6. *Willie Young* Tottenham, Arsenal and Nottingham Forest
7. *Peter Marinello* Hibs, Arsenal, Portsmouth, Motherwell, Fulham and Hearts
8. *Jimmy Logie* Arsenal and Scotland
9. *Ralph Brand* Manchester City, Sunderland and Scotland
10. *Dave Mackay* Tottenham, Derby County, Swindon and Scotland
11. *Eamon Bannon* Hearts, Chelsea, Dundee United and Scotland

Reserves

Harry Thomson Burnley, Blackpool and Barrow
Peter Cormack Hibernian, Nottingham Forest, Liverpool, Bristol City and Scotland
Duncan Forbes Colchester, Norwich City and Torquay

GLASGOW

1. *Dick Beattie* Glasgow Celtic, Portsmouth, Peterborough
2. *Eddie McCreadie* E. Stirling, Chelsea and Scotland
3. *Tommy Gemmell* Glasgow Celtic, Nottingham Forest and Scotland
4. *Bobby Collins* Glasgow Celtic, Everton, Leeds United, Bury, Oldham and Scotland
5. *Kenny Burns* Birmingham City, Nottingham Forest, Leeds and Scotland
6. *Tommy Docherty* Glasgow Celtic, Preston, Arsenal, Chelsea and Scotland
7. *Jimmy Johnstone* Glasgow Celtic, Sheffield United and Scotland
8. *Steve Archibald* Clyde, Aberdeen, Tottenham and Scotland
9. *Kenny Dalglish* Glasgow Celtic, Liverpool and Scotland
10. *Jim Baxter* Glasgow Rangers, Sunderland, Nottingham Forest and Scotland
11. *Willie Johnston* Glasgow Rangers, West Bromwich Albion, Birmingham City, Hearts and Scotland

Reserves

Charlie Wright Glasgow Rangers, Workington, Grimsby, Charlton and Bolton Wanderers
Frank Gray Leeds United, Nottingham Forest and Scotland
Eddie Gray Leeds United and Scotland
Bobby Mitchell T. Lanark, Newcastle and Scotland
Tommy Ring Clyde, Everton, Barnsley and Scotland

GREATER MANCHESTER EXCLUDING THE CITY OF MANCHESTER

1. *Eddie Hopkinson* Oldham, Bolton Wanderers and England
2. *Stan Lynn* Accrington, Aston Villa and Birmingham City
3. *Tommy Banks* Bolton Wanderers and England
4. *Eddie Colman* Manchester United
5. *Roy Gratrix* Blackpool, Manchester City and England 'B'
6. *Henry Cockburn* Manchester United, Bury and England
7. *Francis Lee* Bolton Wanderers, Manchester City, Derby County and England
8. *Tony Brown* West Bromwich Albion, Torquay United and England
9. *Nat Lofthouse* Bolton Wanderers and England
10. *Alan Ball* Blackpool, Everton, Arsenal, Southampton, Bristol Rovers and England
11. *Tommy Lawton* Chelsea, Notts County, Brentford, Arsenal and England

Reserves

Colin McDonald Burnley and England
Don Megson Sheffield Wednesday and Bristol Rovers
Joe Hayes Manchester City, Barnsley and England
Stan Pearson Manchester United, Bury, Chester and England
Eddie Quigley Bury, Sheffield Wednesday, Preston, Blackburn and England 'B'
John Morris Manchester United, Derby County, Leicester City and England
Warren Bradley Manchester United, Bury and England

HANTS, DORSET, WILTS AND OXON

1. *Sam Burton* Swindon
2. *Phil Gunter* Portsmouth and Aldershot
3. *John Trollope* Swindon
4. *Graham Baker* Southampton and Manchester City
5. *Graham Roberts* Tottenham
6. *Ray Barlow* West Bromwich Albion, Birmingham City and England
7. *Mick Channon* Southampton, Manchester City, Newcastle, Bristol Rovers, Norwich and England
8. *Martin Chivers* Southampton, Tottenham, Norwich City, Brighton and England
9. *Ray Crawford* Portsmouth, Ipswich, Wolves, West Bromwich Albion, Charlton, Colchester and England
10. *Terry Paine* Southampton, Hereford and England
11. *David Moss* Swindon and Luton

Reserves

Andy Gosney Portsmouth
Peter Sillett Southampton, Chelsea and England
John Mortimore Chelsea, Queens Park Rangers and Sunderland
Peter Harris Portsmouth and England
Ernie Hunt Swindon, Wolves, Everton, Coventry City and Bristol City
Cliff Holton Arsenal, Watford, Northampton, Crystal Palace, Charlton, and Orient
John Sydenham Southampton and Aldershot

HUMBERSIDE AND N/YORKSHIRE

1. *Ray Clemence* Scunthorpe, Liverpool, Tottenham and England
2. *Jeff Hall* Birmingham City and England
3. *Joe Shaw* Sheffield United
4. *Bill Nicholson* Tottenham and England
5. *Tony Emery* Lincoln City and Mansfield
6. *Ron Flowers* Wolves, Northampton and England
7. *Terry Dyson* Tottenham, Fulham and Colchester
8. *David Mills* Middlesbrough, West Bromwich Albion, Sheffield Wednesday
9. *Bobby Smith* Chelsea, Tottenham, Brighton and England

10. *Derek Kevan* Bradford P.A., West Bromwich Albion, Chelsea, Manchester City, Crystal Palace, Peterborough, Luton, Stockport County and England
11. *Duncan McKenzie* Nottingham Forest, Leeds United, Everton, Chelsea and Blackburn

Reserves

Mark Wallington Walsall and Leicester City
Stuart Gray Nottingham Forest
Peter Daniel Hull City and Wolves
Peter Skipper Hull City, Scunthorpe and Darlington
Stuart Pearson Hull City, Manchester United, West Ham and England
Chris Chilton Hull City and Coventry City
Colin Appleton Leicester, Charlton and Barrow

LANCASHIRE

1. *Frank Swift* Manchester City and England
2. *Jimmy Armfield* Blackpool and England
3. *Bill Slater* Blackpool, Brentford, Wolves and England
4. *Ronnie Clayton* Blackburn and England
5. *Martin Dobson* Bolton, Burnley, Everton and England
6. *Mark Lawrenson* Preston, Brighton, Liverpool and Eire
7. *Bryan Douglas* Blackburn and England
8. *George Eastham* Ards, Newcastle, Arsenal, Stoke and England
9. *Freddie Pickering* Blackburn, Everton, Birmingham City, Blackpool, Brighton and England
10. *Eddie Brown* Preston, Southampton, Coventry City, Birmingham City and Orient
11. *Tom Finney* Preston and England

Reserves

Mike Duxbury Manchester United
Brian Miller Burnley and England
Steve 'Mandy' Hill Blackpool and Tranmere
Dave Wilson Preston, Liverpool, Bradford City, and Southport
Tony Morley Preston, Burnley, Aston Villa and England
Frank Wignall Everton, Nottingham Forest, Wolves, Derby County, Mansfield and England

LEICESTERSHIRE

1. *Peter Shilton* Leicester City, Stoke City, Nottingham Forest, Southampton and England
2. *Steve Whitworth* Leicester City, Sunderland, Bolton and England
3. *Norman Leet* Leicester City
4. *Ken Oliver* Sunderland, Barnsley, Watford, Workington and Bournemouth
5. *Eddie Clamp* Wolves, Arsenal, Stoke, Peterborough and England
6. *Graham Cross* Leicester City, Chesterfield, Brighton, Preston and Lincoln City
7. *Gary Lineker* Leicester City
8. *Andy Peake* Leicester City
9. *Mick Robinson* Preston, Manchester City, Brighton and Eire
10. *Jackie Lee* Leicester City, Derby County, Coventry City and England
11. *Howard Riley* Leicester City, Walsall, Barrow

Reserves

Carl Jayes Leicester City and Northampton
Jeff Blockley Coventry City, Arsenal, Leicester City and Notts County and England
David Hunt Derby County and Notts County
Winston White Leicester City and Hereford
Barrie Thomas Leicester City, Mansfield, Scunthorpe, Newcastle and Barnsley

MANCHESTER

1. *Joe Corrigan* Manchester City and England
2. *Keith Newton* Blackburn, Everton, Burnley and England
3. *Roger Byrne* Manchester United and England
4. *Nobby Stiles* Manchester United, Middlesbrough, Preston and England
5. *Harry Johnston* Blackpool and England
6. *Don Welsh* Torquay, Charlton and England
7. *Dennis Viollet* Manchester United, Stoke and England
8. *Peter Dobing* Blackburn, Manchester City and Stoke
9. *Neil Young* Manchester City, Preston and Rochdale

10. *Stan Bowles* Manchester City, Crewe, Carlisle, Queens Park Rangers, Nottingham Forest, Orient, Brentford and England
11. *Dave Wagstaffe* Manchester City, Wolves, Blackburn and Blackpool

Reserves

Alex Williams Manchester City
John Aston Manchester United and England
Wilf McGuinness Manchester United and England
Mike Doyle Manchester City, Stoke, Bolton and England
Tony Towers Manchester City, Sunderland, Birmingham and England
Doug Holden Bolton, Preston and England
Albert Scanlon Manchester United, Newcastle, Lincoln and Mansfield

MERSEYSIDE

1. *Tony Waiters* Blackpool, Burnley and England
2. *Gerry Byrne* Liverpool and England
3. *Billy Eckersley* Blackburn and England
4. *Dennis Mortimer* Coventry and Aston Villa
5. *Roy McFarland* Tranmere, Derby, Bradford City and England
6. *Tommy Caton* Manchester City
7. *Derek Temple* Everton, Preston and England
8. *Steve Coppell* Tranmere, Manchester United and England
9. *Joe Baker* Hibs, Torino, Arsenal, Nottingham Forest, Sunderland and England
10. *Colin Harvey* Everton, Sheffield Wednesday and England
11. *John Connelly* Burnley, Manchester United, Blackburn, Bury and England

Reserves

Jimmy Rimmer Manchester United, Arsenal, Aston Villa and England
Tommy Wright Everton and England
Brian Labone Everton and England
Ian Callaghan Liverpool, Swansea, Crewe and England
Gary Owen Manchester City and West Bromwich Albion

Joe Royle Everton, Manchester City, Bristol City, Norwich and England
Johnny Morrissey Liverpool, Everton and Oldham

NORFOLK, SUFFOLK AND CAMBS

1. *Gary Bailey* Manchester United
2. *Paul Haylock* Norwich
3. *Richard Money* Scunthorpe, Fulham, Liverpool and Luton
4. *Mike Bailey* Charlton, Wolves, Hereford and England
5. *Maurice Norman* Norwich, Tottenham and England
6. *Ron Ashman* Norwich
7. *Barry Bridges* Chelsea, Birmingham, Queens Park Rangers, Millwall, Brighton and England
8. *Bobby Kellard* Southend, Crystal Palace, Ipswich, Portsmouth, Bristol City, Leicester and Torquay
9. *Vic Keeble* Colchester, Newcastle and West Ham
10. *Ted Phillips* Ipswich, Orient, Luton and Colchester
11. *Ian Storey-Moore* Nottingham Forest, Manchester United and England

Reserves

Tony Godden Gillingham and West Bromwich Albion
John King Peterborough and Leicester
Brian Talbot Ipswich, Arsenal and England
Roy Hollis Norwich, Tottenham and Southend
Trevor Whymark Ipswich, Derby, Grimsby and England

NORTHUMBERLAND

1. *Jim Strong* Hartlepool, Chesterfield, Portsmouth, Walsall and Burnley
2. *John Angus* Burnley and England
3. *Stan Milburn* Chesterfield, Leicester, Rochdale and England 'B'
4. *Ray Kennedy* Arsenal, Liverpool, Swansea and England
5. *Jackie Charlton* Leeds and England
6. *Shaun Elliott* Sunderland
7. *Ray Pointer* Burnley, Bury, Coventry, Portsmouth and England
8. *Trevor Steven* Burnley
9. *Jackie Milburn* Newcastle and England

10. *Bobby Charlton* Manchester United, Preston and England
11. *Wilf Grant* Manchester City, Southampton, Cardiff, Ipswich and England 'B'

Reserves

Ray King Newcastle, Orient, Port Vale and England 'B'
Cec Irwin Sunderland
Bobby Ayre Charlton and Reading
Norman Wilkinson Hull and York

NOTTS

1. *Bill Glazier* Crystal Palace, Coventry and Brentford
2. *Danny Thomas* Coventry
3. *Viv Anderson* Nottingham Forest and England
4. *Henry Newton* Nottingham Forest, Everton, Derby and Walsall
5. *Dave Watson* Notts. County, Rotherham, Sunderland, Manchester City, Werder Bremen, Southampton, Stoke and England
6. *Tony Knapp* Leicester, Southampton, Coventry, Bristol City and Tranmere
7. *Gary Birtles* Nottingham Forest, Manchester United and England
8. *Phil Boyer* Derby, York, Bournemouth, Norwich, Southampton, Manchester City and England
9. *Jeff Astle* Notts. County, West Bromwich Albion and England
10. *David Pleat* Nottingham Forest, Luton, Shrewsbury, Exeter and Peterborough
11. *Tony Woodcock* Nottingham Forest, 1. FC. Köln, Arsenal and England

Reserves

Peter Taylor Coventry, Middlesbrough and Port Vale
Brian Kilcline Notts. County
Stuart Boam Mansfield, Middlesbrough and Newcastle
Don Weston Wrexham, Birmingham, Rotherham, Leeds, Huddersfield and Chester
Mick Jones Sheffield United, Leeds and England

SOUTH YORKS

1. *Gordon Banks* Chesterfield, Leicester, Stoke and England
2. *Len Badger* Sheffield United and Chesterfield
3. *Lionel Smith* Arsenal, Watford and England
4. *Redfern Froggatt* Sheffield Wednesday and England
5. *Tony Kay* Sheffield Wednesday, Everton and England
6. *Graham Shaw* Sheffield United, Doncaster and England
7. *Kevin Keegan* Scunthorpe, Liverpool, Hamburg, Southampton, Newcastle and England
8. *Albert Quixall* Sheffield Wednesday, Manchester United, Oldham, Stockport and England
9. *Tommy Taylor* Barnsley, Manchester United and England
10. *Alick Jeffrey* Doncaster and Lincoln
11. *David Pegg* Manchester United and England

Reserves

Alan Hodgkinson Sheffield United and England
Laurie Scott Bradford City, Arsenal, Crystal Palace and England
Sid Normanton Barnsley and Halifax
Mark Jones Manchester United
Johnnie Fantham Sheffield Wednesday, Rotherham and England
Jack Stamps Mansfield, New Brighton, Derby and Shrewsbury
Graham Rix Arsenal and England

STAFFS

1. *Bert Williams* Walsall, Wolves and England
2. *Mike Pejic* Stoke, Everton, Aston Villa and England
3. *David Nish* Leicester, Derby and England
4. *Brian Horton* Walsall, Port Vale, Brighton and Luton
5. *Neil Franklin* Stoke, Hull, Crewe, Stockport and England
6. *Denis Smith* Stoke and York
7. *Stanley Matthews* Stoke, Blackpool and England
8. *Garth Crooks* Stoke and Tottenham
9. *Ronnie Allen* Port Vale, West Bromwich Albion, Crystal Palace and England
10. *Dennis Wilshaw* Wolves, Walsall, Stoke and England
11. *Mark Chamberlain* Port Vale, Stoke and England

Reserves

Jim Arnold Blackburn and Everton
Tony Allen Stoke, Bury and England
Alan Dodd Stoke and Wolves
Roy Sproson Stoke and Port Vale.
Adrian Heath Stoke and Everton
Peter Eastoe Wolves, Swindon, Queens Park Rangers, Everton and West Bromwich Albion
Frank Bowyer Stoke

SWANSEA AND MERTHYR TYDFIL

1. *Gary Sprake* Leeds, Birmingham and Wales
2. *Jeff Hopkins* Fulham
3. *Chris Marustik* Swansea and Wales
4. *Barry Hole* Cardiff, Blackburn, Aston Villa, Swansea and Wales
5. *Ray Daniel* Arsenal, Sunderland, Cardiff, Swansea and Wales
6. *Mel Charles* Leeds, Swansea, Arsenal, Cardiff, Port Vale and Wales
7. *Trevor Ford* Swansea, Aston Villa, Sunderland, Cardiff, Newport and Wales
8. *Ivor Allchurch* Swansea, Newcastle, Cardiff and Wales
9. *John Charles* Leeds, Juventus, Roma, Cardiff and Wales
10. *Gordon Davies* Fulham and Wales
11. *Cliff Jones* Swansea, Tottenham, Fulham and Wales

Reserves

Vic Rouse Millwall, Crystal Palace, Oxford, Orient and Wales
Dud Lewis Swansea
Jeremy Charles Swansea and Wales
Bryn Jones Wolves, Arsenal, Norwich and Wales
Robbie James Swansea and Wales
Terry Medwin Swansea, Tottenham and Wales
Barrie Jones Swansea, Plymouth, Cardiff and Wales

TYNE AND WEAR

1. *Ray Wood* Newcastle, Darlington, Manchester United, Huddersfield, Bradford City, Barnsley and England
2. *Frank Clark* Newcastle and Nottingham Forest

3. *Derek Parkin* Huddersfield, Wolves and Stoke
4. *Bryan Robson* West Bromwich Albion, Manchester United and England
5. *Gerry Young* Sheffield Wednesday and England
6. *Norman Hunter* Leeds, Bristol City, Barnsley and England
7. *Ernie Taylor* Newcastle, Blackpool, Manchester United, Sunderland and England
8. *Raich Carter* Sunderland, Derby and Hull and England
9. *Stan Mortensen* Blackpool, Hull and Southport and England
10. *Mike Hazard* Tottenham Hotspur
11. *Jimmy Mullen* Wolves and England

Reserves

Jimmy Montgomery Sunderland, Birmingham and Nottingham Forest
Alan Kennedy Newcastle and Liverpool
Johnny Dixon Aston Villa
Howard Kendall Preston, Everton, Birmingham, Stoke and Blackburn
Tommy Baldwin Arsenal, Chelsea and Brentford
George Armstrong Arsenal, Leicester and Stockport
Dennis Tueart Sunderland, Manchester City and England

WEST MIDLANDS

1. *Gil Merrick* Birmingham and England
2. *Bobby Thomson* Wolves, Birmingham, Luton, Port Vale and England
3. *Derek Statham* West Bromwich Albion and England
4. *Ken Barnes* Manchester City and Wrexham
5. *Trevor Smith* Birmingham, Walsall and England
6. *Duncan Edwards* Manchester United and England
7. *Don Howe* West Bromwich Albion, Arsenal and England
8. *Arthur Rowley* Wolves, West Bromwich Albion, Fulham, Leicester, Shrewsbury and England 'B'
9. *Jack Rowley* Wolves, Manchester United, Plymouth and England
10. *Alan Clarke* Walsall, Fulham, Leicester, Leeds, Barnsley and England
11. *Alan Hinton* Wolves, Nottingham Forest, Derby and England

Reserves

Reg Matthews Coventry, Chelsea, Derby and England
Len Millard West Bromwich Albion
Jack Pitt Bristol Rovers
Mick Bernard Stoke, Everton and Oldham
Gary Shaw Aston Villa
Wilf Carter West Bromwich Albion, Plymouth and Exeter
Bob Latchford Birmingham, Everton, Swansea and England

WEST YORKS

1. *Ted Sagar* Everton and England
2. *Paul Madeley* Leeds and England
3. *Terry Cooper* Wolves, Leeds, Middlesbrough, Bristol City, Bristol Rovers, Doncaster and England
4. *Kenny Hibbitt* Bradford Park Avenue and Wolves
5. *Peter Swan* Sheffield Wednesday, Bury and England
6. *Ken Armstrong* Chelsea and England
7. *Mike Hellawell* Queens Park Rangers, Birmingham, Sunderland, Huddersfield, Peterborough and England
8. *Len Shackleton* Arsenal, Bradford Park Avenue, Newcastle, Sunderland and England
9. *Frank Worthington* Huddersfield, Leicester, Bolton, Birmingham, Leeds, Sunderland and England
10. *Kevin Hector* Bradford Park Avenue, Derby and England
11. *Tony Galvin* Tottenham and Eire

Reserves

Gordon Livsey Wrexham, Chester and Hartlepool
Cyril Knowles Middlesbrough, Tottenham and England
Trevor Hockey Bradford City, Nottingham Forest, Newcastle, Birmingham. Sheffield United, Norwich, Aston Villa and Wales
Bert Tindill Doncaster, Bristol City and Barnsley
John Radford Arsenal, West Ham, Blackburn and England
Jim Iley Sheffield United, Tottenham, Nottingham Forest, Newcastle and Peterborough
Colin Grainger Wrexham, Sheffield United, Sunderland, Leeds, Port Vale, Doncaster and England

3 ENGLAND NO. 9'S BORN IN BOLTON

1. *Tommy Lawton*   2. *Nat Lofthouse*   3. *Paul Mariner*

6 ENGLAND LEADERS BORN IN MIDDLESBROUGH

1. *John Calvey*
2. *George Elliott*
3. *Micky Fenton*
4. *Don Revie*
5. *Brian Clough*
6. *Alan Peacock*

7 CHANNEL ISLANDERS TO PLAY REGULAR LEAGUE FOOTBALL SINCE WORLD WAR II

1. *Ray De Grucy* – Over 70 appearances at Full Back for Grimsby.
2. *Len Duquemin* – 114 goals in 275 League appearances for Tottenham during the 'Push and Run' era.
3. *Billy Farmer* – Around 50 games between the posts for Forest.
4. *Ron Farmer* – Battling Wing Half with over 350 matches for Coventry and the Nottingham Clubs.
5. *Chris Jones** – Hit 37 goals in 164 League games for Tottenham before moving in 1982–83 to first Manchester City then back to London and Crystal Palace.
6. *Bill Spurdle* – Clocked up 14 years in the Football League playing close on 400 times for Oldham, Manchester City and Port Vale as a Wing Half or Inside Forward. Became the first Channel Islander to play in a post-war F.A. Cup Final when he lined up for the 'The Citizens' against Newcastle in May, 1955.
7. *Bill Whare* – One club servant to Nottingham Forest whose most memorable moment would have arrived in the 1959 F.A. Cup Final triumph over Luton. A fine Right Back whose career lasted for 11 years at the City ground.

* England U.21 Cap.

54 ONE-CLUB PLAYERS WHO SERVED THEIR HOME TOWN CLUB FOR MORE THAN TEN YEARS SINCE WORLD WAR II

1.	*Jimmy Armfield*	Blackpool	1954–1970	Full Back
2.	*Jack Bailey*	Bristol City	1938–1956	Left Back
3.	*Colin Baker*	Cardiff City	1953–1965	Wing Half
4.	*Harry Bamford*	Bristol Rovers	1946–1958	Utility Player
5.	*Geoff Bradford*	Bristol Rovers	1949–1963	Inside Forward
6.	*Shay Brennan*	Manchester United	1957–1969	Full Back
7.	*Brian Bulless*	Hull City	1952–1963	Full Back
8.	*Sam Burton*	Swindon Town	1946–1961	Goalkeeper
9.	*Gerry Byrne*	Liverpool	1957–1968	Full Back
10.	*Anthony Cook*	Bristol City	1952–1963	Goalkeeper
11.	*Ian Cooper*	Bradford City	1965–1976	Full Back
12.	*Bryan Douglas*	Blackburn Rovers	1954–1968	Outside Right
13.	*Tom Finney*	Preston North End	1946–1959	Winger
14.	*John Forrest*	Bury	1967–1980	Goalkeeper
15.	*Redfern Froggatt*	Sheffield Wednesday	1946–1959	Inside Forward
16.	*Harry Griffiths*	Swansea	1949–1963	Outside Right
17.	*Gladstone Guest*	Rotherham	1946–1956	Inside Forward
18.	*Ivor Guy*	Bristol City	1946–1956	Full Back
19.	*Alan Harrington*	Cardiff City	1952–1965	Full Back
20.	*Peter Harris*	Portsmouth	1946–1959	Right Winger
21.	*Alan Hodgkinson*	Sheffield United	1954–1970	Goalkeeper
22.	*Ken Hodder*	Stockport County	1951–1963	Centre Half
23.	*Barry Jackson*	York City	1958–1969	Centre Half
24.	*Keith Jobling*	Grimsby Town	1953–1968	Wing Half
25.	*Ken Johnson*	Hartlepools United	1949–1963	Inside Forward
26.	*Pat Jones*	Plymouth Argyle	1946–1957	Full Back
27.	*Brian Kinsey*	Charlton Athletic	1956–1970	Full Back
28.	*Eric Lee*	Chester	1946–1956	Centre Half
29.	*Paul Madeley*	Leeds United	1963–1980	Defender
30.	*Jack Marsh*	Stoke City	1967–1978	Full Back
31.	*Geoff Merrick*	Bristol City	1967–1980	Centre Back
32.	*Gil Merrick*	Birmingham City	1946–1959	Goalkeeper
33.	*Ron Moran*	Liverpool	1952–1964	Full Back
34.	*William Morley*	Nottingham Forest	1946–1958	Wing Half
35.	*Frank Mountford*	Stoke City	1946–1957	Centre Half

36. *John Ogilvie*	Workington	1962–1974	Full Back
37. *Gordon Parr*	Bristol City	1957–1971	Half Back
38. *Jack Parry*	Derby County	1948–1965	Wing Half
39. *Tommy Powell*	Derby County	1948–1961	Outside Right
40. *John Rowland*	Newport County	1958–1968	Wing Half
41. *John Sellars*	Stoke City	1946–1957	Half Back
42. *Stuart Taylor*	Bristol Rovers	1965–1979	Centre Back
43. *Geoff Thomas*	Swansea City	1964–1975	Midfielder
44. *Ron Thompson*	Carlisle United	1951–1963	Wing Half
45. *Graham Vearncombe*	Cardiff City	1952–1963	Goalkeeper
46. *John Watling*	Bristol Rovers	1947–1961	Outside Left
47. *John Watts*	Birmingham City	1951–1962	Wing Half
48. *Len Weare*	Newport County	1955–1969	Goalkeeper
49. *James Wheeler*	Reading	1952–1966	Inside Forward
50. *David Williams*	Newport County	1960–1972	Half Back
51. *Herbie Williams*	Swansea Town	1958–1974	Central Defender
52. *Gordon Williams*	Swindon Town	1958–1974	Wing Half
53. *Peter Wright*	Colchester	1952–1963	Inside/Outside Left
54. *Ray Young*	Derby County	1953–1965	Centre Half

10 ENGLAND REPRESENTATIVES WHO WHERE BORN OUTSIDE THE BRITISH ISLES

1. *Luther Blissett* – England Full International Striker, 1982–83, born in Jamaica.

2. *Terry Butcher* – England Full International Centre Back, 1981–83, born in Singapore.

3. *Nigel Callaghan* – England Under 21 Winger, 1982–83, born in Singapore.

4. *Bob Hazell* – England Under 21 Stopper, 1978–79, born in Jamaica.

5. *Ian Hesford* – England Under 21 Goalkeeper, 1981–83, born in Noola, Kenya.

6. *Craig Johnston* – England Under 21 Midfielder, 1980–81, born in South Africa.

7. *Bill Perry* – England Left Winger, 1955–56, born in South Africa, (Johannesburg).

8. *Cyrille Regis* – England Centre Forward, 1981–83, born in French Guyana.

9. *Wilf Smith* – England Under 23 Full Back, 1969–71, born in Neumunster, West Germany.

10. *Colin Viljoen* – England Midfielder, 1974–75, born in South Africa, (Johannesburg).

5 INTERNATIONALS WHO QUALIFIED THROUGH PARENTAGE TO PLAY FOR SCOTLAND

1. *Alex Cropley* – Aldershot born Midfielder who won 2 Caps 1971–72, while with Hibs.
2. *David Harvey* – Leeds born Goalkeeper who won 16 Caps from 1972–76, while with his home town club.
3. *John Hewie* – South African born Full Back who received 16 Caps between 1955 and 1960. He was serving Charlton Athletic.
4. *Bruce Rioch* – Another native of Aldershot who gained 24 Scotland call-ups during service with Derby County and Everton. The only non-Scot to Captain his adopted country.
5. *Bob Wilson* – One of several fine Goalkeepers to emanate from Chesterfield. The Arsenal No. 1 was awarded 2 Scotland Caps during 1971–72.

8 INTERNATIONALS WHO QUALIFIED THROUGH PARENTAGE TO PLAY FOR WALES

1. *George Berry* – A German-born black Centre Back who won 4 Welsh Caps between May and November, 1979, while with Wolves.
2. *Ian Evans* – Dominant Centre Back from Egham, Surrey, who acquired 13 Caps for Wales between 1975 and 1977 while with Crystal Palace before terrible injury put him out of the game for nearly 2 years.
3. *Trevor Hockey* – Squat powerful Midfield hard man who although originating from Keighley, Yorkshire, qualified for Wales under a new F.I.F.A. rule introduced in 1971, allowing footballers to turn out for the 'Land of Their Father'. Won 9 Caps from October, 1971, to September, 1973.
4. *Kenny Jackett* – Intelligent utility player who in playing for his home town club Watford has shone at Left Back, in Midfield and as a Left-Sided Centre Back. Just turned 21 he

could be a regular for years in the red shirt of Wales.

5. *Dave Jones* – Resolute Centre Back who gave splendid service to Bournemouth, Norwich and Nottingham Forest. Was awarded 8 Caps between 1975 and 1979.

6. *David Phillips* – Born in Welberg, West Germany, he is currently being switched between a Midfield role and Full Back for both his club Plymouth Argyle and Wales Under 21's.

7. *John Phillips* – A useful Goalkeeper who unfortunately has for the major part of his career been understudy to Peter Bonetti and Nicky Johns. Originating from Shrewsbury, with whom he started, he won 4 Caps for Wales between 1972 and 1977 while at Chelsea.

8. *Paul Price* – An outstanding competitor for Luton and Wales as Sweeper. Although in and out of the first team at Tottenham he nevertheless makes an ideal Captain of his adopted country. He originally hails from St. Albans.

28 INTERNATIONALS WHOSE PARENTAGE QUALIFIED THEM FOR EIRE

1. *Jeff Chandler* An impish Midfield forager originally from Hammersmith who won two Eire Caps in 1980–81 while with Leeds United. After beginning at Blackpool his career went sadly awry at Leeds, but he is now returning to the form he showed as a teenager, with Bolton.

2. *John Dempsey* A commanding and skilful London born Centre Half whose authoritative play for Fulham and later, Chelsea, won him 19 Caps for Eire, the land of his father.

3. *Terry Donovan* A Scouse Striker whose consistent markmanship in Aston Villa reserves, and occasionally in the first team, was sufficient to win him a call up to the Eire team in the early 1980's. He qualified for Eire through his father, Donal, himself an Eire international Full Back.

4. *Tony Galvin* Huddersfield born Left Flank player who emerged as an ace among the team of Spurs stars in the early 1980's. A bargain buy from Goole Town, his brilliant attacking play and great courage helped him to become an integral part of the most stylish English team. Because of Ron Greenwood's hesitancy, Eire stepped in to reward Tony with national honours in 1982–83.

5. *Tony Grealish* Midfield organizer and hard man in the

Trevor Hockey mould, his biting tackles and aggressive running with the ball endeared him firstly to Orient, then Luton fans. At Brighton he has now shown himself to have the same qualities as his predecessor, fellow bearded player Brian Horton. Had won 30 Caps by the autumn of 1982.

6. *Austin Hayes* Diminutive Striker whose highlight to date is an appearance in the 1979 League Cup Final for Southampton. He moved to Millwall in 1981 after fewer than 40 League and Cup games. His solitary Eire Cap was won in 1979 against Denmark.

7. *Ron Healey* An under-rated Goalkeeper who, after loan spells with Coventry and Preston, settled down to give valuable service over 9 years to Cardiff City. Leaving his home town club, Manchester City, in 1973 for South Wales was the best thing that could happen to young Healey as it enabled him to claim a first team position that he so richly deserved. His father's country awarded him 2 Caps in the late 1970's.

8. *Chris Hughton* This black West Ham born Full Back who trained as a lift engineer while playing in Tottenham's Youth and Reserve teams, shot to prominence in 1979–80 when he played 39 games in his first season as a professional. His pace, close control and attacking skills, have made him into one of Britain's best Full Backs. A regular Eire player since his first Cap against the United States in October, 1979.

9. *Mick Kearns* Oxfordshire born Goalkeeper who, in a career spanning Oxford, Walsall and Wolves, has gained 18 Eire Caps between 1970–80.

10. *Tony Kinsella* Essex born Midfielder who won Eire under 21 Caps while with Millwall. Since leaving the Den in 1981 he has played for Tampa Bay Rowdies in America and Ipswich Town. A player whose early potential has never been fulfilled.

11. *Mark Lawrenson* In terms of versatility undoubtedly Britain's best player, able to slot in effectively at Left, Right or Center Midfield, at Full Back or as a stopper.

Unquestionably he is also the most able 'Libero' in the Football League, although Ante Rajkovic of Swansea pushes him close. Beginning his career at Preston, his own town, he played for two seasons (1975–7) before moving to Brighton for £110,000. Eire claimed him during 1976–7 season and, excepting injuries, he has kept his place ever since. He should win his 25th cap sometime in 1984. After four years and more than 250 games for the 'Gulls' during which he helped Brighton to Division

One for the first time, he moved in a £900,000 transfer to Liverpool. He won League Championship and League Cup medals in 1981–2, his first season at Liverpool, and many more will be won by this bearded six-footer who Bob Paisley and Alan Mullery both regard as Britain's most complete player.

12. *Andy Massey* A London born Midfielder or Full Back who over the last three seasons has become a vital cog in the Lion's side. Through parental qualifications he has appeared in the Emerald shirts at Youth and under 21 levels.

13. *Jim McDonagh* Rotherham born Custodian whose eligibility to play for Eire has been in question. While with his home town club, in the early 1970's, he played Youth football for England, so 'Seamus' was indeed fortunate to be allowed an international call-up, especially when considering the Eamon O'Keefe case. A highly capable Goalkeeper with over 400 appearances behind him.

14. *Paul McGrath* Dominant Ealing born black Centre Back whose splendid form with St. Patrick's Athletic in the League of Ireland prompted Manchester United to pay £30,000 for him as a competitor for a defensive slot. Showing immense promise in 1982–83 he looks likely to be the first choice Eire reserve to the O'Leary–Lawrenson partnership.

15. *Jerry Murphy* His role as an elegant and creative Midfielder in Crystal Palace's Youth Cup winning sides and first team, won him accolades far and plenty, and 3 Eire Caps into the bargain in 1979–80. His form was affected like several other Palace players when the 'Team of the Eighties' went through internal strife and dropped into the depths of the 2nd Division.

16. *Brendan O'Callaghan* Intelligent Bradford born Stopper or Central Striker who has won several Eire Caps since his first appearance during 1978–79 against West Germany. Has bagged over a century of goals in just under 400 first team appearances for Doncaster and Stoke.

17. *Kevin O'Callaghan* Great acceleration and nimble footwork are this young Winger's trade marks. Since his £250,000 transfer from his local club Millwall in 1980, he has never held down a regular place with Ipswich due to the clubs successful 4–3–1–2 formation. He won his first Eire Caps in 1980–81 season and is likely over the next several years to vie with Tottenham's Tony Galvin (Q.V.) for a place in the Eire team.

18. *Sean O'Driscoll* Ubiquitous Midfielder whose form since signing for Fulham from Alvechurch at the close of the 1970's,

has been constantly effective. One of the unsung heroes of the 'Cottagers' push to the 1st Division. He earned his first three Eire Caps on the tour of the America's in May, 1982.

19. *David O'Leary* Along with Lawrenson he forms possibly the best central defensive partnership at international level. Born in London in 1958, he was capped by Eire early in his career. Under the steady guidance of Arsenal coach Don Howe, O'Leary has become Arsenal's Captain and the most outstanding No. 5 in the Football League. From his first season at age 17, when he played over 30 games, he has been a gilt-edged footballer who never panics under pressure or resorts to rough tatics. When his current contract expires many leading European clubs will probably be after him.

20. *John Pender* A native of Luton, this sturdy Centre Back proved to be Wolves' newest star, when in 1982–83 he formed such a promising partnership at the heart of defence, with newcomer Alan Dodd. A winner of Eire Youth Caps he seems destined to win full honours in the future.

21. *Gerry Peyton* This more than useful Goalkeeper has proved to be Fulham's best number one, since Gibraltar-born Tony Macedo. He began his Goalkeeping apprenticeship at Atherstone, under the watchful eye and careful guidance of former Birmingham and England stalwart Gil Merrick. He has gained over 20 Caps since moving South from Burnley in the mid 1970's.

22. *Mick Robinson* A powerful Centre Forward whose prowess in attack for Preston in the late 1970's led Malcolm Allison to splash out £756,000 for him in July, 1979. Although used at Manchester City as a target man, which Robinson admits to having disliked, he scored 8 times in 30 appearances before moving to Brighton for little over half his previous transfer fee. At the Goldstone ground, free from Maine Road pressures, he has scored quite freely and, although Leicester born, was rewarded with a regular place in the Eire side because his great grandmother came from Southern Ireland.

23. *Kevin Sheedy* One that got away from Liverpool's stable! This Welsh-born, sometimes brilliant Midfield orchestrator until this last season had little opportunity to show his abundant talent to the viewing public. Beginning with Hereford, his precocious skills soon brought him to the attention of Liverpool, who promptly whisked him away to Merseyside. Three League appearances in four seasons were understandably not enough

for a player wishing to build a case for inclusion in the Eire side, and Liverpool were forced to sell him to neighbours Everton, for a knock down £60,000.

24. *John Sheridan* Lancashire born Midfielder who on his first team displays during 1982–83 looks to be one of the first home grown talents of any real quality for some years in the Leeds United set up. Already an Eire Under 21 player he could well figure in Eire Senior squads over the next couple of years.

25. *Gary Waddock* An impressive dynamo and battler in the middle of the park for Queens Park Rangers since his first appearance in late 1979. He has taken over from club mate Tony Currie as the most essential member of the Rangers Midfield, providing the grit, solidity and no little amount of skill. A more than useful back up to the Eire side since his first Cap in 1979–80.

26. *Mickey Walsh* For the last three seasons this Striker who hails from Chorley has played his football in Portugal with F.C. Porto. A consistent marksman with his first club Blackpool, he had few occasions and little time to enjoy any degree of consistency at Everton and Queens Park Rangers before moving to warmer climes. Has played for Eire on a dozen occasions.

27. *Mike Walsh* Mancunian Centre Back who won Eire honours on the 1982 South American tour due to the absence of the Arsenal, Liverpool and Manchester United retinue.

28. *Robert Wilson* Clever Londoner, whose skill on the ball and strong runs have had his manager, Malcolm MacDonald, demanding his inclusion in the Eire squad. A certain star of the future in what looks likely to be the best Fulham side of all time.

15 DOUBLE/TREBLE INTERNATIONALS

1. *Jose 'Mazzola' Altafini*	Brazil and Italy
2. *Ruben Cano*	Argentina and Spain
3. *John Hawley Edwards*	England and Wales
4. *Robert Evans*	Wales and England
5. *Alcide Ghiggia*	Uruguay and Italy
6. *Ladislao Kubala*	Spain, Hungary and Czechoslovakia
7. *Julio Libonatti*	Argentina and Italy

8.	*Luisito Monti*	Argentina and Italy
9.	*Raimondo Orsi*	Argentina and Italy
10.	*Ferenc Puskas*	Hungary and Spain
11.	*John Reynolds*	Ireland and England
12.	*José Santamaria*	Uruguay and Spain
13.	*Juan Schiaffino*	Uruguay and Italy
14.	*Omar Sivori*	Argentina and Italy
15.	*Alfredo Di Stefano*	Argentina, Colombia and Spain

28 PLAYERS BORN IN ONE COUNTRY BUT CAPPED BY ANOTHER

		Place of Birth	Country Played For
1.	*Bobby Almond*	London, England	New Zealand
2.	*Michele Andreolo*	Uruguay	Italy
3.	*Miguel Bernardo ('Migueli')*	Ceuta, N/Africa	Spain
4.	*Mario Coluna*	Mozambique	Portugal
5.	*Alberto da Costa Pereira*	Portugese E/Africa	Portugal
6.	*Eusebio*	Mozambique	Portugal
7.	*Just Fontaine*	Morocco	France
8.	*Claudio Gentile*	Tripoli, Libya	Italy
9.	*Jordao*	Angola	Portugal
10.	*Bernd Krauss*	Dortmund, W/Germany	Austria
11.	*Jean-François Larios*	Sidi-bel-Abbes	France
12.	*Christian Lopez*	Algeria	France
13.	*Juan Lozano*	Spain	Belgium
14.	*Jimmy Mackay*	Scotland	Australia
15.	*Roberto Martinez*	Argentina	Spain
16.	*Eddie McIlvenny*	Scotland	U.S.A.
17.	*Néné*	W / Africa	Portugal
18.	*Raimondo Ponte*	Italy	Switzerland
19.	*Ramon Quiroga*	Argentina	Peru
20.	*Jose 'Pirri' Sanchez*	Ceuta, N/Africa	Spain
21.	*Branko Segota*	Yugoslavia	Canada
22.	*Steve Sumner*	Preston, England	New Zealand
23.	*Simon Tahamata*	The Moluccas	Holland
24.	*Jean Tigana*	Martinique	France
25.	*Marius Tresor*	Guadaloupe	France
26.	*Giuseppe Wilson*	Darlington, England	Italy
27.	*Peter Wilson*	Middlesbrough, England	Australia
28.	*Steve Wooddin*	Liverpool, England	New Zealand

Clubs

12 ORIGINAL LEAGUE MEMBERS 1888

1. Aston Villa
2. Blackburn Rovers
3. Bolton Wanderers
4. Burnley
5. Derby County
6. Everton
7. Notts County
8. Preston North End
9. Stoke City
10. West Bromwich Albion
11. Wolverhampton Wanderers
12. Accrington Stanley

12 ORIGINAL MEMBERS OF 2nd DIVISION (1892–3)

1. Ardwick
2. Bootle
3. Burslem Port Vale
4. Burton Swifts
5. Crewe Alexandra
6. Darwen
7. Grimsby Town
8. Lincoln City
9. Northwich Victoria
10. Sheffield United
11. Small Heath
12. Wallsend Town Swifts

22 ORIGINAL MEMBERS OF 3rd DIVISION SOUTH (1920–21)

1. Brentford
2. Brighton and Hove Albion
3. Bristol Rovers
4. Crystal Palace
5. Exeter City
6. Gillingham
7. Grimsby Town
8. Luton Town
9. Merthyr Town
10. Millwall Athletic
11. Newport County
12. Northampton Town
13. Norwich City
14. Plymouth Argyle
15. Portsmouth
16. Queen's Park Rangers
17. Reading
18. Southampton
19. Southend United
20. Swansea Town
21. Swindon Town
22. Watford

Crystal Palace won promotion in 1920–21, the only year of the 3rd Division South's existence and Grimsby Town, as the next list shows, competed in the 3rd Division North during the following season. The other 20 Clubs formed along with newcomers Aberdare Athletic and Charlton Athletic the 3rd Division (South) in 1921–22.

THE 20 ORIGINAL MEMBERS OF 3rd DIVISION NORTH (1921–2)

1. *Accrington Stanley*
2. *Ashington*
3. *Barrow*
4. *Chesterfield*
5. *Crewe Alexandra*
6. *Darlington*
7. *Durham City*
8. *Grimsby Town*
9. *Halifax Town*
10. *Hartlepools United*
11. *Lincoln City*
12. *Nelson*
13. *Rochdale*
14. *Southport*
15. *Staleybridge Celtic*
16. *Stockport County*
17. *Tranmere Rovers*
18. *Walsall*
19. *Wigan Borough*
20. *Wrexham*

24 LEAGUE CLUBS THAT FORMED ORIGINAL DIVISION 4 (1958–1959)

1. *Aldershot*
2. *Barrow*
3. *Bradford Park Avenue*
4. *Carlisle*
5. *Chester*
6. *Coventry City*
7. *Crewe Alexandra*
8. *Crystal Palace*
9. *Darlington*
10. *Exeter City*
11. *Gateshead*
12. *Gillingham*
13. *Hartlepools United*
14. *Millwall*
15. *Northampton*
16. *Oldham Athletic*
17. *Port Vale*
18. *Shrewsbury Town*
19. *Southport*
20. *Torquay United*
21. *Walsall*
22. *Watford*
23. *Workington*
24. *York City*

ADDITIONS TO LEAGUE SINCE 1930

1.	*Chester*	1931	3N
2.	*Mansfield Town*	1931	3S
3.	*Ipswich Town*	1938	3S
4.	*Colchester United*	1950	3S

5.	*Scunthorpe United*	1950	3N
6.	*Shrewsbury Town*	1950	3N
7.	*Peterborough United*	1960	4
8.	*Oxford United*	1962	4
9.	*Cambridge United*	1970	4
10.	*Hereford United*	1972	4
11.	*Wimbledon*	1977	4
12.	*Wigan Athletic*	1978	4

THE 24 CLUBS THAT LOST ENGLISH FOOTBALL LEAGUE STATUS

Their last league season is in brackets. Unless signified clubs were all voted out of the League

1. *Bootle* (1892–93)
2. *Middlesbrough Ironopolis* (1893–94)
3. *Northwich Victoria* (1893–94)
4. *Burton Wanderers* (1896–97)
5. *Darwen* (1898–99)
6. *Loughborough* (1899–1900)
7. *Burton United (Ex-Swifts)* (1906–07)
8. *Gainsborough Trinity* (1911–12)
9. *Glossop North End** (1914–15)
10. *Staleybridge Celtic** (1922–23)
11. *Aberdare Athletic* (1926–27)
12. *Durham City* (1927–28)
13. *Ashington* (1928–29)
14. *Merthyr Town* (1928–29)
15. *Nelson* (1930–31)
16. *Thames°* (1931–32)
17. *Wigan Borough** (1931–32)
18. *New Brighton** (1900–01) (1950–51)
19. *Gateshead* (1959–60)
20. *Accrington Stanley** (1892–93) (1961–2)
21. *Bradford Park Avenue* (1969–70)
22. *Barrow* (1971–72)
23. *Workington* (1976–77)
24. *Southport* (1977–78)

* Resigned.
° Decided not to apply for re-election.

Numerous current League members have lost League status at one time or another, but all have been re-admitted.

THE 10 FOUNDER MEMBERS OF THE SCOTTISH LEAGUE (1890–91)

1. *Abercorn*
2. *Cambuslang*
3. *Celtic**
4. *Cowlairs*
5. *Dumbarton**
6. *Hearts**
7. *Rangers**
8. *St Mirren**
9. *Third Lanark*
10. *Vale of Leven*

* Ever present in the Scottish League.

26 FORMER SCOTTISH LEAGUE CLUBS

1.	*Cambuslang*	1890–1892
2.	*Third Lanark*	1890–1967
3.	*Abercorn*	1890–1915
4.	*Vale of Leven*	1890–92, 1905–15, 1921–24
5.	*Cowlairs*	1890–91, 1893–95
6.	*Leith*	1891–1915, 1927–40, 1947–48
7.	*Renton*	1891–98 (Resigned)
8.	*St. Bernard's*	1893–1915, 1921–40
9.	*Port Glasgow Athletic*	1893–1911
10.	*Northern*	1893–94
11.	*Dundee Wanderers*	1894–95
12.	*Linthouse*	1895–1900
13.	*Arthurlie*	1901–15, 1924–29 (Resigned)
14.	*Ayr Parkhouse*	1903–04, 1906–10
15.	*Dundee Hibs.* (Later Dundee United)	1910–15, 1921–23
16.	*Lochgelly*	1914–15
17.	*Armadale*	1921–32
18.	*Bathgate*	1921–28
19.	*Bo'ness*	1921–32
20.	*Broxburn*	1921–26
21.	*Kings' Park*	1921–40
22.	*Lochgelly United*	1921–24
23.	*Clackmannan*	1921–22
24.	*Johnston*	1912–15, 1921–25
25.	*Nithsdale*	1925–27
26.	*Edinburgh City*	1931–40

THE 5 CURRENT 1st DIVISION CLUBS
THAT COMPETED IN THE LEAGUE
FOR MORE THAN 50 YEARS BEFORE
REACHING THE TOP BRACKET

1.	*Watford*	62 years	They reached Division One in 1982
2.	*Swansea City*	61 years	,,	,,	,,	,,	,, 1981
3.	*Brighton*	59 years	,,	,,	,,	,,	,, 1979
4.	*Luton Town*	58 years	,,	,,	,,	,,	,, 1955
5.	*Norwich City*	52 years	,,	,,	,,	,,	,, 1972

THE 6 OLDEST LEAGUE MEMBERS
STILL TO ACHIEVE 1st DIVISION STATUS

with date of original League membership

1. *Lincoln*, 1892
2. *Port Vale*, 1892
3. *Walsall*, 1892
4. *Rotherham*, 1893
5. *Barnsley*, 1898
6. *Chesterfield*, 1899

THE 8 CLUBS WITHOUT EXPERIENCE
OF 1st DIVISION FOOTBALL TO
ENJOY THE LONGEST TIME IN THE
2nd DIVISION

1. *Barnsley*, 51 years
2. *Hull City*, 49 years
3. *Lincoln City*, 38 years
4. *Plymouth Argyle*, 35 years
5. *Chesterfield*, 27 years
6. *Rotherham United*, 26 years
7. *Stockport County*, 25 years
8. *Port Vale*, 20 years

10 CLUBS WITH MORE THAN 40
YEARS IN THE LOWEST DIVISION

1.	*Stockport County*	62 yrs out of 71 yrs in the League
2.	*Crewe Alexandra*	57 yrs out of 59 yrs in the League
3.	*Hartlepool*	54 yrs out of 55 yrs in the League
4.	*Darlington*	52 yrs out of 55 yrs in the League
5.	*Rochdale*	49 yrs out of 55 yrs in the League
6.	*Newport County*	47 yrs out of 55 yrs in the League
7.	*Halifax Town*	43 yrs out of 55 yrs in the League

8. *Aldershot*   41 yrs out of 44 yrs in the League
9. *Torquay United* 41 yrs out of 49 yrs in the League
10. *Walsall*   41 yrs out of 63 yrs in the League

THE 12 CURRENT LEAGUE CLUBS
THAT WERE FORMED BEFORE 1877

1. *Notts County*, 1862
2. *Stoke City*, 1863
3. *Nottingham Forest*, 1865
4. *Chesterfield*, 1866
5. *Sheffield Wednesday*, 1867
6. *Reading*, 1871
7. *Wrexham*, 1873
8. *Aston Villa*, 1874
9. *Bolton Wanderers*, 1874
10. *Birmingham City*, 1875
11. *Blackburn Rovers*, 1875
12. *Middlesbrough*, 1876

THE 16 LEAGUE CLUBS TO HAVE
PLAYED MORE THAN 50 SEASONS IN
DIVISION 1

1915–19 and 1936–46, as war years, do not count towards
these totals

1. *Everton* 80 out of 84
2. *Aston Villa* 73
3. *Liverpool* 68
4. *Swindon Town* 67
5. *Arsenal* 66
6. *West Bromwich Albion* 65
7. *Manchester City* 63
8. *Manchester United* 58
9. *Wolves* 58
10. *Sheffield United* 55
11. *Blackburn Rovers* 54
12. *Derby County* 54
13. *Newcastle United* 54
14. *Burnley* 51
15. *Sheffield Wednesday* 51
16. *Stoke City* 50

Tottenham, in 1984/85, should become the 17th club to have
played more than 50 seasons in Division 1.

THE 11 CLUBS TO HAVE PLAYED
MORE THAN 25 CONSECUTIVE
YEARS IN THE HIGHEST DIVISION

1915–19 and 1939–46, as war years, do not count towards
these totals

1. *Arsenal*   57 seasons 1919–1983
2. *Sunderland*   57   ,,   1890–1958
3. *Aston Villa*   44   ,,   1888–1936
4. *Blackburn Rovers* 44   ,,   1888–1936

103

5.	*Everton*	38	,,	1888–1930 and 29 seasons from 1954 to present
6.	*Liverpool*	38	,,	1905–1954
7.	*Sheffield United*	37	,,	1893–1934
8.	*Newcastle United*	32	,,	1898–1934
9.	*Manchester United*	29	,,	1938–1974
10.	*Tottenham*	27	,,	1950–1977
11.	*Wolves*	26	,,	1932–1965

THE 14 FOOTBALL LEAGUE CLUBS NEVER TO HAVE PLAYED BELOW DIVISIONS 1 AND 2

1. *Arsenal*
2. *Aston Villa*
3. *Birmingham City*
4. *Chelsea*
5. *Everton*
6. *Leicester City*
7. *Liverpool*
8. *Manchester City*
9. *Manchester United*
10. *Newcastle United*
11. *Sunderland*
12. *Tottenham Hotspur*
13. *West Bromwich Albion*
14. *West Ham United*

THE 10 EVER PRESENT CLUBS OF THE FOOTBALL LEAGUE (1888–1983)

1. *Aston Villa*
2. *Blackburn Rovers*
3. *Bolton Wanderers*
4. *Burnley*
5. *Derby County*
6. *Everton*
7. *Notts County*
8. *Preston North End*
9. *West Bromwich Albion*
10. *Wolves*

THE 5 EVER-PRESENTS OF THE SCOTTISH LEAGUE

1. *Celtic*
2. *Dumbarton*
3. *Hearts*
4. *Rangers*
5. *St Mirren*

THE 4 EVER-PRESENTS OF THE BUNDESLIGA 1964–83

1. *1. FC. Köln*
2. *Eintracht Frankfurt*
3. *Hamburger S.V.*
4. *1. FC. Kaiserslautern*

THE 22 CLUBS TO OCCUPY TOP THREE PLACINGS IN DIVISION 1 SINCE THE WAR

1. *Liverpool* 15 times
2. *Manchester United* 15 times
3. *Tottenham Hotspur* 10 times
4. *Wolves* 10 times
5. *Leeds United* 8 times
6. *Arsenal* 7 times
7. *Ipswich* 6 times
8. *Burnley* 5 times
9. *Everton* 5 times
10. *Derby County* 4 times
11. *Chelsea* 3 times
12. *Nottingham Forest* 3 times
13. *Portsmouth* 3 times
14. *Preston North End* 3 times
15. *Blackpool* 2 times
16. *Manchester City* 2 times
17. *West Bromwich Albion* 2 times
18. *Aston Villa* 1 time
19. *Huddersfield Town* 1 time
20. *Queens Park Rangers* 1 time
21. *Sheffield Wednesday* 1 time
22. *Sunderland* 1 time

THE 7 CLUBS WHOSE FIRST PERIOD IN DIVISION I AFTER PROMOTION STRETCHED TO MORE THAN 16 YEARS

1. *Sheffield United*	37 seasons	–	1893–1934
2. *Newcastle United*	32 ,,	–	1898–1934
3. *Huddersfield Town*	25 ,,	–	1920–1952
4. *Portsmouth*	25 ,,	–	1927–1959
5. *Middlesbrough*	18 ,,	–	1902–1924
6. *Bury*	17 ,,	–	1895–1912
7. *Coventry City*	16 ,,	–	1967–1983 with more seasons to come

Sunderland, Blackburn Rovers and Aston Villa spent 55, 44 and 44 years respectively in Division 1 after election to, or original membership of, the League.

THE 22 CURRENT 1st DIVISION CLUBS' LENGTH OF STAY IN DIVISION I (TO 1982–83).

1. *Arsenal*
promoted in 1919 Consecutive seasons in Division 1: 56
2. *Everton*
promoted in 1954 Consecutive seasons in Division 1: 28
3. *Liverpool*
promoted in 1962 Consecutive seasons in Division 1: 20
4. *Manchester City*
promoted in 1966 Consecutive seasons in Division 1: 16
5. *Coventry City*
promoted in 1967 Consecutive seasons in Division 1: 15
6. *Ipswich*
promoted in 1968 Consecutive seasons in Division 1: 14
7. *Aston Villa*
promoted in 1975 Consecutive seasons in Division 1: 7
8. *Manchester United*
promoted in 1975 Consecutive seasons in Division 1: 7
9. *West Bromwich Albion*
promoted in 1976 Consecutive seasons in Division 1: 6
10. *Nottingham Forest*
promoted in 1977 Consecutive seasons in Division 1: 5
11. *Southampton*
promoted in 1978 Consecutive seasons in Division 1: 4
12. *Tottenham*
promoted in 1978 Consecutive seasons in Division 1: 4
13. *Brighton*
promoted in 1979 Consecutive seasons in Division 1: 3
14. *Stoke City*
promoted in 1979 Consecutive seasons in Division 1: 3
15. *Birmingham City*
promoted in 1980 Consecutive seasons in Division 1: 2
16. *Sunderland*
promoted in 1980 Consecutive seasons in Division 1: 2
17. *Notts County*
promoted in 1981 Consecutive seasons in Division 1: 1
18. *Swansea City*
promoted in 1981 Consecutive seasons in Division 1: 1

19. *West Ham United*
promoted in 1981 Consecutive seasons in Division 1: 1
20. *Luton*
promoted in 1982 Consecutive seasons in Division 1: –
21. *Watford*
promoted in 1982 Consecutive seasons in Division 1: –
22. *Norwich*
promoted in 1982 Consecutive seasons in Division 1: –

THE 22 CURRENT 2ND DIVISION CLUBS' LENGTH OF STAY IN DIVISION 2 (to 1982–83)

1. *Oldham* 1974 8
2. *Cambridge United* 1978 4
3. *Newcastle* 1978 4
4. *Chelsea* 1979 3
5. *Queens Park Rangers* 1979 3
6. *Shrewsbury* 1979 3
7. *Blackburn* 1980 2
8. *Bolton* 1980 2
9. *Derby* 1980 2
10. *Grimsby* 1980 2
11. *Sheffield Wednesday* 1980 2
12. *Barnsley* 1981 1
13. *Charlton* 1981 1
14. *Crystal Palace* 1981 1
15. *Leicester* 1981 1
16. *Rotherham* 1981 1
17. *Burnley* 1982 –
18. *Carlisle* 1982 –
19. *Fulham* 1982 –
20. *Leeds* 1982 –
21. *Middlesbrough* 1982 –
22. *Wolves* 1982 –

THE 24 CURRENT 3rd DIVISION CLUBS' LENGTH OF STAY IN DIVISION 3 (TO 1982–83)

1. *Chesterfield* 1970 12
2. *Gillingham* 1974 8
3. *Oxford* 1976 6
4. *Exeter* 1977 5
5. *Plymouth* 1977 5
6. *Brentford* 1978 4
7. *Millwall* 1979 3
8. *Reading* 1979 3
9. *Huddersfield* 1980 2
10. *Newport* 1980 2
11. *Portsmouth* 1980 2
12. *Walsall* 1980 2
13. *Bristol Rovers* 1981 1
14. *Doncaster* 1981 1
15. *Lincoln* 1981 1
16. *Preston* 1981 1
17. *Southend United* 1981 1
18. *Bournemouth* 1982 –
19. *Bradford City* 1982 –
20. *Cardiff* 1982 –

21. *Orient* 1981 –
22. *Sheffield United* 1982 –
23. *Wigan* 1982 –
24. *Wrexham* 1982 –

THE 24 CURRENT 4TH DIVISION CLUBS' LENGTH OF STAY IN DIVISION 4 (1982–83)

1. *Darlington* 1967 15
2. *Crewe* 1969 13
3. *Hartlepool* 1969 13
4. *Stockport County* 1970 12
5. *Torquay* 1972 10
6. *Scunthorpe* 1973 9
7. *Rochdale* 1974 8
8. *Aldershot* 1976 6
9. *Halifax* 1976 6
10. *Northampton* 1977 5
11. *York* 1977 5
12. *Hereford* 1978 4
13. *Port Vale* 1978 4
14. *Peterborough* 1979 3
15. *Tranmere* 1979 3
16. *Bury* 1980 2
17. *Mansfield* 1980 2
18. *Blackpool* 1981 1
19. *Colchester* 1981 1
20. *Hull* 1981 1
21. *Bristol City* 1982 –
22. *Chester* 1982 –
23. *Swindon* 1982 –
24. *Wimbledon* 1982 –

THE 10 CURRENT SCOTTISH PREMIER LEAGUE CLUBS' LENGTH OF STAY IN THE TOP DIVISION (TO 1982–83)

1. *Celtic** 1890–91 85
2. *Rangers** 1890–91 85
3. *Aberdeen*° 1905–06 70
4. *Dundee United*°
   1960–61 23
5. *St. Mirren* 1977–78 6
6. *Morton* 1978–79 5
7. *Dundee* 1981–82 1
8. *Hibernian* 1981–82 1
9. *Kilmarnock* 1982–83 –
10. *Motherwell* 1982–83 –

* Scottish League Division 1 and Premier Division ever present 1891–1983.
° Scottish Premier League ever present 1975–83.

19 CLUBS WHO HAVE PROVIDED MORE THAN 50 INTERNATIONALS BETWEEN THE 4 UNITED KINGDOM AND EIRE NATIONAL SIDES

		England	Scotland	Wales	N.I.	Eire	TOTAL
1.	Everton	43	19	19	17	13	111
2.	Manchester United	33	17	10	20	17	97
3.	Aston Villa	47	9	16	8	7	87
4.	Arsenal	33	14	14	11	9	81
5.	Liverpool	35	18	12	3	3	71
6.	Tottenham Hotspur	36	7	15	7	5	70
7.	Manchester City	31	10	14	10	4	69
8.	Derby County	36	9	6	9	6	66
9.	West Bromwich Albion	39	4	12	4	6	65
10.	Newcastle United	19	24	10	9	2	64
11.	Blackburn Rovers	38	4	8	7	4	61
12.	Leeds United	20	11	11	11	6	59
13.	Cardiff City	–	2	48	7	2	59
14.	Sheffield Wednesday	36	7	5	7	2	57
15.	Sunderland	20	22	3	9	3	57
16.	Wolverhampton Wanderers	32	4	9	8	4	57
17.	Chelsea	28	10	4	8	3	53
18.	Middlesbrough	20	12	11	6	3	52
19.	Nottingham Forest	27	6	7	9	2	51

9 OLDEST SCOTTISH CLUBS

1.	Queens Park	1867	5.	Rangers	1873
2.	Kilmarnock	1869	6.	Hamilton	1874
3.	Stranraer	1870	7.	Hearts	1874
4.	Dumbarton	1872	8.	Morton	1874
		9.	Hibernian		1875

THE 9 SCOTTISH LEAGUE CLUBS
FOUNDED IN THE 20th CENTURY

1.	*Meadowbank Thistle*	1974 – Founded as Works team Ferranti Thistle in 1943
2.	*Clydebank*	1965 – Formerly the 'Clydebank Junior Club'
3.	*Stirling Albion*	1945
4.	*Dundee United*	1923 – They had been Dundee Hibernian for 14 years
5.	*Queen of the South*	1919
6.	*Ayr United*	1910
7.	*Brechin City*	1906
8.	*Aberdeen*	1903
9.	*East Fife*	1903

THE 8 OLDEST BUNDESLIGA CLUBS

1.	*Hamburger SV*	September, 1887
2.	*Hertha BSC Berlin*	July, 1982
3.	*VfB Stuttgart*	September, 1893
4.	*Karlsruher SC*	November, 1894
5.	*Fortuna Düsseldorf*	May, 1895
6.	*Eintracht Braunschweig*	December, 1895
7.	*Hannover 96*	April, 1896
8.	*Union Solingen*	October, 1897

THE 11 FOOTBALL LEAGUE CLUBS
WITH FEWEST MANAGERS
SINCE 1945.

1.	*West Ham*	4	6.	*Wimbledon*	6
2.	*Liverpool*	5	7.	*Stoke City*	7
3.	*Wigan Athletic*	5	8.	*Oxford United*	7
4.	*Southampton*	5	9.	*Arsenal*	7
5.	*Tottenham Hotspur*	6	10.	*Manchester United*	7
	11.	*Nottingham Forest*	7		

THE 7 FOOTBALL LEAGUE CLUBS
WITH MOST MANAGERS SINCE 1945

1.	*Walsall*	20	3.	*Stockport County*	19
2.	*Halifax Town*	19	4.	*Crystal Palace*	18

THE 3 FORMER LEAGUE CHAMPIONS
TO HAVE APPEARED IN DIVISION 4

1. *Sheffield United*   4th Division status 1981–82
2. *Portsmouth*   4th Division status 1978–80
3. *Huddersfield Town*   4th Division status 1975–80

THE 7 F.A. CUP WINNERS WHO HAVE
SPENT TIME IN DIVISION 4

1. *Notts County*   1959–60 and 1964–71
2. *Bradford City*   1961–69 and 1972–77 and
                     1978–82
3. *Barnsley*   1965–68 and 1972–79
4. *Bury*   1971–74 and 1980–
5. *Huddersfield Town*   1975–80
6. *Portsmouth*   1978–80
7. *Sheffield United*   1981–82

THE 110 CLUBS THAT HAVE
PROVIDED ENGLAND WITH
PLAYERS

From 1870 to February, 1983

Although the likes of Liverpool, Manchester United, Everton, Tottenham and Arsenal all got off to a slow start during the pre-First World War period in supplying England with players, they are now leading the way. Today more than ever it seems important to play for a fashionable club.

As can be seen only 5 non U.K. clubs have supplied England national players Keegan, Woodcock, Cunningham, Watson from the late 1970's and Gerry Hitchens from 1962.

	Caps	Total Appearance
1. *Accrington*	3	7
2. *Arsenal*	33	257
3. *Aston Villa*	47	186
4. *Barnes*	1	1
5. *Barnsley*	1	1

	Caps	Total Appearance
6. *Birmingham City*	14	113
7. *Birmingham Excelsior*	1	1
8. *Blackburn Olympic*	1	1
9. *Blackburn Rovers*	38	251
10. *Blackpool*	11	144
11. *Bolton Wanderers*	25	111
12. *Bradford Park Avenue*	1	1
13. *Bradford City*	3	8
14. *Brentford*	2	2
15. *Brighton and Hove Albion*	3	5
16. *Bristol City*	4	34
17. *Bristol Rovers*	1	1
18. *Burnley*	25	84
19. *Bury*	6	11
20. *Cambridge University*	26	56
21. *Casuals*	5	6
22. *Charlton Athletic*	7	11
23. *Chelsea*	28	156
24. *Clapham Rovers*	8	28
25. *Clapton*	3	4
26. *Clapton Orient*	2	4
27. *Corinthians*	16	51
28. *Coventry City*	1	5
29. *Crewe Alexandra*	1	1
30. *Crystal Palace (19th century)*	4	6
31. *Crystal Palace (Present)*	5	16
32. *Darwen*	4	7
33. *Derby County*	36	214
34. *Dulwich Hamlet*	2	4
35. *Everton*	43	252
36. *Fulham*	9	105
37. *Great Lever*	1	1
38. *Grimsby Town*	3	3
39. *Hamburger S.V. (West Germany)*	1	26
40. *Hendon*	1	2
41. *Hertfordshire Rangers*	2	2
42. *Hibernian*	1	5

	Caps	Total Appearance
43. *Huddersfield Town*	21	138
44. *Inter Milan (Italy)*	1	4
45. *Ipswich Town*	11	113
46. *1. FC. Köln (West Germany)*	1	18
47. *Leeds United*	20	205
48. *Leicester City*	12	99
49. *Leyton*	1	2
50. *Liverpool*	35	420
51. *Liverpool Ramblers*	1	1
52. *Luton Town*	7	16
53. *Manchester City*	31	257
54. *Manchester United*	33	422 including Bobby Charlton 106 appearances
55. *Middlesbrough*	20	99
56. *Millwall*	8	10
57. *New Brighton Tower*	1	3
58. *Newcastle United*	19	73
59. *Norwich City*	2	2
60. *Nottingham Forest*	27	91
61. *Notts County*	17	56
62. *Notts Rangers*	1	1
63. *Old Brightonians*	2	5
64. *Old Carthusians*	8	32
65. *Old Etonians*	6	14
66. *Old Foresters*	2	4
67. *Oldham Athletic*	3	5
68. *Old Harrovians*	3	3
69. *Old Malvernians*	2	4
70. *Old Westminsters*	6	22
71. *Owlerton*	1	1
72. *Oxford City*	1	1
73. *Oxford University*	22	40
74. *Pilgrims*	1	6
75. *Portsmouth*	10	77
76. *Preston North End*	14	120 including Tom Finney 76 Caps
77. *Queens Park Rangers*	8	38

	Caps	Total Appearance
78. Reading	2	5
79. Real Madrid (Spain)	1	3
80. Royal Engineers	6	7
81. Saltley College	1	1
82. Sheffield	1	1
83. Sheffield Albion	2	6
84. Sheffield Heeley	1	7
85. Sheffield United	33	98
86. Sheffield Wednesday	36	209
87. Shropshire Wanderers	1	1
88. Southampton	18	121
89. South Shields	1	1
90. Stafford Road	1	1
91. Stockport County	1	1
91. Stoke City	22	125
93. Sunderland	20	80
94. 1st Surrey Rifles	1	2
95. Swifts	8	31
96. Swindon Town	1	11
97. Thursday Wanderers	1	1
98. Tottenham Hotspur	36	324
99. Tufnell Park	1	1
100. Upton Park	3	7
101. Uxbridge	1	2
102. Walsall Town Swifts	2	3
103. Wanderers	15	23
104. Watford	1	2
105. Wednesbury Old Athletic	1	4
106. Wednesbury Strollers	1	1
107. Werder Bremen (West Germany)	1	1
108. West Bromwich Albion	39	184
109. West Ham United	21	302 including Bobby Moore 108 appearances
110. Wolverhampton Wanderers	32	292 including Billy Wright 105 appearances

THE 120 CLUBS TO PROVIDE
SCOTLAND WITH NATIONAL TEAM
PLAYERS TO FEBRUARY, 1983

1.	*Abercorn*	6	39.	*Dumbreck*	1
2.	*Aberdeen*	33	40.	*Dundee*	33
3.	*Airdrie*	17	41.	*Dundee United*	4
4.	*Albion Rovers*	1	42.	*Dunfermline*	3
5.	*Alexandra Athletic*	1	43.	*Dyke Bar*	1
6.	*Alloa Athletic*	1	44.	*Eastern*	3
7.	*Annbank*	1	45.	*East Fife*	6
8.	*Arbroath*	1	46.	*East Stirling*	3
9.	*Arsenal*	14	47.	*Edinburgh University*	1
10.	*Arthurlie*	4	48.	*Everton*	19
11.	*Aston Villa*	9	49.	*Falkirk*	12
12.	*Ayr United*	8	50.	*Fulham*	2
13.	*Barnsley*	1	51.	*Glasgow University*	1
14.	*Battlefield*	1	52.	*Granville*	1
15.	*Beith*	1	53.	*Greenock Morton*	1
16.	*Birmingham City*	6	54.	*Hamilton Academicals*	2
17.	*Blackburn Rovers*	4	55.	*Hearts*	56
18.	*Blackpool*	9	56.	*Hibernian*	45
19.	*Bolton Wanderers*	4	57.	*Huddersfield*	4
20.	*Bradford P.A.*	1	58.	*Hull*	1
21.	*Bradford City*	1	59.	*Hurlford*	2
22.	*Brentford*	4	60.	*Ipswich*	3
23.	*Burnley*	3	61.	*Kilbirnie*	1
24.	*Bury*	1	62.	*Kilmarnock Athletic*	1
25.	*Caledonian*	1	63.	*Kilmarnock*	23
26.	*Cambuslang*	7	64.	*Leeds United*	11
27.	*Cardiff City*	2	65.	*Leicester City*	6
28.	*Cartvale*	2	66.	*Leicester Fosse*	1
29.	*Celtic*	92	67.	*Leith Athletic*	2
30.	*Charlton Athletic*	1	68.	*Linthouse*	1
31.	*Chelsea*	10	69.	*Liverpool*	18
32.	*Clyde*	11	70.	*Llanelly*	1
33.	*Clydesdale*	6	71.	*Luton Town*	1
34.	*Coventry City*	5	72.	*Manchester City*	10
35.	*Cowdenbeath*	3	73.	*Manchester United*	17
36.	*Cowlairs*	3	74.	*Mauchline*	1
37.	*Derby County*	9	75.	*Middlesbrough*	12
38.	*Dumbarton*	21	76.	*A.C. Milan (Italy)*	1

77.	*Moffat*	2	100.	*Royal Albert*	1
78.	*Montrose*	2	101.	*Royal Engineers*	2
79.	*Morton*	8	102.	*St. Bernards*	8
80.	*Mossend Swifts*	2	103.	*St. Johnstone*	2
81.	*Motherwell*	26	104.	*St. Mirren*	26
82.	*Newcastle United*	24	105.	*Sheffield Wednesday*	7
83.	*Newmilnes*	1	106.	*Sheffield United*	3
84.	*Norwich City*	2	107.	*Southampton*	2
85.	*Nottingham Forest*	6	108.	*South Weston*	1
86.	*Oldham Athletic*	2	109.	*Stoke City*	2
87.	*Partick Thistle*	21	110.	*Sunderland*	22
88.	*Pilgrims*	1	111.	*Swindon Town*	1
89.	*Pollokshields Athletic*	3	112.	*Third Lanark*	34
90.	*Port Glasgow Athletic*	1	113.	*Torino (Italy)*	1
91.	*Portsmouth*	4	114.	*Tottenham Hotspur*	7
92.	*Preston North End*	12	115.	*Vale of Leven*	15
93.	*Queen of the South*	2	116.	*Wanderers*	1
94.	*Queens Park*	75	117.	*West Bromwich Albion*	4
95.	*Queens Park Rangers*	1	118.	*West Ham United*	2
96.	*Raith Rovers*	4	119.	*Wolverhampton*	
97.	*Rangers*	116		*Wanderers*	4
98.	*Renfrew*	1	120.	*Woolwich Arsenal*	3
99.	*Renton*	12			

THE 161 CLUBS FROM WHOM WALES HAVE SELECTED PLAYERS TO FEBRUARY, 1983

1.	*Aberanan*	1	14.	*Blackpool*	4
2.	*Aberdare Athletic*	4	15.	*Bolton Wanderers*	12
3.	*Aberystwyth*	8	16.	*Bootle*	4
4.	*Ardwick – later*		17.	*Bradford City*	3
	Mancester City	1	18.	*Brecon*	1
5.	*Arsenal*	14	19.	*Brentford*	3
6.	*Aston Villa*	16	20.	*Brighton and Hove*	
7.	*Bangor*	12		*Albion*	3
8.	*Barmouth*	1	21.	*Bristol City*	3
9.	*Barnsley*	1	22.	*Bristol Rovers*	3
10.	*Beringen (Belgium)*	1	23.	*Brymbo*	1
11.	*Berwyn Rangers*	4	24.	*Builth*	1
12.	*Birmingham City*	16	25.	*Burnley*	4
13.	*Blackburn Rovers*	8	26.	*Burton Swifts*	1

27. Burton United	1	69. Liverpool	12
28. Caernarvon	1	70. Liverpool Marine	1
29. Cambridge University	3	71. Llanberis	1
30. Cardiff City	48	72. Llandrindod Wells	1
31. Cardiff Corinthians	3	73. Llandudno	2
32. Charlton Athletic	8	74. Llanelly	2
33. Chelsea	4	75. Llangollen	1
34. Chester	5	76. London Welsh	2
35. Chirk	20	77. Lovells Athletic	1
36. Civil Service	1	78. Luton Town	2
37. Clapton	2	79. Manchester Central	1
38. Clapton Orient	4	80. Manchester City	14
39. Colwyn Bay	1	81. Manchester United	10
40. Corinthians	3	82. Merthyr Tydfil	2
41. Corwen	1	83. Middlesbrough	10
42. Coventry City	8	84. Millwall	4
43. Crewe Alexandra	8	85. Mold	1
44. Crusaders	1	86. Motherwell	1
45. Crystal Palace	12	87. Nelson	1
46. Derby County	6	88. North End (of Belfast)	1
47. Derby School Staff	1	89. New Brighton Tower	1
48. Doncaster	1	90. Newcastle United	10
49. Druids	32	91. Newport County	9
50. East Stirling	1	92. Newton Heath	7
51. Everton	19	93. Newton White Star	1
52. Fulham	4	94. Newtown	12
53. Glossop N/E	1	95. Newtown Excelsior	1
54. Grimsby Town	4	96. Northampton Town	4
55. Hearts	1	97. Norwich City	5
56. Hereford United	2	98. Northwich Victoria	1
57. Hibernian	1	99. Notts County	4
58. Huddersfield	4	100. Nottingham Forest	7
59. Hull City	2	101. Nunhead	1
60. Ipswich Town	3	102. Oldham Athletic	3
61. Juventus	1	103. Oswestry	27
62. Leeds United	11	104. Oswestry White Star	1
63. Leicester City	6	105. Oxford United	1
64. Leicester Fosse	2	106. Oxford University	5
65. Leyton	1	107. Park Grove	1
66. Leyton Orient	1	108. Peterborough United	2
67. Lincoln City	1	109. Plymouth Argyle	5
68. Linfield	1	110. Port Vale	1

111. Presteigne	1	139. Sunderland	3
112. Preston North End	6	140. Swansea City	14
113. Portsmouth	3	141. Swansea Town	36
114. P.S.V. Eindhoven		142. Swifts	1
(Holland)	1	143. Swindon Town	2
115. Queens Park	1	144. Tottenham Hotspur	15
116. Queens Park Rangers	2	145. Tranmere Rovers	3
117. Reading	1	146. Treharris	1
118. Rhos	2	147. Vancouver White Caps	
119. Rhostyllen	1	(Canada)	1
120. Rhyl	3	148. Walsall	2
121. Rotherham County	1	149. Wanderers	1
122. Rotherham United	2	150. Watford	3
123. Ruabon	1	151. Wellingborough	
124. Ruthin	6	Grammar School	1
125. Ruthin G.S.	1	152. Welshpool	1
126. St. Helen's Rec.	1	153. West Bromwich Albion	
127. St. Thomas's	1		12
128. Sheffield United	9	154. West Ham United	4
129. Sheffield Wednesday	5	155. Winstay	1
130. Shrewsbury	8	156. Wolverhampton	
131. Shrewsbury Engineers	2	Wanderers	9
132. Shropshire Wanderers	1	157. Woolwich Arsenal	1
133. Small Heath	2	158. Wrexham	77
134. Southampton	3	159. Wrexham Civil	
135. Southend United	2	Service	1
136. Southport Central	1	160. Wrexham Olympic	2
137. South Liverpool	1	161. Wynstay	2
138. Stoke City	12		

THE 136 CLUBS FROM WHOM NORTHERN IRELAND HAVE SELECTED PLAYERS

1. Aberdeen	3	9. Ballymena	3
2. Aidrieonians	3	10. Barnsley	3
3. Aldershot	1	11. Barrow	1
4. Alexander	1	12. Belfast Athletic	1
5. Ards	3	13. Belfast Celtic	28
6. Arsenal	11	14. Belfast Y.M.C.A.	4
7. Aston Villa	8	15. Birmingham City	3
8. Avoniel	1	16. Blackburn Rovers	7

17.	*Blackpool*	4	
18.	*Bohemians*	16	
19.	*Bolton Wanderers*	3	
20.	*Bo'ness*	1	
21.	*Bradford City*	7	
22.	*Bradford Park Avenue*	4	
23.	*Brentford*	4	
24.	*Brighton and Hove Albion*	7	
25.	*Bristol Rovers*	2	
26.	*Burnley*	12	
27.	*Bury*	3	
28.	*Cambridge United*	1	
29.	*Cardiff City*	7	
30.	*Carlisle United*	1	
31.	*Celtic*	7	
32.	*Charlton Athletic*	1	
33.	*Chelsea*	8	
34.	*Chelmsford City*	1	
35.	*Chesterfield*	2	
36.	*Clarence*	2	
37.	*Cliftonville*	62	
38.	*Clyde*	4	
39.	*Coleraine*	10	
40.	*Connah's Quay*	1	
41.	*Coventry City*	5	
42.	*Crusaders*	2	
43.	*Crystal Palace*	1	
44.	*Derby County*	9	
45.	*Derry C.*	4	
46.	*Distillery*	58	
47.	*Doncaster Rovers*	6	
48.	*Dublin Association*	2	
49.	*Dublin Freebooters*	3	
50.	*Dublin University*	8	
51.	*Dundee*	3	
52.	*Dunfermline Athletic*	1	
53.	*Everton*	17	
54.	*Falkirk*	4	
55.	*Fulham*	8	
56.	*Glenavon*	12	
57.	*Glentoran*	36	

58.	*Glossop North End*	1	
59.	*Grimsby Town*	3	
60.	*Hearts*	1	
61.	*Hertford*	1	
62.	*Hibernian*	4	
63.	*Huddersfield Town*	8	
64.	*Hull City*	8	
65.	*Ipswich Town*	3	
66.	*Kilmarnock*	1	
67.	*Knock*	4	
68.	*Knock and Down Athletic*	1	
69.	*Leeds United*	11	
70.	*Leicester City*	5	
71.	*Leyton*	1	
72.	*Ligoniel*	1	
73.	*Limavady*	6	
74.	*Linfield*	56	
75.	*Linfield Athletic*	1	
76.	*Liverpool*	3	
77.	*London Caledonians*	1	
78.	*Luton Town*	7	
79.	*Manchester City*	10	
80.	*Manchester United*	20	
81.	*Mansfield Town*	1	
82.	*Middlesbrough*	6	
83.	*Millwall*	4	
84.	*Motherwell*	1	
85.	*Morton*	1	
86.	*Moyola Park*	4	
87.	*New Brighton*	1	
88.	*Newcastle United*	9	
89.	*New York Cosmos (U.S.A.)*	1	
90.	*Norwich City*	3	
91.	*Nottingham Forest*	9	
92.	*Oldham Athletic*	4	
93.	*Old Park*	2	
94.	*Oxford United*	2	
95.	*Partick Thistle*	1	
96.	*Peterborough*	1	
97.	*Pontypridd*	1	

98.	Portadown	3	118.	Stoke City	6
99.	Portsmouth	9	119.	Sunderland	8
100.	Port Vale	2	120.	Swansea Town/City	7
101.	Preston North End	3	121.	Swindon Town	3
102.	Queen's Island	4	122.	Toronto Blizzard	
103.	Queens Park Rangers	6		(Canada)	1
104.	Rangers	9	123.	Tottenham Hotspur	7
105.	Reading	2	124.	Tranmere Rovers	1
106.	Rossall School	1	125.	Tulsa Roughnecks	
107.	Sheffield Wednesday	7		(U.S.A.)	2
108.	Sheffield United	3	126.	Ulster	11
109.	Shelbourne	5	127.	Walsall	1
110.	Shrewsbury	2	128.	Watford	2
111.	Southampton	4	129.	Wellington Park	2
112.	Southend United	3	130.	West Bromwich Albion	4
113.	Southport	2	131.	West Down	1
114.	Sparta Rotterdam		132.	West Ham United	1
	(Holland)	2	133.	Woolwich Athletic	1
115.	St. Columb's Court	2	134.	Wolves	8
116.	St. Johnstone	1	135.	Y.M.C.A.	3
117.	St. Mirren	2	136.	York City	10

THE 106 CLUBS TO PROVIDE EIRE INTERNATIONALS TO FEBRUARY, 1983

1.	Aberdeen	2	16.	Brideville	2
2.	Arsenal	9	17.	Brighton and Hove	
3.	Aston Villa	7		Albion	5
4.	Barnsley	1	18.	Bristol City	1
5.	Belfast Celtic	3	19.	Bristol Rovers	2
6.	Birmingham City	5	20.	Bury	1
7.	Blackburn Rovers	4	21.	Cardiff City	2
8.	Blackpool	1	22.	Celtic	7
9.	Bohemians	19	23.	Charlton Athletic	2
10.	Bolton Wanderers	3	24.	Chelsea	3
11.	Bo'ness	1	25.	Clyde	2
12.	Bournemouth and		26.	Coleraine	1
	Boscombe Athletic	1	27.	Cork	9
13.	Bradford	1	28.	Cork Athletic	1
14.	Bray Unknowns	1	29.	Cork Bohemians	1
15.	Brentford	1	30.	Cork Hibernian	2

31. Cork United	3	70. Newport County	1
32. Coventry City	3	71. Northampton Town	1
33. Crystal Palace	1	72. Norwich City	2
34. Derby County	6	73. Notts County	4
35. Derry City	1	74. Nottingham Forest	2
36. Dolphin	4	75. Oldham Athletic	1
37. Doncaster Rovers	3	76. Orient	1
38. Drogheda United	3	77. Oxford United	1
39. Drumcondra	13	78. Peterborough United	1
40. Dumbarton	1	79. Philadelphia Fury	
41. Dundalk	11	(U.S.A.)	1
42. Everton	13	80. Porto	1
43. Exeter City	1	81. Portsmouth	2
44. Falkirk	1	82. Preston North End	8
45. Fordsons	6	83. Queens Park Rangers	6
46. Fortuna Köln (West		84. Shamrock Rovers	60
Germany)	1	85. Sheffield United	2
47. Fulham	7	86. Sheffield Wednesday	2
48. Gillingham	1	87. Shelbourne	22
49. Glentoran	1	88. Sligo Rovers	1
50. Grimsby Town	1	89. Southampton	5
51. Hartlepools United	1	90. Southend United	3
52. Hibernian	2	91. St. James Gate	8
53. Huddersfield	3	92. St. Patricks Athletic	6
54. Ipswich Town	3	93. Stoke City	2
55. Jacobs	1	94. Sunderland	3
56. Juventus (Italy)	1	95. Swansea Town	3
57. Leeds United	6	96. Swindon	1
58. Leicester City	1	97. Tottenham Hotspur	5
59. Limerick	6	98. Tranmere Rovers	1
60. Lincoln City	3	99. Vancouver Whitecaps	
61. Liverpool	3	(Can).	1
62. Luton	6	100. Walsall	4
63. Manchester City	4	101. Waterford	7
64. Manchester United	17	102. Watford	1
65. Middlesbrough	3	103. West Bromwich Albion	6
66. Millwall	4	104. West Ham United	7
67. Minnesota Kicks		105. Wolves	4
(U.S.A.)	1	106. York City	1
68. Newcastle United	2		
69. Neuchatel Xamax			
(Switzerland)	1		

THE 49 CLUBS TO PROVIDE
INTERNATIONAL PLAYERS WHILE
IN THE 3RD OR 4TH DIVISIONS

		Country	Division
1. *Aldershot*	Peter Scott	N.I.	4
2. *Barnsley*	Pat Kelly	N.I.	3N
	A. Richards	Wales	3N
3. *Barrow*	Billy Millar	N.I.	3N
4. *Bournemouth*	Tommy Godwin	Eire	3
5. *Bradford City*	Bobby Campbell	N.I.	4
6. *Bradford Park Avenue*	R. W. Matthews	Wales	3N
	Mike McGrath	Eire	4
7. *Brighton and Hove Albion*	Jack Jenkins	Wales	3S
	Peter O'Sullivan	Wales	3
	Joe Kinnear	Eire	3
8. *Bristol City*	R. W. Matthews	Wales	3S
9. *Bristol Rovers*	H. R. Buckle	N.I.	3S
	Matt O'Mahoney	Eire and N.I.	3S
	Joe Haverty	Eire	3
	Wayne Jones	Wales	3
10. *Burnley*	Tommy Cassidy	N.I.	3
	Billy Hamilton	N.I.	3
11. *Bury*	Derek Spence	N.I.	3
12. *Chester*	Albert Gray	Wales	3N
	Ian Edwards	Wales	3
13. *Coventry City*	Leslie Jones	Wales	3S
	Hugh Bane	N.I.	3
	Billy Humphries	N.I.	3
	Reg Matthews	England	3S
14. *Crewe Alexandra*	Fred Keenor	Wales	3N
15. *Crystal Palace*	Vic Rouse	Wales	4
	Johnny Byrne	England	3
	Peter Taylor	England	3
16. *Doncaster Rovers*	E. Perry	Wales	3N
	Len Graham	N.I.	3
	Alfie Hale	Eire	4
17. *Exeter City*	Dermot Curtis	Eire	4
18. *Fulham*	Jimmy Conway	Eire	3
	Jimmy Dunne	Eire	3
	Gordon Davies	Wales	3
19. *Gillingham*	Damien Richardson	Eire	4
20. *Grimsby Town*	D. J. Collier	Wales	3
	Joe Waters	Eire	3
21. *Hartlepool United*	Ambrose Fogarty	Eire	4

22. *Hereford United*	Brian Evans	Wales	3
23. *Lincoln City*	Con Moulson	Eire	3N
	George Moulson	Eire	3N
24. *Luton Town*	A. Mathieson	N.I.	3S
25. *Mansfield Town*	John McClelland	N.I.	4
26. *Millwall Athletic*	Freddie Fox	England	3S
(Former name of			
Millwall)			
Millwall	Joe Haverty	Eire	3
	Charlie Hurley	Eire	3
	Pat Saward	Eire	3S
	T. Brolly	N.I.	3S
	E. Hinton	N.I.	3S
	Eamonn Dunphy	Eire	3
27. *Newport County*	Fred Cook	Wales	3S
	Jack Nicholls	Wales	3S
	A. R. Hugh	Wales	3S
	Alf Sherwood	Wales	3S
	Harold Williams	Wales	3S
	Billy Thomas	Wales	3S
	T. J. Martin	Wales	3S
	H. A. Duggan	Eire	3S
28. *Northampton Town*	W. Williams	Wales	3S
29. *Norwich City*	M. T. O'Brien	Eire	3S
	Johnny Gavin	Eire	3
	Noel Kinsey	Wales	3
30. *Notts County*	E. Gannon	Eire	3S
	Bill Fallon	Eire	3S
	Con Moulson	Eire	3S
	Tommy Lawton	England	3S
31. *Oldham Athletic*	Tom Davis	N.I.	3N
	Billy Johnston	N.I.	3
32. *Orient (Clapton)*	E. Lawrence	Wales	3S
	T. G. Mills	Wales	3S
33. *Peterborough United*	Ollie Conmy	Eire	3
	Frank Rankmore	Wales	3
	Tony Millington	Wales	4
	Trevor Anderson	N.I.	3
34. *Plymouth Argyle*	Moses Russell	Wales	3S
35. *Port Vale*	Billy Bingham	N.I.	3
	Sammy Morgan	N.I.	3
36. *Preston North End*	John Anderson	Eire	3
37. *Queens Park Rangers*	Ivor Powell	Wales	3S
	Ray Brady	Eire	3
38. *Reading*	D. G. Evans	Wales	3S
	Pat McConnell	N.I.	3S

39. *Rotherham United*	Stanley Davies	Wales	3N
	Ray Mielczarek	Wales	3
40. *Shrewsbury Town*	Jimmy McClaughlin	N.I.	3
41. *Southend United*	J. H. Evans	Wales	3S
	Tommy Canwell	Eire	3S
	C. J. Turner	Eire	3S
	George MacKenzie	Eire	3S
	Sammy McCrory	N.I.	3S
	Derek Spence	N.I.	3
42. *Southport*	Terry Harkin	N.I.	3
43. *Swansea Town (now City)*	W. Davies	Wales	3S
	J. Fowler	Wales	3S
	Billy Hole	Wales	3S
	Ivor Jones	Wales	3S
	E. J. Morley	Wales	3S
	Roy Paul	Wales	3S
	Brian Evans	Wales	4
	Barrie Hole	Wales	3
	Tony Millington	Wales	3
	Herbie Williams	Wales	3
	John Toshack	Wales	3
	Alan Curtis	Wales	4
	Robbie James	Wales	3
44. *Swindon Town*	Norman Uprichard	N.I.	3S
	Rod Thomas	Wales	3
	Trevor Anderson	N.I.	3
45. *Tranmere Rovers*	Albert Gray	Wales	3N
	J. Brown	N.I.	3N
	Tony Rowley	Wales	3
46. *Walsall*	M. T. O'Brien	Eire	3S
	W. R. John	Wales	3S
	R. Griffith	Eire	3N
	Miah Dennehy	Eire	3
	Mick Kearns	Eire	3
47. *Watford*	M. T. O'Brien	Eire	3S
	F. Hoddinott	Wales	3S
	Pat Dennings	N.I.	3
48. *Wrexham*	T. Bamford	Wales	3N
	Rev. H. Davies	Wales	3N
	R. J. Finnigan	Wales	3N
	G. Godding	Wales	3N
	J. Jones	Wales	3N
	A. Lumberg	Wales	3N
	A. W. Mays	Wales	3N
	George Poland	Wales	3N
	W. Rogers	Wales	3N

	A. L. Williams	Wales	3N
	J. T. Williams	Wales	3N
	Dai Davies	Wales	3
	Gareth Davis	Wales	3
	Arfon Griffiths	Wales	3
	Joey Jones	Wales	3
	Brian Lloyd	Wales	3
	Dave Powell	Wales	4
	Dave Smallman	Wales	3
	Mickey Thomas	Wales	3
49. York City	Eamonn Dunphy	Eire	3
	Peter Scott	N.I.	4

12 FOOTBALL LEAGUE CLUBS TO HAVE USED FEWER THAN 18 PLAYERS IN ONE SEASON

1.	Aston Villa	14 (1980–81)	League Champions
2.	Liverpool	14 (1965–66)	League Champions
	Liverpool	15 (1978–79)	League Champions
3.	Huddersfield	16 (1979–80)	Division 4 Champions
4.	Nottingham Forest	16 (1977–78)	League Champions
	Liverpool	16 (1981–82)	League Champions
5.	Tranmere Rovers	16 (1977–78)	
6.	Bristol City	17 (1977–78)	
7.	Darlington	17 (1977–78)	
	Liverpool	17 (1967–68)	3rd in Division 1
	Liverpool	17 (1979–80)	League Champions
8.	Manchester United	17 (1975–76)	3rd in Division 1
9.	Notts County	17 (1978–79)	
	Notts County	17 (1981–82)	
10.	Orient	17 (1977–78)	
11.	Reading	17 (1978–79)	Division 4 Champions
12.	West Bromwich Albion	17 (1977–78)	
	West Bromwich Albion	17 (1978–79)	3rd in Division 1

8 FOOTBALL CLUBS TO HAVE USED 30 OR MORE PLAYERS IN ONE SEASON

1.	Bradford Park Avenue	31	1967–68
2.	Bristol City	30	1981–82
3.	Derby County	31	1977–78
	Derby County	32	1979–80
	Derby County	30	1981–82

4. *Hereford*	42	1978–79
5. *Hull City*	42	1946–47
6. *Newcastle*	35	1977–78
7. *Sheffield Wednesday*	42	1919–20
8. *Stockport County*	32	1975–76

12 CLUBS IN RECENT YEARS TO HAVE USED FOUR OR MORE GOALKEEPERS IN A SEASON

1. *Hereford United (1982–83)*

   John Jackson   Gary Plumley

   Melvin Gwynnett   Kevin Rose

   Drew Brand   Andy Powell

   6 Goalkeepers were used before the halfway point of the season.

2. *Cardiff City (1978–79)*

   Ron Healey   John Davies

   Jim Platt (Loan)   Keith Barber (Loan)

3. *Chelsea (1978–79)*

   Peter Bonetti   John Phillips

   Peter Borota   Bob Iles

4. *Chesterfield (1979–80)*

   Phil Tingay   Mark Kendall (Loan)

   John Turner   Glan Letheran

5. *Crewe Alexandra (1979–80)*

   Bruce Grobbelaar   Kevin Rafferty

   David Felgate (Loan)   John Phillips (Loan)

6. *Crystal Palace (1977–78)*

   Tony Burns   Peter Caswell

   John Burridge   David Fry

7. *Hartlepool United (1978–79)*

   Graham Richardson   John Watson

   Jim Platt (Loan)   Eddie Edgar

8. *Lincoln City (1978–79)*

   Peter Grotier   Chris Turner (Loan)

   Laurie Sivell (Loan)   Ian Turner (Loan)

9. *Rotherham United (1975–76)*

   Tom McAlister   Barry Watling (Loan)

   Jim McDonagh   Graham Haslam

10. *Sheffield United (1979–80)*

    Steve Conroy   Terry Poole

    Derek Richardson   Neil Ramsbottom

11. *Southend (1977–78)*
    Neil Freeman
    John Burridge (Loan)
    Sean Rafter
    Graham Horn
12. *Stockport County (1967–68)*
    Alan Ogley
    Steve Fleet
    Brian Lloyd
    Ken Mulhearn

6 CLUBS TO COMPLETE A SEASON WITH 5 OR MORE EVER-PRESENT PLAYERS

1. *Aston Villa* (1980–81) 1st Division Champions
   Jimmy Rimmer   (GK)   Gordon Cowans   (M)
   Kenny Swain   (FB)   Des Bremner   (M)
   Ken McNaught   (CB)   Tony Morley   (S)
   Dennis Mortimer   (M)

2. *Huddersfield Town* (1952–53) Division 2
   John Wheeler   (GK)   Don McAvoy   (HB)
   Ron Staniforth   (FB)   Len Quested   (HB)
   Laurie Kelly   (FB)   Vic Metcalfe   (OL)
   Bill McGarry   (HB)

The only club whose entire defence were ever-present.

3. *Bristol City* (1975–76) Division 2
   Ray Cashley   (GK)   Trevor Tainton   (M)
   Geoff Merrick   (CB)   Tom Ritchie   (S)
   Gerry Gow   (M)

4. *Orient* (1977–78) Division 2
   John Jackson   (GK)   Glenn Roeder   (SW)
   Bobby Fisher   (FB)   Peter Kitchen   (S)
   Bill Roffey   (FB)

5. *Tranmere Rovers* (1975–76) Division 4
   Dick Johnson   (GK)   Steve Peplow   (MW)
   Ray Mathias   (FB)   Ronnie Moore   (CF)
   David Philpotts   (CB)

6. *Watford* (1967–68) Division 3
   Bob Slater   (GK)   Duncan Welbourne (HB)
   John Williams   (FB)   Stewart Scullion (W)
   Brian Garvey   (CB)

THE 8 CURRENT FOOTBALL LEAGUE
CLUBS NEVER TO HAVE SUPPLIED
AN INTERNATIONAL PLAYER

1. *Colchester United*
2. *Darlington*
3. *Halifax Town*
4. *Rochdale*
5. *Scunthorpe United*
6. *Torquay United*
7. *Wigan Athletic*
8. *Wimbledon*

7 CURRENT OR FAMOUS FORMER
LEAGUE CLUB MOTTOES

Birmingham City	Forward
Bristol Rovers	Virtue and Industry
Cambridge United	United in Endeavour
Nelson	By Industry and Integrity
Peterborough United	Upon This Rock
Scunthorpe United	Unity
Wigan	Progress with Unity

THE 22 NON FIRST DIVISION CLUBS
IN F.A./LEAGUE CUP FINALS.

F.A. Cup

1.	*The Wednesday*	(1889–90)		Non League
2.	*Notts County*	(1893–94)	Winners	2nd Division
3.	*Southampton*	(1899–1900)		Southern League
4.	*Tottenham*	(1900–1901)	Winners	Southern League
	Southampton	(1901–1902)		Southern League
5.	*Bolton*	(1903–1904)		2nd Division
6.	*Wolves*	(1907–1908)	Winners	2nd Division
7.	*Barnsley*	(1909–1910)		2nd Division
	Barnsley	(1911–1912)	Winners	2nd Division
8.	*Huddersfield*	(1919–1920)		2nd Division
	Wolves	(1920–1921)		2nd Division
9.	*West Ham*	(1922–1923)		2nd Division
10.	*West Bromwich Albion*	(1930–1931)	Winners	2nd Division
11.	*Sheffield United*	(1935–1936)		2nd Division
12.	*Burnley*	(1946–1947)		2nd Division
13.	*Leicester City*	(1948–1949)		2nd Division

14.	Preston North End	(1963–1964)		2nd Division
15.	Sunderland	(1972–1973)	Winners	2nd Division
16.	Fulham	(1974–1975)		2nd Division
	Southampton	(1975–1976)	Winners	2nd Division
	West Ham	(1979–1980)	Winners	2nd Division
17.	Queens Park Rangers	(1981–1982)		2nd Division

League Cup

18.	Rotherham	(1960–1961)		2nd Division
19.	Norwich City	(1961–1962)	Winners	2nd Division
20.	Rochdale	(1961–1962)		4th Division
	Queens Park Rangers	(1966–1967)	Winners	3rd Division
21.	Swindon Town	(1968–1969)	Winners	3rd Division
22.	Aston Villa	(1970–1971)		3rd Division
	Aston Villa	(1974–1975)	Winners	2nd Division
	Norwich City	(1974–1975)		2nd Division

THE 4 ENGLISH CLUBS TO HAVE WON THE LEAGUE AND CUP DOUBLE

Preston North End	1888–1889	Tottenham Hotspur	1960–1961
Aston Villa	1896–1897	Arsenal	1970–1971

THE 12 MOST SUCCESSFUL ENGLISH CLUBS OVER THE LAST 10 YEARS (1972–3 TO 1981–2)

Liverpool	318 points	Everton	136 points
Ipswich	199 points	Aston Villa	128 points
Arsenal	178 points	Tottenham	128 points
Leeds United	163 points	Nottingham Forest	118 points
Manchester United	158 points	Derby County	112 points
Manchester City	143 points	Wolves	98 points

The points were accumulated thus:
    32 points League Champions
    26 points League Runners Up
    20 points For 3rd place in the 1st Division, and 1 point less
        for each lower position

6 points For 2nd Division Champions
10 points for F.A. Cup Winners
5 points for F.A. Cup Runners-Up
6 points for League Cup Winners
3 points for League Cup Runners-Up

THE 4 CLUBS TO HAVE HAD MORE THAN 2 LEAGUE CHAMPIONSHIPS SINCE THE WAR

Liverpool	9	*Arsenal*	3
Manchester United	5	*Wolves*	3

THE 14 CLUBS WITH MOST DIVISIONAL TITLE WINS

Liverpool	17	*Sunderland*	7
Aston Villa	9	*Derby County*	6
Manchester United	9	*Grimsby*	6
Sheffield Wednesday	9	*Leicester City*	6
Arsenal	8	*Notts County*	6
Everton	8	*Preston*	6
Manchester City	8	*Wolves*	6

THE 44 LEAGUE CLUBS PROMOTED TO DIVISION I SINCE WORLD WAR II

1. *Birmingham City* 4 times
2. *Leicester City* 4 times
3. *Sheffield Wednesday* 4 times
4. *Luton* 3 times
5. *Manchester City* 3 times
6. *Norwich* 3 times
7. *Sheffield United* 3 times
8. *Sunderland* 3 times
9. *Aston Villa* Twice
10. *Burnley* Twice
11. *Cardiff* Twice
12. *Chelsea* Twice
13. *Crystal Palace* Twice
14. *Fulham* Twice
15. *Huddersfield* Twice
16. *Ipswich Town* Twice
17. *Leeds United* Twice
18. *Newcastle* Twice
19. *Nottingham Forest* Twice
20. *Queens Park Rangers* Twice
21. *Southampton* Twice
22. *Stoke* Twice
23. *Tottenham* Twice
24. *West Bromwich Albion* Twice
25. *West Ham United* Twice
26. *Wolves* Twice
27. *Blackburn* Once only

28. *Blackpool* Once only
29. *Bolton* Once only
30. *Brighton* Once only
31. *Bristol City* Once only
32. *Carlisle* Once only
33. *Coventry* Once only
34. *Derby* Once only
35. *Everton* Once only
36. *Liverpool* Once only
37. *Manchester United* Once only
38. *Middlesbrough* Once only
39. *Northampton* Once only
40. *Notts County* Once only
41. *Orient* Once only
42. *Preston* Once only
43. *Swansea* Once only
44. *Watford* Once only

THE 14 CLUBS TO HAVE WON LEAGUE CHAMPIONSHIPS IN 3 OR MORE DIVISIONS

1. *Brentford*	–	2nd	–	3S	–	4th
2. *Burnley*	1st	2nd	3rd	–	–	–
3. *Coventry*	–	2nd	3rd	3S	–	–
4. *Derby County*	1st	2nd	–	–	3N	–
5. *Grimsby Town*	–	2nd	3rd	–	3N	4th
6. *Huddersfield*	1st	2nd	–	–	–	4th
7. *Ipswich*	1st	2nd	–	3S	–	–
8. *Luton Town*	–	2nd	–	3S	–	4th
9. *Notts County*	–	2nd	–	3S	–	4th
10. *Nottingham Forest*	1st	2nd	–	3S	–	–
11. *Portsmouth*	1st	–	3rd	3S	–	–
12. *Preston North End*	1st	2nd	3rd	–	–	–
13. *Sheffield United*	1st	2nd	–	–	–	4th
14. *Wolves*	1st	2nd	–	–	3N	–

THE 7 CLUBS WITH MOST F.A. CUP WINS

1. *Aston Villa* — 7
2. *Tottenham Hotspur* — 7
3. *Blackburn Rovers* — 6
4. *Newcastle United* — 6
5. *Arsenal* — 5
6. *West Bromwich Albion* — 5
7. *The Wanderers* — 5

THE 5 CLUBS WITH MOST F.A. CUP WINS SINCE THE WAR

1. *Tottenham Hotspur* — 5
2. *Arsenal* — 3
3. *Manchester United* — 3
4. *Newcastle* — 3
5. *West Ham* — 3

THE 6 CLUBS TO HAVE WON THE LEAGUE CUP MORE THAN ONCE (1961–82)

1. *Aston Villa*	3	4. *Nottingham Forest*	2
2. *Liverpool*	2	5. *Tottenham Hotspur*	2
3. *Manchester City*	2	6. *Wolves*	2

THE 9 CLUBS TO HAVE WON THE FOOTBALL LEAGUE CHAMPIONSHIP, THE F.A. CUP AND THE LEAGUE CUP

	League Championships	F.A. Cups	Football League Cups
1. *Liverpool*	13	2	2
2. *Aston Villa*	7	7	3
3. *Wolves*	3	4	2
4. *Tottenham*	2	7	2
5. *Manchester City*	2	4	2
6. *Leeds*	2	1	1
7. *West Bromwich Albion*	1	5	1
8. *Nottingham Forest*	1	2	2
9. *Chelsea*	1	1	1

THE 5 UNITED KINGDOM CLUBS TO HAVE WON INTERNATIONAL AND DOMESTIC TROPHIES IN THE SAME SEASON

1. *Glasgow Celtic* – European Cup winners; Scottish League champions; Scottish Cup and Scottish League Cup winners, 1966–1967
2. *Leeds United* – Inter Cities Fairs Cup and League Cup winners, 1967–1968
3. *Manchester City* – European Cup Winners Cup and League Cup winners, 1969–1970
4. *Liverpool* – UEFA Cup winners and League Champions, 1972–1973
   Liverpool – UEFA Cup winners and League Champions, 1975–1976

Liverpool –	European Cup winners and League Champions, 1976–1977
Liverpool –	European Cup winners and European Super Cup winners, 1977–1978.
5. Nottingham Forest –	European Cup winners and League Cup winners, 1978–1979.
Liverpool –	European Cup winners and League Cup winners, 1980–1981

THE 6 CLUBS WHO RETAINED THE F.A. OR LEAGUE CUP

1.	*The Wanderers* 1871–72 and 1872–73	F.A. Cup
	The Wanderers 1875–76, 1876–77 and 1877–78	F.A. Cup
2.	*Blackburn Rovers* 1883–84, 1884–85 and 1885–86	F.A. Cup
	Blackburn Rovers 1889–90 and 1890–91	F.A. Cup
3.	*Newcastle United* 1950–51 and 1951–52	F.A. Cup
4.	*Tottenham Hotspur* 1960–61 and 1961–62	F.A. Cup
	Tottenham Hotspur 1980–81 and 1981–82	F.A. Cup
5.	*Nottingham Forest* 1977–78 and 1978–79	League Cup
6.	*Liverpool* 1980–81 and 1981–82	League Cup

THE 11 CLUBS TO HAVE WON THE FOOTBALL LEAGUE CHAMPIONSHIP TWO OR MORE YEARS IN SUCCESSION

1. *Preston North End* 1888–89 and 1889–90
2. *Sunderland* 1891–92 and 1892–93
3. *Aston Villa* 1895–96 and 1896–97
   Aston Villa 1898–99 and 1899–1900
4. *The Wednesday* 1902–03 and 1903–04
5. *Liverpool* 1921–22 and 1922–23
6. *Huddersfield Town* 1923–24, 1924–25 and 1925–26
7. *Sheffield Wednesday* 1928–29 and 1929–30
8. *Arsenal* 1932–33, 1933–34 and 1934–35
9. *Portsmouth* 1948–49 and 1949–50
10. *Manchester United* 1955–56 and 1956–57
11. *Wolves* 1957–58 and 1958–59
    Liverpool 1975–76 and 1976–77
    Liverpool 1978–79 and 1979–80
    Liverpool 1981–82 and 1982–83

133

THE 28 F.A. CHARITY SHIELD
WINNERS 1908–1982

1. *Liverpool* 6 plus 3 shared
2. *Tottenham* 4 plus 2 shared
3. *Manchester United* 5 plus 3 shared
4. *Arsenal* 7
5. *Wolves* 1 plus 3 shared
6. *Aston Villa* 1 shared
7. *Nottingham Forest* 1
8. *Derby County* 1
9. *Burnley* 1 plus 1 shared
10. *Manchester City* 3
11. *Leicester City* 1
12. *Everton* 4
13. *Leeds United* 1
14. *West Ham United* 1 shared
15. *Bolton Wanderers* 1
16. *Chelsea* 1
17. *West Bromwich Albion* 1 plus 1 shared
18. *1950 World Cup Team* 1
19. *Portsmouth* 1 shared
20. *Sunderland* 1
21. *Sheffield Wednesday* 1
22. *Professionals* 4
23. *Cardiff City* 1
24. *Amateurs* 2
25. *Huddersfield* 1
26. *Blackburn Rovers* 1
27. *Brighton and Hove Albion* 1
28. *Newcastle* 1

On nine occasions the games have been drawn, on all but one of these (Liverpool v. Leeds United in 1974, which was settled on penalties) the outcome has been that the trophy was held by each club for six months.

THE 9 SCOTTISH LEAGUE
CHAMPIONS (1891–1982)

1. *Dumbarton*	2	4. *Rangers*	36	7. *Motherwell*	1
2. *Celtic*	33	5. *Hibernian*	4	8. *Aberdeen*	3
3. *Hearts*	4	6. *Third Lanark*	1	9. *Kilmarnock*	1

THE 22 SCOTTISH F.A. CUP WINNERS
(1874–1982)

1.	*Queens Park*	10	8. *Celtic*	26	15. *Morton*		1
2.	*Vale of Leven*	3	9. *Rangers*	24	16. *Airdrionians*		1
3.	*Dumbarton*	1	10. *St. Bernard's*	1	17. *St. Mirren*		2
4.	*Renton*	2	11. *Dundee*	1	18. *East Fife*		1
5.	*Hibernian*	2	12. *Falkirk*	2	19. *Clyde*		2
6.	*Third Lanark*	2	13. *Kilmarnock*	2	20. *Aberdeen*		3
7.	*Hearts*	5	14. *Partick Thistle*	1	21. *Motherwell*		1
					22. *Dunfermline*		2

THE 10 SCOTTISH LEAGUE CUP
WINNERS (1947–1982)

1.	*Rangers*	11	6. *Aberdeen*		2
2.	*East Fife*	3	7. *Celtic*		8
3.	*Motherwell*	1	8. *Partick Thistle*		1
4.	*Dundee*	3	9. *Hibernian*		1
5.	*Hearts*	4	10. *Dundee United*		2

THE 3 SCOTTISH DOUBLE OR
TREBLE WINNERS

1.	*Rangers*	4 trebles
2.	*Celtic*	2 trebles
	Celtic	8 League and Scottish Cup Doubles
	Rangers	7 League and Scottish Cup Doubles
	Celtic	3 Scottish League and League Cup Doubles
3.	*Hearts*	1 Scottish League and League Cup Double
	Rangers	1 Scottish League and League Cup Double
	Rangers	2 Cup Doubles
	Celtic	1 Cup Double

THE 11 ITALIAN LEAGUE AND CUP
WINNING CLUBS SINCE 1945/1946

	League Championships	Cup Wins
1. Torino	5	2
2. Juventus (of Turin)	13	4
3. A.C. Milan	7	4
4. Inter-Milan	7	2
5. Fiorentina	2	3
6. Bologna	1	2
7. Cagliari	1	–
8. Lazio	1	1
9. Napoli	–	2
10. Atalanta	–	1
11. A.S. Roma	–	4

THE 20 WEST GERMAN LEAGUE AND
CUP WINNING CLUBS SINCE 1948

	League Championships	Cup Wins
1. 1. FC. Nürnberg	3	1
2. VfR Mannheim	1	–
3. VfB Stuttgart	2	2
4. 1. FC. Kaiserslautern	2	–
5. Hannover 96	1	–
6. Rot-Weiss Essen	1	1
7. Karlsruhe S.C.	–	2
8. Borussia Dortmund	3	1
9. Schalke 04	1	1
10. Eintracht Frankfurt	1	3
11. Schwarz-Weiss Essen	–	1
12. Hamburger S.V.	3	2
13. 1. FC. Köln	3	3
14. Werder Bremen	1	1
15. München 1860	1	1
16. Bayern München	6	6
17. Eintracht Braunschweig	1	–
18. Borussia Mönchengladbach	5	2
19. Kickers Offenbach	–	1
20. Fortuna Düsseldorf	–	2

THE 23 DUTCH LEAGUE AND CUP WINNING CLUBS SINCE WORLD WAR II

	League Championships	Cup Wins
1. Haarlem	1	–
2. Ajax Amsterdam	13	6
3. B.V.V. Scheidam	1	–
4. S.V.V. Scheidam	1	–
5. Wageningen	–	1
6. Quick Nijmegen	–	1
7. Limburgia	1	–
8. P.S.V. Eindhoven	5	3
9. Willem II Tilburg	2	1
10. R.C.H. Haarlem	1	–
11. Eindhoven	1	–
12. Rapid J.C. Haarlem	1	–
13. DOS Utrecht	1	–
14. Fortuna Geleen	–	2
15. Sparta Rotterdam	1	3
16. V.V.V. Groningen	–	1
17. Feyenoord	6	3
18. D.W.S. Amsterdam	1	–
19. A.D.O. Den Haag	–	1
20. N.A.C. Breda	–	1
21. F.C. Den Haag	–	1
22. Twente Enschede	–	1
23. A.Z. 67 Alkmaar	1	3

THE 14 BELGIAN LEAGUE AND CUP
WINNERS SINCE WORLD WAR II

	League Championships	Cup Wins
1. Malines	2	–
2. Anderlecht	17	5
3. F.C. Liège	2	–
4. Standard Liège	7	4
5. Antwerp	1	1
6. Tournai	–	1
7. Lierse S.K.	1	1
8. La Gantoise	–	1
9. F.C. Bruges	5	3
10. Beerschot	–	2
11. Waregem	–	1
12. R.W.D. Molenbeek	1	–
13. Beveren	1	1
14. Waterschei	–	2

THE 9 SPANISH LEAGUE AND CUP
WINNERS SINCE THE WAR

	League Championships	Cup Wins
1. Sevilla	1	1
2. Valencia	2	4
3. Barcelona	7	10
4. Atlético Madrid	6	5
5. Real Madrid	18	8
6. Atlético Bilbao	1	6
7. Real Zaragoza	–	2
8. Real Betis (of Seville)	–	1
9. Real Sociedad	2	–

THE 8 PORTUGUESE LEAGUE AND
CUP WINNERS SINCE THE WAR

	League Championships	Cup Wins
1. *Belenenses*	1	1
2. *Sporting Lisbon*	14	9
3. *Benfica*	18	14
4. *F.C. Porto*	4	4
5. *Leixoes*	–	1
6. *Vitoria Setubal*	–	2
7. *Sporting Braga*	–	1
8. *Boavista*	–	3

56 EUROPEAN LEAGUE AND CUP
DOUBLE WINNERS SINCE THE WAR

1. *Rapid Vienna*	Austria	3
2. *Wacker Vienna*	Austria	1
3. *F.K. Austria*	Austria	3
4. *Linz A.S.K.*	Austria	1
5. *Admira Energie*	Austria	1
6. *T.S. Innsbruck*	Austria	2
7. *Austria/W.A.C.*	Austria	1
8. *Anderlecht*	Belgium	2
9. *F.C. Bruges*	Belgium	1
10. *Levski Sofia*	Bulgaria	4
11. *C.S.K.A Sofia (formerly C.D.N.A.)*	Bulgaria	8
12. *Levski Spartak*	Bulgaria	3
13. *Dukla Prague*	Czechoslovakia	2
14. *Spartak Trnava*	Czechoslovakia	1
15. *Slovan Bratislava*	Czechoslovakia	1
16. *Lille O.S.C.*	France	1
17. *Stade de Reims*	France	1
18. *A.S. Monaco*	France	1
19. *Saint Etienne*	France	4
20. *Olympique Marseille*	France	1
21. *Dynamo Dresden*	East Germany	2
22. *Bayern München*	West Germany	1
23. *1 FC. Köln*	West Germany	1
24. *Ujpest Dozsa*	Hungary	4
25. *Ferencvaros*	Hungary	1

26. *Shamrock Rovers*	Eire	1
27. *Juventus*	Italy	1
28. *Feyenoord*	Netherlands	2
29. *Ajax Amsterdam*	Netherlands	3
30. *P.S.V. Eindhoven*	Netherlands	1
31. *A.Z. '67 Alkmaar*	Netherlands	1
32. *Legia Warsaw*	Poland	2
33. *Gornik Zabrze*	Poland	3
34. *Ruch Chorzow*	Poland	1
35. *Sporting Lisbon*	Portugal	3
36. *Benfica*	Portugal	6
37. *F.C. Porto*	Portugal	1
38. *Barcelona*	Spain	3
39. *Atlético Bilbao*	Spain	1
40. *Real Madrid*	Spain	3
41. *Malmö F.F.*	Sweden	6
42. *Öster Vaxto*	Sweden	1
43. *Grasshoppers Zurich*	Switzerland	2
44. *La Chaux-de-Fonds*	Switzerland	2
45. *Young Boys Berne*	Switzerland	1
46. *F.C. Zurich*	Switzerland	2
47. *F.C. Basle*	Switzerland	1
48. *Servette*	Switzerland	1
49. *O.S.K.A. Moscow*	U.S.S.R.	2
50. *Spartak Moscow*	U.S.S.R.	1
51. *Torpedo Moscow*	U.S.S.R.	1
52. *Dynamo Kiev*	U.S.S.R.	2
53. *Ararat Erevan*	U.S.S.R.	1
54. *Partizan Belgrade*	Yugoslavia	1
55. *Red Star Belgrade*	Yugoslavia	4
56. *Hajduk Split*	Yugoslavia	2

THE 7 CLUBS WITH MOST EUROPEAN TROPHIES

1. *Real Madrid*	6 European Champions Cups – 6
2. *Liverpool*	3 European Champions Cups – 5
	2 U.E.F.A. Cups
3. *Barcelona*	2 European Cup Winners Cups – 5
	3 U.E.F.A. Cups
4. *Bayern München*	3 European Champions Cups – 4
	1 European Cup Winners Cup

5. *Ajax Amsterdam*   3 European Champion Cups – 3
6. *A.C. Milan*   2 European Champions Cup – 3
                         1 European Cup Winners Cup
7. *Valencia*   1 European Cup Winners Cup – 3
                         2 U.E.F.A. Cups

THE 12 CLUBS TO APPEAR IN MOST EUROPEAN FINALS

1. *Real Madrid*   10 finals   7. *Borussia Mönchengladbach*
2. *Barcelona*   8 finals   5 finals
3. *Liverpool*   6 finals   8. *Leeds*   5 finals
4. *A.C. Milan*   5 finals   9. *Ajax Amsterdam* 4 finals
5. *Benfica*   5 finals   10. *Hamburger S.V.* 4 finals
6. *Byern München*   5 finals   11. *Juventus*   4 finals
                  12. *Valencia*   4 finals

THE 4 CLUBS TO APPEAR IN A FINAL OF ALL 3 EUROPEAN TROPHIES

1. *Barcelona* – In 1969, by playing against Slovan Bratislava in the Final of the European Cup Winners Cup they became the first club to compete in all 3 European Finals.

2. *Leeds United* – Having already won 2 Fairs Cup Finals and lost a Cup Winners Cup Final they became only the second club to compete in all 3 European Trophy Finals when they played at the Parc de Prince, Paris, in 1975 against Bayern München.

3. *Liverpool* – Their first European Cup triumph over Borussia Mönchengladbach in Rome in 1977 was the 3rd different European Final in which they played.

4. *Hamburger S.V.* – In 1982 their 2-legged U.E.F.A. Cup Final against I.F.K. Gothenburg meant that they became a member of the prestigious foursome to have played in all three European Trophy Finals.

Barcelona and Leeds appeared in Fairs Cup Finals while Liverpool and Hamburger S.V. appeared in the UEFA Cup.

THE 17 BRITISH CLUBS TO APPEAR
IN EUROPEAN TROPHY FINALS

1.	*London**	Inter-Cities Fairs Cup					1958
2.	*Birmingham City*	,,	,,	,,	,,		1960
	Birmingham City	,,	,,	,,	,,		1961
3.	*Rangers*	Cup Winners Cup					1960
4.	*Tottenham Hotspur*	,,	,,	,,		Winners	1965
5.	*West Ham United*	,,	,,	,,		Winners	1965
6.	*Liverpool*	,,	,,	,,			1966
7.	*Leeds United*	Inter-Cities Fairs Cup					1967
	Rangers	Cup Winners Cup					1967
8.	*Celtic*	Champions Cup				Winners	1967
	Leeds United	Inter-Cities Fairs Cup				Winners	1968
9.	*Manchester United*	Champions Cup				Winners	1968
10.	*Newcastle United*	Inter-Cities Fairs Cup				Winners	1969
11.	*Manchester City*	Cup Winners Cup				Winners	1970
12.	*Arsenal*	Inter-Cities Fairs Cup				Winners	1970
	Celtic	Champions Cup					1970
13.	*Chelsea*	Cup Winners Cup				Winners	1971
	Leeds United	Inter-Cities Fairs Cup				Winners	1971
	Tottenham Hotspur	UEFA Cup				Winners	1972
14.	*Wolves*	UEFA Cup					1972
	Rangers	Cup Winners Cup				Winners	1972
	Leeds United	Cup Winners Cup					1973
	Liverpool	UEFA Cup				Winners	1973
	Tottenham Hotspur	UEFA Cup					1974
	Leeds United	Champions Cup					1975
	West Ham United	Cup Winners Cup					1976
	Liverpool	Champions Cup				Winners	1977
	Liverpool	Champions Cup				Winners	1978
15.	*Nottingham Forest*	Champions Cup				Winners	1979
	Arsenal	Cup Winners Cup					1980
	Nottingham Forest	Champions Cup				Winners	1980
16.	*Ipswich Town*	UEFA Cup				Winners	1981
	Liverpool	Champions Cup				Winners	1981
17.	*Aston Villa*	Champions Cup				Winners	1982

* A side selected from the best of London's players – a practice
discontinued in subsequent Fairs Cups.

THE 9 CLUBS TO SUCCESSFULLY
DEFEND EUROPEAN TROPHIES

1. *Real Madrid* – Won the European Cup 5 times in succession from 1956–60 (incl.) They appeared in 8 of the first 11 finals.
2. *Barcelona* – Won the 1958 and 1960 Fairs Cup Finals. (The 1960 Fairs Cup had begun in 1959.)
3. *Benfica* – Victors in 1962 for the second year running.
4. *Valencia* – 1963 saw the Spanish club carry off the Fairs Cup for the second year in succession.
5. *Inter Milan* – Brazilian Jair scored the goal against Benfica in 1965 which saw the Italians retain the European Cup.
6. *Ajax Amsterdam* – In 1973 they became the first club to gain a hat trick of European Cup Final wins since Real Madrid's 3rd successive triumph in 1958.
7. *Bayern München* – The best West German Team ever, their run of 3 Champion's Cup successes 1974–76 was brought to an end when Dynamo Kiev knocked them out in the 1976–77 Quarter-finals.
8. *Liverpool* – Won Europe's Premier Club competition for the second year in succession in 1978 when they beat F.C. Bruges 1–0 in one of the most boring ever Finals.
9. *Nottingham Forest* – Against the odds, Hamburg were much the better side, Forest won through a Kaltz error and a little inspiration from John Robertson. This second consecutive European Cup Final victory for Forest was the fourth out of six English victories from 1977–82.

Although no clubs have retained the European Cup Winners Cup, 4 clubs Fiorentina, Atlético Madrid, A.C. Milan and Anderlecht have all reached the Final as holders, the last named winning the Cup again in their 3rd successive final.

THE 2 CLUBS TO REACH AN F.A. CUP
FINAL AND BE RELEGATED IN THE
SAME SEASON

1. *Manchester City* 1925–26
   Lost 1–0 to Bolton in the Cup Final and finished 21st in the League.
2. *Leicester City* 1968–1969
   Lost 1–0 to Manchester City and finished 21st in the League.

THE 3 CLUBS TO REACH AN F.A. CUP FINAL AND BE PROMOTED IN THE SAME SEASON

1. *Huddersfield Town* 1919–1920
   Lost 1–0 to Aston Villa in the Cup Final, 2nd Division runners up.
2. *West Ham United* 1922–1923
   Lost 2–0 to Bolton, 2nd Division runners up.
3. *West Bromwich Albion* 1930–1931
   Won 2–1 against Birmingham City, 2nd Division runners up.

THE 4 CLUBS TO PLAY IN AN F.A. CUP FINAL THE SEASON AFTER WINNING PROMOTION

1. *Burnley* Promoted 1912–1913.
   Cup Winners 1913–1914 beating Liverpool 1–0.
2. *Tottenham* Promoted 1919–1920 as 2nd Division Champions.
   Cup Winners 1920–1921 beating Wolves 1–0.
3. *Birmingham City* Promoted 1954–1955 as 2nd Division Champions. Cup runners up 1955–1956, lost to Manchester 3–1.
4. *Leeds United* Promoted 1963–1964 as 2nd Division Champions. Cup runners up 1964–1965, lost to Liverpool 2–1.

THE 3 CLUBS THAT WON THE 1ST DIVISION CHAMPIONSHIP IN THEIR FIRST SEASON AFTER PROMOTION

1. *Tottenham* 1949–50 2nd Division Champions, 1950–51 1st Division Champions
2. *Ipswich* 1960–61 2nd Division Champions, 1961–62 1st Division Champions
3. *Nottingham Forest* 1976–77 3rd in Division 2, 1977–78 1st Division Champions

THE 29 CLUBS TO HAVE MADE
APPLICATIONS FOR RE-ELECTION
TO THE FOOTBALL LEAGUE SINCE 1959

	Applications				*Division*
Hartlepool	9	plus	3	made from	3N
Barrow	6	,,	5	,,	,,
				,,	,,
				,,	,,	3N
Crewe Alexandra	6	,,	3	,,	,,	3N
Darlington	5	,,	3	,,	,,	3N
Lincoln City	5				
Workington	5	,,	2	,,	,,	3N
Rochdale	5	,,	4	,,	,,	3N
Bradford Park Avenue	4	,,	1	,,	,,	3N
Chester	4	,,	2	,,	,,	3N
Halifax Town	4	,,	6	,,	,,	3N
Newport County	4	,,	6	,,	,,	3S
Stockport County	4				
Doncaster Rovers	3				
Northampton Town	3				
Bradford City	2	,,	1	,,	,,	3N
Hereford United	2				
Oldham Athletic	2				
Scunthorpe United	2				
Aldershot	1	,,	2	,,	,,	3S
Colchester United	1	,,	2	,,	,,	3S
Exeter City	1	,,	6	,,	,,	3S
Gateshead	1	,,	1	,,	,,	3N
Grimsby Town	1	,,	1	,,	,,	3N
Swansea City	1				
Tranmere Rovers	1	,,	2	,,	,,	3N
Wrexham	1				
Port Vale	1	because of expulsion in 1968			

7 CURRENT LEADING 1ST OR 2ND
DIVISION CLUBS THAT HAVE HAD
TO APPLY FOR RE-ELECTION

Swansea City   *Queens Park Rangers*
Norwich City   *Oldham Athletic*
Brighton   *Charlton Athletic*
Watford

8 CLUBS THAT WERE 1st DIVISION CHAMPIONS ONE SEASON AND BATTLERS AGAINST RELEGATION THE NEXT.

1. *Sheffield United* Champions 1897–98 – 16th out of 18 clubs 1898–99
2. *Aston Villa* Champions 1899–1900 – 15th out of 18 clubs 1900–01
3. *Liverpool* Champions 1905–06 – 15th out of 20 clubs 1906–07
4. *Manchester United* Champions 1907–08 – 13th out of 20 clubs 1908–9
   Manchester United Champions 1910–11 – 13th out of 20 clubs 1911–12
5. *Everton* Champions 1927–28 – 18th out of 22 clubs 1928–29
6. *Manchester City* Champions 1936–37 – 21st Relegated 1937–38
7. *Chelsea* Champions 1954–55 – 16th 1955–56
8. *Ipswich Town* Champions 1961–62 – 17th 1962–63

THE 2 BRITISH CLUBS TO PROVIDE THE GREATEST NUMBER OF PLAYERS AT ONE TIME FOR DIFFERENT NATIONAL SIDES

1. *Arsenal*: 7 of their players helped make up the England team that beat Italy 3–2 at Highbury in November, 1934. Namely: Frank Moss in goal; George Male and Eddie Hapgood at Full Back; Wilf Copping at Left Half; Ray Bowden and Cliff Bastin as Inside Forwards and Ted Drake as leader of the attack. The other 4 players were: Cliff Britton of Everton and John Barker of Derby at Right Half and Centre Half respectively; Stanley Matthews as a mere stripling of 19 on the Right Wing and Manchester City's Eric Brook at Outside Left.

2. *Queen Park*: 10 of the all conquering Queens Park team plus a player later to join them took the field against England in the first British International Football match in 1872. This milestone took place in Glasgow, but ended a disappointing 0–0 draw. The team selected was: R. Gardiner (GK); W. Ker of Granville (RB); J. Taylor (LB); J. J. Thomson, James Smith and Rob Smith (HB's); R. Leckie (OR); A. Rhind (IR); W.

W. McKinnon (CF); J. B. Weir (IL) and D. N. Wotherspoon (OL).

THE 3 CLUBS WHO MISSED THE 'DOUBLE' BY LOSING THE CUP FINAL

1. *Newcastle* 1904–05 'The Magpies' lost 2–0 to Aston Villa at Crystal Palace.
2. *Sunderland* 1912–13 Sunderland lost their chance of a double when League runners up Aston Villa beat them 1–0 in a replayed Final. This was the only Cup Final to involve the top two League clubs.
3. *Liverpool* 1976–77 Manchester United's 2–1 defeat of Champions Liverpool prevented 'The Anfielders' from becoming only the 5th club to capture the League and Cup Double.

THE 2 NON-ENGLISH CLUBS TO REACH THE ENGLISH CUP FINAL

1. *Queens Park*: The Glaswegians lost in 1883–1884 and 1884–1885 to Blackburn Rovers. These are the only occasions on which two clubs have played each other in two consecutive Finals. Queens Park were Scottish Cup Winners when they travelled to the Kennington Oval for the first of these Finals. The earlier Cup Final defeat by Blackburn Rovers, was the 18th game that Queens Park had 'played' in the F.A. Cup Competition, but the first they lost on a pitch. Because of travelling difficulties and the small number of entries to the early F.A. Cup Competitions they had received 9 byes and had scratched on 4 occasions. However, in 1883–84 their F.A. Cup form was quite breathtaking, including a 6–1 defeat of Aston Villa and a 4–1 semi-final defeat of Cup holders Blackburn Olympic.

2. *Cardiff City* In 1927 they became the first and only club to take the F.A. Cup out of England when they beat Arsenal 1–0. Hugh Ferguson's goal was enough to beat 'The Gunners' and the result was ample compensation for their previous disappointing final display against Sheffield United two years previously when they lost 1–0.

10 CLUBS OUTSIDE OF ENGLAND AND WALES TO ENTER THE F.A. CUP COMPETITION

1. *Queens Park* (Q.V.) Their second game against Nottingham Forest in 1884–85 was the only F.A. Cup Semi-final to be held beyond the borders of England. The replayed Semi-final, after a 1–1 draw, took place at Merchiston Castle School in Edinburgh. Home territory paid off for 'The Spiders' who recorded a handsome 3–0 victory.

2. *Clydesdale* In 1876 were one of Scotland's premier sides (Scottish Cup runners up, 1874). But they never took the opportunity to test their mettle against tougher English opposition, scratching before the First Round of the 1875–76 F.A. Cup.

3. *Glasgow Rangers* While not being over-stretched on other fronts – the Scottish League had not yet started – Rangers competed only occasionally in the F.A. Cup. However, a good draw and good play saw them reach a Semi-final in 1886–87.

4. *Cliftonville* An 11–1 thrashing by Scotland's Partick Thistle in the Third Round of the 1886–87 F.A. Cup, persuaded the Irish Club that perhaps they were out of their depth. They did not enter the competition again.

5. *Cowlairs* A brief sojourn into the F.A. Cup was climaxed by a 3–2 defeat at the hands of fellow Scottish club, Rangers, in 1886–87.

6. *Partick Thistle* Aided by weak opponents, Cliftonville, and a bye, they reached the last 16 in their first excursion into English football in 1886–87.

7. *Renton* Another Scottish club to meet with little success in the rigours of English competition, they went down 2–0 to Preston North End in the 1886–87 season.

8. *Linfield* They only played once, scratching shortly before playing Nottingham Forest, in their First Round replay in 1888–89. However, the game due against Forest was played as a friendly in Linfield, Northern Ireland.

9. *Belfast Distillery* A crushing 10–1 defeat at the hands of Bolton Wanderers put paid to any hopes that they could make an impression across the Irish Sea.

10. *Crusaders* Their ambition of a good F.A. Cup run was thwarted when they twice crashed in the First Round to less than brilliant opposition, Birmingham St. George's and Accrington Stanley in 1891 and 1892 respectively.

THE 5 EARLIEST F.A. CUP COMPETITORS OF THE PRESENT FOOTBALL LEAGUE CLUBS

1. *Notts County*   1877–78
2. *Reading*   1877–78
3. *Nottingham Forest* 1878–79
4. *Blackburn Rovers* 1879–80
5. *Aston Villa*   1879–80

THE 10 FORMER SOUTHERN LEAGUE CLUBS WHO BEGAN 1983 IN DIVISION I

1. *Brighton and Hove Albion* 1901–1920
2. *Coventry City*   1910–1919
3. *Ipswich Town*   1938
4. *Luton Town*   1895–1896
5. *Norwich City*   1905–1920
6. *Southampton*   1894–1920
7. *Swansea*   1920
8. *Tottenham Hotspur* 1896–1908
9. *Watford*   1904–1920
10. *West Ham*   1898–1920

THE 17 CLUBS WHO REACHED THE QUARTER FINALS OF THE F.A. CUP SINCE WORLD WAR II WHILE PLAYING IN THE 3RD OR 4TH DIVISION

	Division	Quarter Finals
1. *Barnsley*	3	1961
2. *Bradford City*	4	1976
3. *Bournemouth*	3S	1957
4. *Colchester United*	4	1971
5. *Coventry City*	3	1963
6. *Exeter City*	3	1981
7. *Hull City*	3N	1949
8. *Mansfield Town*	3	1969
9. *Norwich City*	3	1959 (Semi-Final)
10. *Orient*	3S	1954
11. *Oxford United*	4	1964
12. *Peterborough United*	3	1965
13. *Port Vale*	3N	1954 (Semi-Final)
14. *Queens Park Rangers*	3S	1948
15. *Shrewsbury Town*	3	1979
16. *Wrexham*	3	1974
17. *York City*	3N	1955

THE 13 CLUBS THAT TOTTENHAM HOTSPUR PLAYED ON THE WAY TO THEIR RECORD RUN OF 18 UNBEATEN F.A. CUP TIES IN 1983

1. *Queens Park Rangers –* Twice
2. *Hull City*
3. *Coventry City*
4. *Exeter City*
5. *Wolves – Twice*
6. *Manchester City – Twice*
7. *Arsenal*
8. *Leeds United*
9. *Aston Villa*
10. *Chelsea*
11. *Leicester City* *Queen Park Rangers –* Twice
12. *Southampton*
13. *West Bromwich Albion*

THE 22 CLUBS WITH THE BEST FOOTBALL LEAGUE RECORD SINCE ITS INCEPTION

	played	won	drawn	lost	points
1. *Everton*	3074	1270	734	1070	3291
2. *Liverpool*	2690	1180	661	849	3047
3. *Aston Villa*	2690	1199	601	980	3014
4. *Arsenal*	2690	1127	692	871	2966
5. *Sunderland*	2568	1064	574	930	2713
6. *Manchester City*	2528	980	609	939	2584
7. *Manchester United*	2334	979	583	772	2563
8. *West Bromwich Albion*	2484	939	584	948	2486
9. *Newcastle*	2340	928	546	866	2402
10. *Wolves*	2228	905	495	828	2315
11. *Bolton*	2308	868	513	927	2249
12. *Sheffield United*	2154	810	508	836	2128
13. *Tottenham*	1950	792	468	690	2072
14. *Derby County*	2048	793	479	776	2065
15. *Burnley*	1982	784	447	751	2015
16. *Sheffield Wednesday*	1982	771	444	767	1986
17. *Chelsea*	2076	726	532	818	1984
18. *Blackburn*	2024	755	467	802	1977
19. *Preston*	1720	671	390	659	1732
20. *Middlesbrough*	1826	644	433	749	1729
21. *Birmingham*	1914	619	470	825	1718
22. *Stoke*	1866	630	446	790	1718

THE 5 CLUBS TO HAVE
SPENT FEWEST SEASONS IN
DIVISION 1 TO 1983.

1. *Carlisle*	1	4. *Swansea**	2
2. *Northampton*	1	5. *Watford**	1
3. *Orient*	1		

* Currently in this division.

THE 10 CLUBS TO HAVE SPENT MOST
SEASONS IN DIVISION 2 TO 1983

1. *Barnsley**	47	6. *Nottingham Forest*	36
2. *Fulham**	45	7. *Orient*	41
3. *Grimsby**	41	8. *Preston*	32
4. *Hull*	49	9. *Southampton*	34
5. *Leicester*	44	10. *Swansea*	33

*Currently in this division.

THE 9 CLUBS TO HAVE SERVED
THE SHORTEST TIME IN
DIVISION 2 TO 1983

1. *Crewe*	4	6. *Northampton*	3
2. *Darlington*	2	7. *Reading*	5
3. *Everton*	4	8. *Tranmere*	1
4. *Hereford*	1	9. *York*	2
5. *Mansfield*	1		

THE 8 CLUBS TO HAVE
ACCUMULATED THE MOST YEARS
IN DIVISION 3 1958–59 TO 1983

1. *Gillingham**	16	5. *Reading**	10
2. *Mansfield*	15	6. *Shrewsbury*	19
3. *Norwich*	14	7. *Southend**	17
4. *Plymouth**	14	8. *Swindon*	18

*Currently in this division.

THE 13 CLUBS TO HAVE SERVED
THE LEAST TIME IN DIVISION 3
1958–59 TO 1983

1. *Aldershot*	3	8. *Darlington*	1
2 *Aston Villa*	2	9. *Middlesbrough*	1
3. *Blackpool*	3	10. *Shrewsbury*	3
4. *Bolton*	2	11. *Southampton*	3
5. *Burnley*	2	12. *Wigan**	1
6. *Cambridge*	2	13. *Wimbledon*	2
7. *Crewe*	2		

* Currently in this division.

THE 8 CLUBS WITH MOST YEARS IN
THE DIVISION 3N 1921–22 TO 1958

1. *Halifax**	30	5. *Stockport*	25
2. *Hartlepool**	30	6. *Tranmere*	29
3. *Rochdale**	30	7. *Wrexham**	30
4. *Rotherham*	21	8. *York*	22

THE 5 CLUBS TO HAVE SPENT THE
FEWEST YEARS IN DIVISION 3N
1921–22 TO 1958

1. *Coventry City*	1	4. *Stoke City*	1
2. *Derby County*	2	5. *Wolves*	1
3. *Shrewsbury*	1		

THE 14 CLUBS WITH MOST SEASONS
IN DIVISION 3S 1921–22 TO 1958

1. *Bournemouth*	28	8. *Northampton**	30
2. *Brighton**	30	9. *Queens Parks Rangers*	26
3. *Crystal Palace*	26	10. *Reading*	25
4. *Exeter City**	30	11. *Southend**	30
5. *Gillingham*	25	12. *Swindon**	30
6. *Millwall*	21	13. *Torquay*	24
7. *Newport County*	28	14. *Watford**	*30*

* *Ever present.*

THE 3 CLUBS TO HAVE SERVED THE SHORTEST PERIOD IN DIVISION 3S 1921–22 TO 1958

1. *Fulham* 4 seasons   2. *Mansfield Town* 4 seasons
3. *Nottingham Forest* 2 seasons

THE 10 CLUBS TO HAVE SERVED MOST YEARS IN THE THIRD DIVISIONS 1920–83

1. *Bristol Rovers**	40	6. *Reading**	44
2. *Bournemouth**	45	7. *Swindon*	48
(40 successive years)		8. *Tranmere*	42
3. *Exeter**	41	9. *Watford*	44
4. *Gillingham**	42	10. *Wrexham**	43
5. *Halifax*	42		

* Currently in this division.

9 CLUBS WITH THE MOST YEARS IN DIVISION 4 1958–59 TO 1983

1. *Chester**	18	6. *Rochdale**	19
2. *Crewe**	23	7. *Stockport**	21
3. *Darlington**	24	8. *Torquay**	17
4. *Hartlepool**	24	9. *York City**	17
5. *Newport*	18		

* Currently in this Division.

10 CLUBS TO HAVE SERVED THE SHORTEST PERIOD IN DIVISION 4 1958–59 TO 1983

1. *Brighton*	2	6. *Rotherham*	2
2. *Coventry City*	1	7. *Sheffield United*	1
3. *Hull*	2	8. *Shrewsbury Town*	2
4. *Oxford*	3	9. *Swindon Town*	1
5. *Portsmouth*	2	10. *Walsall*	3

THE 18 CLUBS WHO ESCAPED DEFEAT IN THEIR OPENING F.A. CUP-TIE EACH SEASON FOR THE LONGEST PERIOD

1.	*Rotherham*	1965–80	16 seasons
2.	*Preston*	1932–49	12 ,,
3.	*Chelsea*	1963–73	11 ,,
4.	*Liverpool*	1967–77	11 ,,
5.	*Queens Park Rangers*	1957–67	11 ,,
6.	*Sheffield United*	1958–68	11 ,,
7.	*Torquay*	1955–65	11 ,,
8.	*Tottenham*	1952–62	11 ,,
9.	*Norwich*	1947–56	10 ,,
10.	*Walsall*	1966–75	10 ,,
11.	*Wolves*	1937–52	10 ,,
	Chelsea	1939–53	9 ,,
12.	*Crystal Palace*	1957–65	9 ,,
13.	*Newcastle*	1950–58	9 ,,
14.	*Sheffield Wednesday*	1888–96	9 ,,
	Tottenham	1965–73	9 ,,
15.	*Watford*	1966–74	9 ,,
16.	*West Bromwich Albion*	1935–49	9 ,,
	West Bromwich Albion	1952–60	9 ,,
17.	*Everton*	1962–69	8 ,,
18.	*Swindon*	1947–54	8 ,,
	Sheffield United	1935–47	7 ,,
	Swindon	1966–72	7 ,,
	Tottenham	1933–39	7 ,,

THE 10 CLUBS WHO HAVE FAILED OVER THE LONGEST PERIOD TO WIN AN F.A. CUP-TIE

1. *Rochdale* 1929–39 11 seasons
2. *Leeds United* 1953–62 10 seasons
3. *Southport* 1970–77 8 seasons
4. *Blackpool* 1961–67 7 seasons
5. *Northampton* 1963–69 7 seasons
6. *Norwich* 1969–75 7 seasons

7. *Sheffield United* 1907–13 7 seasons
8. *Cardiff City* 1960–65 6 seasons
9. *Derby* 1964–69 6 seasons
10. *Lincoln* 1955–60 6 seasons

3 CLUBS WHOSE CONTINUED FIRST ROUND DISMISSALS IN THE LEAGUE CUP MUST HAVE MADE THEM FEEL LIKE QUITTING THE COMPETITION

1. *Aldershot* 1972–80 9 seasons
2. *Peterborough* 1961–66 6 seasons
3. *Hartlepool* 1961–65 5 seasons

THE 4–5 CLUBS IN EACH DIVISION TO HAVE ACCUMULATED MOST POINTS IN ONE SEASON

		Points	Possible Points	Season
Division 1	*Liverpool**	87	126	1981–82
	Liverpool	68	84	1978–79
	Leeds	67	84	1973–74
	Tottenham	66	84	1960–61
	Everton	66	84	1969–70
Division 2	*Luton**	88	126	1981–82
	Tottenham	70	84	1919–20
	Bristol City	66	76	1905–06
	West Ham	66	84	1980–81
Division 3	*Burnley**	80	138	1981–82
	Aston Villa	70	92	1971–72
	Hull	69	92	1965–66
	Bury	68	92	1960–61
Division 3N	*Doncaster*	72	84	1946–47
	Rotherham	71	92	1950–51
	Lincoln	69	92	1951–52
	Port Vale	69	92	1953–54
Division 3S	*Nottingham Forest*	70	92	1950–51
	Bristol City	70	92	1954–55

* Under new system of 3 points for a win.

		Points	Possible Points	Season
	Plymouth Argyle	68	84	1929–30
	Cardiff City	66	84	1946–47
	Plymouth Argyle	66	92	1951–52
	Leyton Orient	66	92	1955–56
Division 4	Sheffield United*	96	138	1981–82
	Lincoln City	74	92	1975–76
	Watford	71	92	1977–78
	Notts County	69	92	1970–71

* Under new system of 3 points for a win.

THE 2 SCOTTISH CLUBS IN THE FIRST AND SECOND DIVISION TO HAVE ACCUMULATED MOST POINTS IN ONE SEASON

1st Division	Rangers	76	84	1920–21
	Rangers	71	84	1919–20
	Celtic	67	84	1915–16
	Celtic	67	84	1921–22
	Rangers	67	84	1928–29
2nd Division	Morton	69	76	1966–67
	Morton	67	76	1963–64
	Motherwell	64	72	1968–69

THE 4–5 CLUBS IN EACH DIVISION WITH THE SMALLEST HAUL OF POINTS IN ONE SEASON

		Points	Games	Season
Division 1	Glossop N.E.	18	34	1899–1900
	Notts County	18	34	1904–05
	Woolwich Arsenal	18	38	1912–13
	Leeds United	18	42	1946–47
	Queens Park Rangers	18	42	1968–69
Division 2	Loughborough	8	34	1899–1900
	Doncaster Rovers	8	34	1904–05
	Northwich Victoria	9	28	1893–94
	Darwen	9	34	1898–99

Barnsley with 18 points in 1952–53 and Watford with 19 points in 1971–72 were the only Division 2 clubs since the war to fail to reach 20 points.

Division 3	Rochdale	21	46	1973–74
	Newport	22	42	1961–62
	Stockport	23	46	1969–70
	Lincoln City	25	46	1978–79
Division 3N	Rochdale	11	40	1931–32
	Barrow	18	42	1925–26
	Nelson	19	42	1930–31
	Accrington Stanley	20	42	1938–39
Division 3S	Merthyr Tydfil	21	42	1924–25
	Merthyr Tydfil	21	42	1929–30
	Queens Park Rangers	21	42	1925–26
	Thames	23	42	1931–32
	Aldershot	23	42	1936–37
Division 4	Workington	19	46	1976–77
	Bradford P.A.	20	46	1968–69
	Workington	21	46	1975–76
	Barrow	22	46	1970–71
	Bradford P.A.	23	46	1967–68
	Bradford P.A.	23	46	1969–70
	Rochdale	24	46	1977–78

THE 5 FIRST DIVISION CLUBS TO WIN THE CHAMPIONSHIP WITH FEWEST POINTS SINCE 1946

1.	Chelsea	52 points		1954–55
2.	Portsmouth*	53	,,	1949–50
3.	Derby County	53	,,	1974–75
4.	Arsenal*	54	,,	1952–53
5.	Burnley	55	,,	1959–60

* Won Championship on goal average.

4 FIRST DIVISION CHAMPIONS WITH BIGGEST WINNING MARGINS FROM LEAGUE RUNNERS-UP

1. *Everton* 9 points from Leeds 1969–70
2. *Tottenham* 8 points from Sheffield Wednesday 1960–61
3. *Liverpool* 8 points ahead from Nottingham Forest 1978–79
4. *Nottingham Forest* 7 points more than Liverpool 1977–78

4 SECOND DIVISION CHAMPIONS WITH BIGGEST WINNING MARGINS FROM LEAGUE RUNNERS-UP

1. *Middlesbrough* 15 points more than Luton in 1973–74
2. *West Ham United* 13 points ahead of Notts County in 1980–81
3. *Tottenham Hotspur* 9 points better off than Sheffield Wednesday in 1949–50
4. *Bury* 9 points clear of Notts County in 1894–95

5 SECOND DIVISION CHAMPIONS WITH FEWEST POINTS – SINCE 1946

1. *Sheffield Wednesday*	53 points		1951–52
2. *Stoke City*	53	,,	1962–63
3. *Birmingham City*	54	,,	1954–55
4. *Leicester City*	55	,,	1970–71
5. *Sheffield Wednesday*	55	,,	1979–80

4 THIRD DIVISION CHAMPIONS WITH FEWEST POINTS

1. *Oxford United*	57 points		1967–68
2. *Coventry City*	60	,,	1963–64
3. *Carlisle United*	60	,,	1964–65
4. *Blackburn Rovers*	60	,,	1974–75

4 THIRD DIVISION CHAMPIONS WITH BIGGEST WINNING MARGINS

1. *Queens Park Rangers* 12 points more than Middlesbrough 1966–67
2. *Bury* 6 points clear of Walsall 1960–61

3. *Hereford United* 6 points ahead of Cardiff 1975–76
4. *Aston Villa* 5 points ahead of Brighton 1971–72

3 FOURTH DIVISION CHAMPIONS WITH FEWEST POINTS

1. *Millwall*	56 points	1961–62
2. *Doncaster Rovers**	59 ,,	1965–66
3. *Doncaster Rovers*	59 ,,	1968–69

* Won on goal average.

4 FOURTH DIVISION CHAMPIONS WITH BIGGEST POINTS MARGIN FROM RUNNERS-UP

1. *Watford* 11 points ahead of Southend 1977–78
2. *Notts County* 9 points ahead of Bournemouth 1970–71
3. *Mansfield* 6 points ahead of Shrewsbury 1974–75
4. *Lincoln* 6 points ahead of Northampton 1975–76

5 CLUBS THAT HAVE BEEN DEMOTED OR PREVENTED FROM ENTERING THEIR FIRST DIVISION BY LEAGUE AUTHORITIES

1. *A.C. Milan* – The club was involved in a bribery scandal.
2. *Lazio* – Also relegated by the Italian F.A. for being involved in the same scandal.
3. *Schalke 04* – Because of financial irregularities.
4. *Rot-Weiss Oberhausen* – Because of financial difficulties.
5. *Castilla (of Madrid)* – They were disallowed from entering the Spanish first division because they are Real Madrid's nursery club and understandably no two clubs so closely connected can compete in the same division.

5 MAJOR CLUBS TO LOSE PROFESSIONAL STATUS OR FOLD ALTOGETHER IN THE LAST 20 YEARS

1. *W.T.K. Budapest* of Hungary
2. *Racing Club Paris* of France

3. *Schwarz-Weiss Essen* of West Germany – amateurized
4. *Xerxes* of Rotterdam, Holland
5. *F.C. Amsterdam* of Holland

50 INTERNATIONAL FOOTBALLERS WHO IN THE PERIOD BETWEEN 1936–74 PLAYED FOR ONE OF FOUR DIFFERENT CLUBS THAT HAVE RECENTLY LANGUISHED FOR A SPELL IN DIVISION 4

Blackpool

1. *Tony Waiters* (England)
2. *Jimmy Armfield* (England)
3. *Eddie Shimwell* (England)
4. *Harry Johnston* (England)
5. *Roy Gratrix* (England 'B')
6. *Hugh Kelly* (Scotland)
7. *Stanley Matthews* (England)
8. *Ernie Taylor* (England)
9. *Stan Mortenson* (England)
10. *Alan Ball* (England)
11. *Bill Perry* (England)
12. *George Farm* (Scotland)
13. *Peter Doherty* (Northern Ireland)
14. *Fred Pickering* (Ex England)

Bury

15. *Arthur Evans* (England Youth)
16. *Bill Gorman* (Eire)
17. *Tony Allen* (Ex England)
18. *Bobby Collins* (Ex Scotland)
19. *Peter Swan* (Ex England)
20. *Ray Parry* (Ex England)
21. *John Connelly* (Ex England)
22. *Ray Pointer* (Ex England)
23. *Stan Pearson* (Ex England)
24. *Eddie Quigley* (Ex England 'B')
25. *Brian Pilkington* (Ex England)

Hull City

26. *Billy Bly* (No apologises for including the best uncapped Goalkeeper of his time 1946–59)
27. *Sam Weaver* (England)
28. *Alan Jarvis* (Wales)
29. *Don Revie* (Ex England)
30. *Neil Franklin* (Ex England)

31. *Terry Neill* (Northern Ireland) Holds record international appearances whilst with Hull
32. *Jackie Sewell* (Ex England)
33. *Wilf Mannion* (Ex England)

34. *Stan Mortenson* (Ex England)
35. *Raich Carter* (Ex England)
36. *Dally Duncan* (Ex Scotland) Outside Left

Portsmouth

37. *Norman Uprichard* (Northern Ireland)
38. *Jimmy Scoular* (Scotland)
39. *Phil Roberts* (Wales)
40. *Len Phillips* (England)
41. *Jack Froggatt* (England)
42. *Jimmy Dickinson* (England)
43. *Peter Harris* (England)
44. *Norman Piper* (England under 23)

45. *Ron Davies* (Wales)
46. *Derek Dougan* (Northern Ireland)
47. *John Henderson* (Scotland)
48. *Ray Pointer* (Ex England)
49. *Reg Flewin* (England Wartime International)
50. *Phil Gunter* (England 'B')

'Ex' denotes that the player appeared for his country before he joined Division 4.

Soccer Beat – And Other Fields of Entertainment

16 FAMOUS RECORDS OF RECENT YEARS

1. 1970 *Back Home* – England World Cup Squad, reached No. 1 June, 1970.
2. 1971 *Good Old Arsenal* – Arsenal F.C. First Team Squad, reached No. 16 in June, 1971.
3. 1972 *Blue Is The Colour* – Chelsea, reached No. 5 in April, 1972.

4. 1972 *Leeds United* – Leeds United F.C., reached No. 10 in May/June, 1972.
5. 1973 *Nice One Cyril* – The Cockerel Chorus, reached No. 14 in April, 1973.
6. 1975 *I'm Forever Blowing Bubbles* – West Ham United Cup Squad, reached No. 31 in May, 1975.
7. 1977 *We Can Do It* – an E.P. by the Liverpool Football team, reached No. 15 in June, 1977.
8. 1978 *We've Got The Whole World In Our Hands* – Nottingham Forest F.C and Paper Lace, reached No. 24 in March, 1978.
9. 1981 *Ossie's Dream* (Spurs are on their way to Wembley) – The Tottenham Hotspur F.A. Cup Final Squad. 'B' side *Glory, Glory, Tottenham Hotspur*.
10. 1982 *Argentine Melody* (*Cancion De Argentina*) – San Jose (Andrew Lloyd Webber).
11. 1982 *El Mundial* – Placido Domingo.
12. 1982 *Tottenham, Tottenham* – 'B' side 'Spurs Medley' by the Tottenham Hotspur F.A. Cup Final Squad 1981–82.
13. 1982 *We Have A Dream* – with the 'B' side *Wrap Up the Cup*, the Scottish World Cup Squad with the voice of John Gordon Sinclair.
14. 1982 *This Time We'll Get it Right* – The England World Cup Team. C/W *We'll Fly the Flag* – the England World Cup Squad.
15. 1982 *Yer Man* – Dana and the Northern Ireland World Cup Squad.
16. 1983 *The Tigers Are Back* – Hull City Football Club.

It is not only in Britain that the recording of popular tunes by football clubs has become popular. France, Italy, Germany, Brazil and Chile are just five other counries whose teams are not reluctant to seek musical success. The West German World Cup Squad had a hit of sorts in 1982 with *Olé España*.

8 RECORDS THAT COULD HAVE HAD FOOTBALL CONNECTIONS

1. *Football Crazy* – Robin Hall and Jimmy McGregor's 1950's hit.
2. *Feet Up* – Guy Mitchell, No. 2 in 1952.

3. *Foot Prints in the Snow* – Johnny Duncan and the Blue Grass Boys, No. 27 in 1957.
4. *Footsteps* – Steve Lawrence, No. 4 in 1960.
5. *Rubber Ball* – Bobby Vee, No. 4 in 1961.
6. *Foot Tapper* – The Shadows, No. 1 in 1963.
7. *Ball of Confusion* – The Temptations, No. 7 in 1970.
8. *Kicks* – The U.K. Subs, No. 36 in 1979.

6 FILMS THAT HAVE CENTRED AROUND SOCCER

1. *Goal! World Cup '66* – (Columbia 1966) narrated by Nigel Patrick from a script by Brian Glanville.
2. *Goal! Goal! Another Goal!* – (A Len Film 1968).
3. *The Goalkeeper's Fear of the Penalty** – Wim Wenders' *Die Angst des Tormans beim Elf Meter* made in 1971.
4. *Yesterday's Hero* – (Columbia/EMI/Warner 1979) starring Ian McShane, son of ex footballer, Harry.
5. *Gregory's Girl* – 1980. Directed by Bill Forsyth and starring John Gordon Sinclair.
6. *Escape to Victory* – (Lorimar 1981) a John Houston film which takes place in a P.O.W. camp in Germany.

* This film involves the trials and tribulations of a Goalkeeper's private life.

THE 11 INTERNATIONAL FOOTBALLERS TO PLAY IN *ESCAPE TO VICTORY*

This film starred Michael Caine and Sylvestor Stallone as prisoners of war who participate in a soccer match against their captors. To ensure authentic football sequences the help of the following was enlisted.

1. *Osvaldo Ardiles* – Argentina
2. *Kazimierz Deyna* – Poland
3. *Soren Lindsted* – Denmark
4. *Bobby Moore* – England
5. *Russell Osman* – England
6. *Pelé*– Brazil
7. *Co Prins* – Netherlands
8. *Mike Summerbee* – England
9. *Hallvar Thoresen* – Norway
10. *Paul Van Himst* – Belgium
11. *John Wark* – Scotland

3 FORMER FOOTBALLERS WHO MADE THE 'BIG TIME' AS SINGERS

1. *Julio Iglesias* – Once a Real Madrid Youth and Reserve Goalkeeper.
2. *Des O'Connor* – Once on the books of Northampton Town.
3. *Rod Stewart* – Ex-Brentford apprentice.

3 GUITAR PLAYING FOOTBALL INTERNATIONALS

1. *Miguel Brindisi* – Argentina
2. *Martin Buchan* – Scotland
3. *Terry Neill* – Northern Ireland

6 PLAYERS WHO HAVE WAXED LYRICAL

1. *Les Barrett* – Recorded in mid 60's with his brother Paul. They were a footballing Paul and Barry Ryan.
2. *Alan Birchenall* – A good singer whose football restricted his appearances.
3. *Colin Grainger* – Popular singer on the club and cinema circuit in the early 60's. Once appeared on the same bill as The Beatles. Two records – *Are You* and *This I Know*.
4. *Kevin Keegan* – His record *Head over Heels in Love* (not his first) reached No. 31 in 1979.
5. *Francisco Marinho* – Put his voice on wax in the mid 70's at the height of his footballing fame.
6. *Terry Venables* – Sang with the Joe Loss Orchestra at the Hammersmith Palais.

18 TELEVISION FOOTBALL COMMENTATORS AND REPORTERS

B.B.C
1. *David Coleman*
2. *Kevin Cosgrave*
3. *Barry Davies*
4. *Tony Gubba*
5. *Desmond Lynham*
6. *Archie McPherson*
7. *John Motson*

I.T.V.
10. *David Burton*
11. *John Helm*
12. *Hugh Johns*
13. *Brian Moore*
14. *Jim Rosenthal*
15. *Gerald Sinstadt*
16. *Roger Tames*

8. *Alan Parry*
9. *Kenneth Wolstenholme*
   (Former)

17. *Martin Tyler*
18. *Elton Welsby*

20 LEADING FOOTBALL WRITERS AND JOURNALISTS OF THE 1980's

1. *Eric Batty*
2. *Danny Blanchflower* – Sunday Express
3. *Richard Bott* – Sunday Express
4. *Patrick Collins* – News of the World
5. *Reg Drury* – News of the World
6. *André Duclos*
7. *Paul Gardner*
8. *Brian Glanville* – Sunday Times
9. *Rob Hughes* – Mail on Sunday
10. *Mike Langley* – Sunday People
11. *Hugh McIlvanney* – Observer
12. *David Miller* – Daily Express
13. *James Mossop* – Sunday Express
14. *Tony Pullein*
15. *Keir Radnedge*
16. *Jack Rollin*
17. *Arthur Rotmill*
18. *Leslie Vernon*
19. *Julie Welch* – Observer
20. *Ian Wooldridge* – Daily Mail

Where no newspaper is specified this signifies that the writer has no particular allegiance to any one paper or magazine.

In the Family

20 PAIRS OF BROTHERS TO WIN INTERNATIONAL HONOURS

In brackets no. of Caps as at August, 1982

1. *Rüdiger* (19) and *Volker Abramczik* (School and Youth) – West Germany
2. *Ivor* (68) and *Len* (11) *Allchurch* – Wales

3. *Klaus* (24) and *Thomas* (2 'B') *Allofs* – West Germany
4. *Franco* (1) and *Giuseppe* (6) *Baresi* – Italy
5. *Danny* (56)and *Jackie* (12) *Blanchflower* – Northern Ireland
6. *Ray* (2) and *Liam* (36) *Brady* – Eire
7. *John* (38) and *Mel* (31) *Charles* – Wales
8. *Bobby* (106) and *Jackie* (35) *Charlton* – England
9. *Pat* (5) and *Tony* (32) *Dunne* – Eire
10. *Bernd* (19) and *Karl-Heinz* (42) *Förster* – West Germany
11. *Alan* (17) and *John* (2) *Hansen* – Scotland
12. *Uli* (22) and *Dieter* (2) *Hoeness* – West Germany
13. *Dave* (11) and *John* (1) *Hollins* – Wales and England respectively
14. *Bobby* (8) and *Willie* (23) *Irvine* – Northern Ireland
15. *Cyril* (4) and *Peter* (4 u.23) *Knowles* – England
16. *Bobby, Danny* and *Sammy Lenarduzzi* (no. of caps unknown) – Canada
17. *Eduard* (1) and *Johnny* (15) *Metgod* – Netherlands
18. *Arthur* (6) and *Jack* (1 'B') *Rowley* – England
19. *Alex* (16) and *Jimmy* (1) *Scott* – Scotland
20. *Fritz* (61) and *Otmar* (21) *Walter* – West Germany

7 FATHERS AND THEIR SONS TO WIN INTERNATIONAL HONOURS

1. *John* (17) and *John Jnr.* (I u.23) *Aston* – England
2. *Mel* (31) and *Jeremy* (5) *Charles* – Wales
3. *George R.* (1) and *George E.* (19) *Eastham* – England
4. *Alec* (1) and *David* (5) *Herd* – Scotland
5. *Con* (30) and *Mick* (48) *Martin* – Eire
6. *Joe* (2) and *Joe Jnr.* (I u. 21) *McBride* – Scotland
7. *Bobby* (29) and *Tommy* (20) *Walker* – Scotland

4 BROTHERS-IN-LAW TO WIN INTERNATIONAL HONOURS

1. *Johnny Giles* (50) and *Nobby Stiles* (28) – Eire and England respectively
2. *Colin Grainger* (7) and *Jim Iley* (I u.23) – England

166

7 UNCLES AND THEIR NEPHEWS TO HAVE MADE A MAJOR IMPRESSION IN THE FOOTBALL LEAGUE

Uncle listed first

1. *Les Allen* – Chelsea, Tottenham, Q.P.R. and England u.23
   Paul Allen – West Ham and England Youth
2. *Billy Butler* – Bolton and England
   Dennis Butler – Bolton and Rochdale
3. *Jimmy Dugdale* – W.B.A., Aston Villa, Q.P.R., and England 'B'
   Alan Dugdale – Coventry, Charlton and England Youth
4. *Roy Paul* – Swansea, Manchester City and Wales
   Alan Curtis – Swansea, Leeds and Wales
5. *Ellis Rimmer* – Tranmere, Sheffield Wednesday, Ipswich and England
   Warwick Rimmer – Bolton and Crewe
6. *Roy Sproson* – Stoke and Port Vale
   Phil Sproson – Port Vale
7. *Tommy Wright* – Everton and England
   Billy Wright – Everton and England u.21

17 PAIRS OF BROTHERS TO HAVE PLAYED MORE THAN 300 LEAGUE GAMES EACH

Elder brother listed first

			appearances
1.	*Les Allen*	– Chelsea, Tottenham, Q.P.R. and England u.23	301
	Dennis Allen	– Charlton, Reading and Bournemouth	357
2.	*Alan Buckley*	Nottingham Forest, Walsall and Birmingham	404
	Steve Buckley	Luton and Derby County	297*
3.	*Tom Callender*	Lincoln City and Gateshead	439
	Jack Callender	Gateshead	470
4.	*Jack Charlton*	Leeds United and England	629

* Passed the 300 total during 1982–83.

Bobby Charlton	Manchester United, Preston and England	644
5. *Frank Clarke*	Shrewsbury, Q.P.R., Ipswich and Carlisle	448
Allan Clarke	Walsall, Fulham, Leicester, Leeds, Barnsley and England	573
6. *Eddie Gray*	Leeds United and Scotland	427
Frankie Gray	Leeds United, Nottingham Forest and Scotland	311
7. *Terry Hibbitt*	Leeds, Newcastle and Birmingham	385
Ken Hibbitt	Bradford Park Avenue and Wolves	426
8. *Ralph Hunt*	Portsmouth, Bournemouth, Norwich, Derby, Grimsby, Swindon, Port Vale, Newport and Chesterfield	373
Dennis Hunt	Gillingham and Brentford	333
9. *Keith Kennedy*	Newcastle, Bury and Mansfield	406
Alan Kennedy	Newcastle, Liverpool and England u.23.	285*
10. *Tom McAnearney*	Sheffield Wednesday, Peterborough and Aldershot	469
Jimmy McAnearney	Sheffield Wednesday, Plymouth, Watford and Bradford City	306
11. *Chris Nicholl*	Burnley, Halifax, Luton, Aston Villa, Southampton and Northen Ireland	536
Terry Nicholl	Crewe, Sheffield United, Southend and Gillingham	302
12. *Jack Parry*	Derby County	478
Ray Parry	Bolton, Blackpool, Bury and England	544
13. *Jack Rowley*	Wolves, Manchester United, Plymouth and England	373
Arthur Rowley	Wolves, W.B.A., Fulham, Leicester, Shrewsbury and England 'B'	619

* Passed the 300 total during 1982–83.

14.	*Graham Shaw*	Sheffield United, Doncaster and England	464
	Bernard Shaw	Sheffield United, Wolves, Sheffield Wednesday and England u.23	356
15.	*Tony Wagstaff*	Sheffield United and Reading	315
	Barry Wagstaff	Sheffield United, Reading and Rotherham	364
16.	*John White*	Aldershot and Bristol City	425
	Len White	Rotherham, Newcastle, Huddersfield, Stockport and English F.L.	444
17.	*David Worthington*	Halifax, Barrow, Grimsby and Southend	491
	Frank Worthington	Huddersfield, Leicester, Bolton, Birmingham, Leeds, Sunderland and England	557

6 PAIRS OF TWINS WHO HAVE PLAYED IN THE FOOTBALL LEAGUE

1. *Mike Betts* – Blackpool and Bury.
   Stuart Betts – Blackpool, Halifax and Crewe.
2. *George Fisher* – Millwall, Fulham and Colchester.
   John Fisher – Millwall and Bournemouth.
3. *Paul Futcher* – Chester, Luton, Manchester City, Oldham, Derby and England u.21.
   Ron Futcher – Chester, Luton, Manchester City, and Southampton (on trial).
4. *David Jackson* – Wrexham, Bradford City, Tranmere and Halifax.
   Peter Jackson – Wrexham, Bradford City and Tranmere.
5. *Ian Morgan* – Q.P.R. and Watford.
   Roger Morgan – Q.P.R., Tottenham and England u.23.
6. *Alf Stephens* – Leeds and Swindon.
   John Stephens – Leeds, Swindon, West Ham, and Cardiff.

4 BROTHERS WHO HAVE APPEARED WITH THEIR TWIN IN A FULL INTERNATIONAL TEAM

1. *Erwin Kremers* – Schalke 04 and West Germany.
   Helmut Kremers – Schalke 04 and West Germany.

2. *Willie Van der Kerkhof* – PSV Eindhoven and West
   Germany.
   Rene Van der Kerkhof – PSV Eindhoven and West
   Germany.
3. *Zlatko Vujovic* – Hajuk Split and Yugoslavia.
   Zoran Vujovic – Hajduk Split and Yugoslavia.
4. *Fritz Walter* –1. FC. Kaiserslautern and West Germany.
   Ottmar Walter – 1. FC. Kaiserslautern and West Germany.

20 PLAYERS WHO DIDN'T MATCH UP
TO THEIR ELDER BROTHERS

Younger brother	*Older brother*
1. *Denis Allen* – Charlton, Reading and Bournemouth. Half Back.	*Les Allen* – Chelsea, Tottenham, and Q.P.R. Spurs League and Cup Double Forward and England u.23.
2. *Peter Berry* – Crystal Palace and Ipswich. Forward.	*Johnny Berry* – Birmingham, Manchester United and England Outside Right, dreadfully injured in the Munich Air Disaster.
3. *Kevin Bremner* – Colchester and Millwall. Striker.	*Des Bremner* – Hibs, Aston Villa and Scotland Midfielder.
4. *George Buchan* – Aberdeen, Manchester United, Mossley and Glossop. Utility Attacker.	*Martin Buchan* – Countless honours with Aberdeen and Manchester United. Winner of 34 Scotland Caps.
5. *John Conway* – Bohemians, Fulham and Swiss 1st Division. Forward.	*Jimmy Conway* – Bohemians, Fulham, Manchester City, Portland Timbers. Capped 19 times for Eire.
6. *Paul Davies* – Arsenal and Charlton. Centre Forward.	*Ron Davies* – 29 times Capped Welshman.
7. *David Drinkell* – Grimsby Schoolboy and Apprentice. Centre Forward.	*Kevin Drinkell* – Grimsby, Highly rated Centre Forward.

170

8. *Peter Firmani* – Charlton in fewer than 40 games. Full Back.

Eddie Firmani – Charlton, Sampdoria and Southend, first rate scorer of goals especially in Italy. Forward.

9. *John Flowers* – Stoke, Doncaster and Port Vale. Half Back.

Ron Flowers – Wolves and Northampton 49 times Capped Wing Half.

10. *Steve Francis* – Q.P.R. Schoolboy and Apprentice. Midfielder.

Gerry Francis – Q.P.R. Crystal Palace, Coventry and England Midfielder 12 times.

11. *Trevor Gould* – Coventry, Northampton and Bedford. Full Back/Midfielder.

Bobby Gould (Q.V. Nomads) 8 clubs including Coventry, Arsenal and Wolves. Striker.

12. *Nigel Hart* – Wigan, Leicester, Blackpool and Rochdale. Centre Back.

Paul Hart – Stockport, Blackpool and Leeds. Centre Back.

13. *John Hilaire* – Millwall Schoolboy and Apprentice. Winger.

Vince Hilaire – Crystal Palace and England u.21 Midfielder.

14. *Billy Hughes* – Sunderland, Derby, Leicester and Enderby Town. Forward.

John Hughes 'Yogi Bear' – Celtic, Crystal Palace and Scotland Striker.

15. *Bryn Jones* – Swansea, Newport, Bournemouth, Northampton and Watford. Inside Forward.

Cliff Jones – Spurs, Fulham and Wales. International Winger.

16. *Greg MacKenzie* – Chelsea Apprentice. Full Back.

Steve MacKenzie – Crystal Palace, Manchester City, West Brom and England u.21. Midfielder.

17. *Terry Nicholl* – Crewe, Sheffield United Southend and Gillingham. Midfielder.

Chris Nicholl – Burnley, Witton, Halifax, Luton, Aston Villa, Southampton and N. Ireland Centre Half

18. *Mel Pejic* – Stoke and Hereford. Full Back.

Mike Pejic – Stoke, Everton, Aston Villa and England. Full Back.

19. *Tom White* – Aberdeen, Crystal Palace, Blackpool, Bury and Crewe. Forward.

John White – Alloa, Falkirk, Tottenham and Scotland Midfielder.

20. *Steve Wilkins* – Chelsea and Dagenham. Midfielder.

Ray Wilkins – Chelsea, Manchester United and England Midfielder.

6 FOOTBALLERS' RELATIONS

1. *Roy Dwight* – Fulham and Nottingham Forest, Coventry and Millwall Winger, who broke a leg in the 1959 F.A. Cup Final.

Uncle of *Reginald Hercules Dwight*, also known as *Elton John*.

2. *Steve Gatting* – Arsenal and Brighton Sweeper.

Brother of *Mike*, Middlesex and England cricketer.

3. *Harry McShane* – Blackburn, Huddersfield, Bolton, Manchester United and Oldham Right Winger.

Father of *Ian McShane*, the actor (he played Disraeli on television).

4. *Dave Sexton* – Luton, West Ham, Orient, Brighton and Crystal Palace schemer. Now a manager.

Son of *Archie* renowned A.B.A. Middleweight boxer.

5. *Steve Sherwood* – Chelsea and Watford Goalkeeper.

Brother of Olympic athlete, *John*.

6. *Fred Steele* – Stoke, Mansfield, Port Vale and England Centre Forward.

Uncle of *David Steele*, Northants and England cricketer.

3 FOOTBALLING FAMILIES

1. *The Milburns and the Charltons*

Four *Milburn* brothers – *George* (Chesterfield and Leeds Full Back), *Jim* (Ashington, Leeds and Bradford P.A. Full Back), *John* (Leeds, Norwich and Bradford City Full Back) and *Stan* (Ashington, Chesterfield, Leicester, Rochdale and England 'B') – cousins to – *Jackie Milburn* (Ashington, Newcastle and England) – and also cousins to the *Charlton* brothers – *Jack*

(Leeds and England) and *Bobby* (Manchester United, Preston and England)

2. *The Moores*

Norman Moore (Grimsby, Hull, Blackburn and Bury Centre Forward) brother of *Tom* (Grimsby) and father of *Kevin* (Grimsby Full Back), *David* (Grimsby Full Back) and *Andy* (Grimsby Centre Back)

3. *The Seymours and the Phillipses*

Tommy Seymour (Pre-war Shrewsbury Full Back) father-in-law of *Roy Phillips* (1940s Shrewsbury Centre Forward) father of *John Phillips* (Shrewsbury and – currently – Crystal Palace Goalkeeper)

THE 15 PAIRS OF BROTHERS WHO PLAYED FOR THE SAME CLUB DURING 1982–83

1. *Chris* (Centre Back) and *Gerhardt* (Midfielder) *Ampofo* – West Ham
2. *Neville* (Striker) and *Mark* (Winger) *Chamberlain* – Stoke
3. *Dave* (Midfielder) and *Jim* (Full Back) *Collins* – Derby
4. *Eddie* (Midfielder) and *Frankie* (Full Back) *Gray* – Leeds
5. *Danny* (Striker) and *Andy* (Defender) *Greaves* – Southend
6. *Brian* (Defender) and *Jimmy* (Striker) *Greenhough* – Rochdale
7. *Glenn* (Midfielder) and *Carl* (Midfielder) *Hoddle* – Tottenham
8. *John** (Midfielder) and *Phil* (Utility) *Linacre* – Hartlepool
9. *Andy* (Centre Back) and *David* (Centre Back) *Linighan* – Hartlepool
10. *Steve* (Midfielder) and *John* (Full Back) *McMahon* – Everton
11. *Kevin* (Full Back), *Dave* (Full Back) and *Andy* (Midfielder) *Moore* – Grimsby
12. *Micky* (Centre Back/MF) and *Marcus* (Goalkeeper) *Phelan* – Burnley

* Now playing in Malta.

173

13. *Peter* (Centre Back) and *Paul* (Midfielder) *Shirtliff* –
Sheffield Wednesday
14. *Glynn* (Full Back) and *Ian* (Midfielder) *Snodin* – Doncaster
15. *Garry†* (Centre Forward) and *Keith* (Striker) *Thompson* –
Coventry

† Now with West Bromwich Albion.

29 CURRENT LEAGUE
FOOTBALLERS WHOSE FATHERS
ALSO PLAYED AT LEAGUE LEVEL

Son		Father
1. *John Armfield*	Manchester United	*Jimmy*
2. *Alan Ball*	Bristol Rovers	*Alan*
3. *Stuart Beavon*	Reading	*Cyril*
4. *Graham Bell*	Preston	*Tom*
5. *Keith Bowen*	Brentford	*Dave*
6. *Shaun Brooks*	Crystal Palace	*Johnny*
7. *Greg Campbell*	West Ham	*Bobby*
8. *Jeremy Charles*	Swansea	*Mel*
9. *Alan Devonshire*	West Ham	*Les*
10. *Gerry Francis*	Coventry	*George*
11. *Roger Gibbins*	Cardiff	*Eddie*
12. *Derek Hales*	Charlton	*Richard*
13. *Mark Hateley*	Coventry	*Tony*
14. *Mark Higgins*	Everton	*John*
15. *Paul Hinshelwood*	Crystal Palace	*Wally*
16. *Kenny Jackett*	Watford	*Frank*
17. *Gary Mabbutt*	Tottenham	*Ray*
Kevin Mabbutt	Crystal Palace	
18. *Joe McBride*	Rotherham	*Joe*
19. *Andy McCulloch*	Sheffield Wednesday	*Adam*
20. *Mick Martin*	Newcastle	*Con*
21. *Gary Megson*	Sheffield Wednesday	*Don*
22. *Gary Mills*	Derby	*Rolly*
23. *Johnny Morrissey*	Everton	*Johnny*
24. *Russell Osman*	Ipswich	*Rex*
25. *Paul Petts*	Shrewsbury	*John*

174

26. *Steve Powell*	Derby	*Tommy*
27. *Gary Rowell*	Sunderland	*John*
28. *Carl Swan*	Doncaster	*Peter*
29. *Neil Webb*	Portsmouth	*Dougie*

10 FATHERS OR UNCLES ON THE MANAGERIAL/COACHING STAFF WHOSE SONS OR NEPHEWS PLAYED FOR THEIR CLUBS (ALBEIT IN MOST CASES BRIEFLY)

1. *Jimmy Bloomfield*
   Orient Manager

   Clive
   released before making the first team.

2. *John Bond*
   Bournemouth, Norwich and Manchester City Manager

   Kevin
   useful First Division Defender who has followed his father around.

3. *Mike Bullock*
   Halifax Coach and then Manager

   Simon
   made 17 appearances before his uncle released him.

4. *Walter Joyce*
   Bolton Coach

   Warren
   young midfielder awaiting a first team opportunity.

5. *George Kirby*
   Halifax Manager

   Simon
   released without a first team appearance.

6. *Billy Lansdowne*
   West Ham Coach

   Billy
   although very successful in the reserves was released in 1981 after only 9 League games.

7. *Bert Loxley*
   Lincoln Physiotherapist

   Tony
   Full Back who made one appearance before leaving as a 19 year old.

8. *Lawrie McMenemy*
   Southampton Manager

   Chris
   although he signed pro. was released that same season. Sean was only on schoolboy forms.

175

9. *Brian Miller*
   Burnley Manager

   David
   Centre Half who is rated highly
   by many. Is still at the club that
   his father left earlier this year.

10. *Dougie Webb*
    Reading
    Physiotherapist

    Neil
    highly talented utility player
    whose £100,000 transfer to
    Portsmouth makes nonsense of
    the nasty statements implying he
    was a first teamer only because
    of his father.

Managers

THE 6 MANAGERS WHO HAVE WON THE LEAGUE CHAMPIONSHIP AS PLAYERS AND AS TEAM BOSSES

	Player	Manager
1. *Ted Drake*	Arsenal 1934, 1935, 1938	Chelsea 1955
2. *Bill Nicholson*	Tottenham 1951	Tottenham 1961
3. *Alf Ramsey*	Tottenham 1951	Ipswich 1962
4. *Joe Mercer*	Everton 1939. Arsenal 1948 and 1953	Manchester City 1968
5. *Dave Mackay*	Tottenham 1961	Derby County 1975
6. *Bob Paisley*	Liverpool 1947	Liverpool 1976, 1977, 1979, 1980 and 1982

THE 12 BRITISH MANAGERS
TO GUIDE TEAMS TO THE
WORLD CUP FINALS

1. *Walter Winterbottom* – England. 1954, lost to Uruguay in Quarter Finals. 1958, lost against Russia in play off for Quarter Final place. 1962, reached Quarter Finals.

2. *Andy Beattie* – Scotland. 1954, last in a group consisting of Uruguay, Austria and Czechoslovakia.

3. *George Raynor* – Sweden. World Cup Final in 1958, runners up to Brazil. Also 3rd place in 1950.

4. *Jimmy Murphy* – Wales, Manchester United's Assistant Manager, he steered Wales to the Quarter Finals in 1958, only losing 1–0 to eventual World Cup winners, Brazil.

5. *Peter Doherty* – Northern Ireland. 1958, lost 4–0 to an outstanding French side in the Quarter Finals.

6. *Matt Busby* – Scotland. 1958, as caretaker Manager guided them to qualification in the 6th World Cup. Near fatal injury in the Munich air disaster prevented him from helping Scotland in Sweden.

7. *Alf Ramsey* – England. The architect of the 1966 home triumph, he then took his country to the Quarter Finals in 1970. Knighted after the 1966 World Cup victory.

8. *Willie Ormond* – Scotland. His team's lack of goal power was its downfall, Brazil and Yugoslavia went through at Scotland's expense to the Quarter Finals in 1974.

9. *Ally MacLeod* – Scotland. A shock 3–1 defeat by Peru, and a 1–1 draw with Iran were Scotland's opening games in the 1978 World Cup when once again Scotland failed to make the Quarter Finals.

10. *Ron Greenwood* – England. Took England to the Quarter Finals in 1982. The draw with Spain was his last match as a manager.

11. *Billy Bingham* – Northern Ireland. He brought amazing success with Northern Ireland's splendid performances. The most outstanding of the three home countries in the 1982 competition.

12. *Jock Stein* – Scotland. Now manager of his country for the second time. In 1966 as stop gap boss Scotland failed to qualify. In 1982 Russia and Brazil's greater class prevented them from making advances in the competition.

8 MANAGERS WHO HAVE COACHED 'FOREIGN' COUNTRIES IN POST-WAR WORLD CUPS

	World Cup Team	Nationality
1. *Gregorio Bundo*	El Salvador 1970	Argentinian
2. *Carlos Alberto*	Kuwait 1982	Brazilian
3. *Guy Cluseau*	Morocco 1970	French
4. *Didi*	Peru 1970	Brazilian
5. *George Raynor*	Sweden 1950 and 1958	English
6. *'Tim' Elba de Padua Lima*	Peru 1982	Brazilian
7. *Blagoye Vidimic*	Zaire 1974	Yugoslav
8. *Jean Vincent*	Cameroon 1982	French

Sad Occasions

THE 18 WORST CROWD DISASTERS

1. *Ayresome Park, Middlesbrough* January, 1980. | Wall near exit collapsed killing a married couple. | Middlesbrough v Manchester United Division 1

2. *Bucaramanga, Colombia* 1981. | A riot prompted police gunfire; 4 people were killed, 2 shot and 2 from beatings. Around 40 injured. | Bucaramanga v Atlético Junior.

3. *Burnden Park, Bolton* March, 1946. | A dividing wall collapsed; 33 died. 400+ were injured. | Bolton v Stoke, F.A. Cup, Quarter Final.

4. *The Zamalek Stadium, Cairo* February, 1974. — A crush by over-eager Egyptian fans at entrances resulted in 60 deaths and as many injuries. — Egypt v Dukla Prague Tour match.

5. *Ibague, Colombia* April, 1981. — Through the collapse of a stand 11 died and many more were injured. — Tolima v Deportivo Cali in Cup Semi-Final.

6. *Ibrox Park, Glasgow* April, 1902. — Large part of West Stand collapsed; 23 were killed, 364 injured. — Scotland v England. The game, a 1–1 draw, was scratched from International records because of the disaster.

7. *Ibrox Park, Glasgow* September, 1961. — A pillar of a stand collapsed killing 3 and injuring 320. — Rangers v Celtic.

8. *Ibrox Park, Glasgow* January, 1971. — 'Fans' colliding on steps caused 66 to lose their lives and injured 100. — Celtic v Rangers. Britain's worst-ever crowd disaster.

9. *Kaisarie, Central Turkey* September, 1971. — A stand collapsed, 44 died and hundreds were injured. — A 3rd Division game, Kaisarie v Siwas.

10. *Karaiskaki Ground, Athens* Early 1981. — A crowd stumbled down steps, 21 dead and over 50 hurt. — Olympiakos v neighbours A.E.K.

11. *Lenin Stadium, Moscow* November, 1982. — Fighting broke out among drunken fans causing panic; 60–100 dead (reports vary) and hundreds injured. — Moscow Spartak v Haarlam (U.E.F.A. Cup Match).

12. *The Alianza Club's Lima Ground, Peru* May, 1964.	Fans were trampled to death at exits after fleeing from police bullets; 318 died, nearly 600 were gravely injured.	Peru v Argentina in an Olympic qualifying game.
13. *Pasual Guerrero Stadium, Cali-Colombia* November, 1982.	Drunken fans caused a panic and many were trampled underfoot; 22 died, over 100 hurt.	Deportivo Cali v America.
14. *Port-au-Prince, Haiti* December, 1976.	6 fans were shot by over eager police.	Haiti v Cuba – World Cup match
15. *River Plate Stadium, Buenos Aires* June, 1968.	Boca 'fans' pelted home supporters with lighted newspapers causing panic; 74 dead, nearly 200 hurt.	River Plate v Boca Juniors.
16. *Santiago, Chile* April, 1961.	Huge crush in over-capacity crowd; 5 died and over 300 required medical attention.	Chile v Brazil (friendly international).
17. *Sao Luis, N. E. Brazil* Spring, 1982.	Police shot into the crowd to stop rioting; 3 died and 25 were badly wounded.	Sao Luis v Fortaleza.
18. *Volksparkstadion, Hamburg* April 1967.	More than 50 people fell from a stand. One died and 15 were injured.	Hamburger S.V. v Bayern München.

THE 6 SOCCER AIR DISASTERS.

These are the number of players killed

1. *Torino* 1949 — 18
2. *Manchester United* 1958 — 8
3. *Denmark 'B'* 1960 — 8
4. *Green Cross* (then a Chilean 1st Division club) 1961 — 8
5. *The Strongest* (Bolivian Champions) 1969 — 16
6. *Pakhtakorer Tashkent* 1979 — 17

THE 8 MANCHESTER UNITED PLAYERS WHO LOST THEIR LIVES IN THE MUNICH AIR DISASTER FEBRUARY, 1958

1. *Geoff Bent*, 25
2. *Roger Byrne*, 29 (Captain)
3. *Eddie Colman*, 21
4. *Duncan Edwards*, 21
5. *Mark Jones*, 24
6. *David Pegg*, 22
7. *Tommy Taylor*,
8. *Liam Whelan*, 2

THE 9 MANCHESTER UNITED PLAYERS TO SURVIVE THE MUNICH AIR DISASTER

1. *Johnny Berry**
2. *Jackie Blanchflower**
3. *Bobby Charlton*
4. *Billy Foulkes*
5. *Harry Gregg*
6. *Ken Morgans*
7. *Albert Scanlon*
8. *Dennis Viollet*
9. *Ray Wood*

* Never played again because of the injuries he sustained.

12 FOOTBALLERS WHO DIED THROUGH ILLNESS AT PLAYING AGE

	Age at Death	Year	Clubs	Illness
1. *Renato Curi*	24	1977	Ascoli	Heart attack in game v Juventus

	Age at Death	Year	Clubs	Illness
2. *Gilbert Dussier*	29	1978	Rochling Volkingen, Nancy, Lille, Waterschei, Luxembourg	Leukaemia
3. *Bobby Finch*	30	1978	Queens Park Rangers	Heart attack
4. *Alan Groves*	29	1978	Southport, Chester, Shrewsbury, Bournemouth, Oldham, Blackpool	Heart failure
5. *Jeff Hall*	29	1959	Birmingham City and England	Polio
6. *Brian Hill*	30	1968	Sheffield Wednesday	Heart trouble
7. *Mel Holden*	26	1981	Preston, Sunderland, Blackpool, Pec Zwolle (Holland)	Multiple sclerosis
8. *Tom McLaren*	29	1978	Port Vale	Heart trouble
9. *Tommy Mehan*	28	1925	Rochdale, Manchester United, Chester	Polio
10. *Pavao*	Late 20's	1978	Porto	Heart failure
11. *Omar Sahnoun*	24	1980	Nantes, Bordeaux and France	Heart attack
12. *Johnny Summers*	34	1962	Fulham, Norwich, Millwall, Charlton	Cancer

19 ACCIDENTAL DEATHS

1. *Georghi Asparoukhov* of Levski Spartak and Bulgaria died 1971, aged 28, in a car crash
2. *Jacques Borel* of St. Etienne died 1980, aged 20, in a car crash.
3. *Peter Canavan* of Ipswich Town and England Youth died 1978, aged 17, in a car crash.

4. *Tommy Cooper* of Port Vale, Derby County, Liverpool and England, died 1940, aged 35 in a motor cycle accident.
5. *Vitalij Daraselia* of Dinamo Tbilisi and the Soviet Union died 1983, aged 25, in a car crash.
6. *Ian Fallis* of Kilmarnock died 1977, in his early twenties, in a car crash.
7. *Peter Houseman* of Chelsea and Oxford died 1977, aged 31, in a car crash.
8. *Bobby McKean* of St. Mirren, Rangers and Scotland died 1979, aged 25, of carbon monoxide poisoning.
9. *Valentino Mazzola* of Venezia, Torino and Italy died 1949, aged 30, in a plane crash at Superga.
10. *Gigi Meroni* of Torino and Italy died 1967, aged 25, when he was knocked down in a road accident.
11. *Georgi Milkov* of Levsky Spartak died 1979, aged 27, in a car crash.
12. *Ermindo Onega* of River Plate, Penarol and Argentina died 1979, aged 37, in a car crash after a veterans' match.
13. *Mladen Ramljak* of Dynamo Zagreb, Feyenoord and Yugoslavia died 1978, in his early thirties, in a car crash.
14. *Luciano Re Cecconi* of Pro Patria, Foggia, Lazio and Italy died 1977, aged 28, shot by a jeweller when pretending to hold up the shop.
15. *Miro Rys* of Chicago Sting, L.A. Aztecs and U.S.A. died 1977, aged 19, in a car crash.
16. *John Thomson* of Celtic and Scotland died 1931, aged 22. A Goalkeeper, he dived at the feet of an onrushing Forward in a Celtic/Rangers match and received a kick in the side of the head.
17. *Jimmy Thorpe* of Sunderland died 1936, aged 22. Also a Goalkeeper, in a match against Chelsea he received a kick in the head which reacted with his diabetic condition and led to his death.
18. *John White* of Alloa, Falkirk, Tottenham and Scotland died 1964, aged 27, struck by lightning on a golf course.
19. *Dave Wiggett* of Lincoln City and Hartlepool died 1978, aged 21, in a car crash.

It is remarkable coincidence that both Asparoukhov (1) and Milkov (11), who played for the same club, in the same position (Centre Forward), and were almost the same age, should die the same death.

24 PLAYERS WHO WERE FORCED INTO EARLY RETIREMENT THROUGH INJURY

	Age at Retirement	Last season before Retirement	Clubs
1. *Mike Bernard*	29	1977–78	Stoke City, Everton, Oldham and England Under 23.
2. *Jackie Blanchflower*	24	1957–58	Manchester United and Northern Ireland
3. *Paul Bradshaw*	24	1977–78	Burnley and Sheffield Wednesday
4. *Terry Bush*	27	1969–70	Bristol City
5. *Paul Cheesley*	23	1976–77	Norwich and Bristol City
6. *Micky Conway*	22	1977–78	Brighton and Swansea
7. *Derek Dooley*	24	1952–53	Lincoln and Sheffield Wednesday
8. *John Fitzpatrick*	26	1972–73	Manchester United
9. *Tony Green*	26	1972–73	Albion Rovers, Blackpool, Newcastle and Scotland
10. *Roly Gregoire*	23	1980–81	Halifax and Sunderland
11. *Bedford Jezzard*	28	1955–56	Fulham and England
12. *Jimmy Kerr*	21	1970–71	Bury and Blackburn
13. *Erwin Kremers*	29	early 1978–79	Schalke 04 and West Germany
14. *Brian Little*	26	1980–81	Aston Villa and England
15. *Malcolm MacDonald*	29	1979–80	Tonbridge, Fulham, Luton, Newcastle, Arsenal and England
16. *Willie Maddren*	28	1978–79	Middlesbrough and England Under 23

184

17.	*John Middleton*	25	1981–82	Nottingham Forest, Derby, and England Under 21
18.	*Jimmy Pearce*	25	1972–73	Tottenham
19.	*Ritchie Powling*	26	1981–82	Arsenal
20.	*John Robson*	27	1979	Derby County, Aston Villa and England Under 23
21.	*Helmut Schön*	25	1940–41	Dresdner S.C. and West Germany
22.	*Paul Stratford*	22	1977–78	Northampton Town
23.	*Tostao*	26	1972–73	Cruzeiro, Vasco da Gama and Brazil
24.	*Tommy Wright*	28	1972–73	Everton and England

Second Sight

12 PLAYERS WHO CAUSE 'DOUBLE VISION'

Only principal clubs are given

1. *Biro-Biro** – Corinthians and Brazil
2. *Paul Bonga Bonga* – One-time Standard Liege and Congo
3. *Didì* – Fluminense, Botafogo and Brazil
4. *Dudu** – Vasco da Gama of Brazil
5. *Néné** – Benfica and Portugal
6. *Pepé** – Salamanca of Spain
7. *Tata** – Portuguesa of Brazil
8. *Toto** – Real Zaragoza of Spain
9. *Vavà* – Vasco da Gama, Atletico Madrid, Palmeiras and Brazil
10. *Xaxa** – Vasco da Gama
11. *Yi Yi** – Sevilla of Spain
12. *Zeze** – Fluminense of Brazil

* Still playing at the end of 1982.

4 WHOSE RELIGION CAME BEFORE FOOTBALL

1. *Willie Bell* – Former Queens Park, Leeds, Leicester, Brighton and Scotland Full Back whose fervent Christianity and disillusionment with football prompted him to resign as Lincoln City manager in October 1978 and join a religious sect in California. Among his duties were to include the running of a soccer team 'The Campus Crusade for Christ'.

2. *Peter Knowles* – Talented Inside Forward who had won England Under 23 honours while with Wolves, his only professional club, for whom he played almost 200 times. Although he retired from the game in 1970 at the age of 24 to become a Jehovah's Witness, Wolves kept his registration in the vain hope that he might one day return. In 1982 Wolves cancelled his registration.

3. *Basil Stonehouse* – One-time Middlesbrough player, whose becoming a Jehovah's Witness was responsible for his finishing with the Northern League game and football in general, arguing that the kicking of people and feelings of anger engendered on the football field were not suitable for a person with deep religious faith.

4. *Bobby Tambling* – A former Chelsea and England player who was finishing his career with Crystal Palace, when in 1974 he decided to quit the game to enable him to spread the gospel as a Jehovah's Witness. He continued to play sporadically, for Cork Celtic among other clubs.

The Sexy Side of Football

JUST 7 OF GEORGE BEST'S GIRLFRIENDS

1. *Sinead Cusack*   – Actress
2. *Mary Fullaway*   – George's landlady and friend
3. *Eva Haraldsted*   – Danish girl who sued for breach of promise

4. *Angela MacDonald Janes*	– Later to become his wife
5. *Carolyn Moore*	– Ex Beauty Queen
6. *Mary Stavin*	– Ex Swedish Miss World
7. *Marjorie Wallace*	– Ex American Miss World

7 'MODEL' PROFESSIONALS OF INTERNATIONAL STATUS

1. *Derek Dougan* – Fashion model once voted amongst Britain's Best Dressed Men.
2. *Gerry Francis* – Modelling for a newspaper at the time of his England Captaincy.
3. *Glenn Hoddle* – Male model for newspapers.
4. *Kevin Keegan* – Models sports wear and other clothes.
5. *Shep Messing* – Cosmos and Boston Goalkeeper who gave the NASL unique 'exposure' as a nude centrefold in 'Viva' magazine.
6. *John O'Rourke* – Former England under 23 Striker whose slim build and elegance have made him an ideal model for a number of years.
7. *Ray Wilkins* – Fashion model, including work with a national industrial clothing and tool firm.

20 'SEXY' PLAYERS

British	Foreigners
1. *Garth Crooks*	11. *Thomas Allofs* – West Germany
2. *Kevin Dillon*	12. *Manfred Kaltz* – West Germany
3. *Andy Gray*	13. *Kurt Jara* – Austria
4. *Asa Hartford*	14. *Hansi Müller* – West Germany
5. *Russell Osman*	15. *Michel Platini* – France
6. *Nicky Pickering*	16. *Paolo Rossi* – Italy
7. *Bryan Robson*	17. *Werner Roth* – U.S.A.
8. *Gary Shaw*	18. *Marco Tardelli* – Italy
9. *Peter Shilton*	19. *'Zico'* – Brazil
10. *Graeme Souness*	20. *Patricio Yanez* – Chile

'Show Biz'

2 'ALL TIME GREAT' SHOW BIZ ELEVENS. DAVID (DIDDY) HAMILTON'S CHOICE

1. *Jess Conrad*

6. *Des O'Connor*

3. *Tony Selby*

5. *Sean Connery*

2. *Jim Davidson*

8. *Jimmy Tarbuck*

4. *Robert Powell*

10. *Dennis Waterman*

7. *Tommy Steele*

9. *Rod Stewart*

11. *Richard O'Sullivan*

THIS SHOW BIZ ELEVEN WAS SELECTED BY A RADIO ONE D.J. – GUESS WHO?

11. *Flipper*　　10. *Lassie*　　8. *Kermit*　　7. *Miss Piggy*

6. *Sooty*　　　　9. *Orville*　　4. *Roger the Dog*
　　　　　　　　(Captain)

3. *Basil Brush*　　5. *Sweep*　　2. *Andy Pandy*

1. *Champion the Wonder Horse*

Reserves
Bill and Ben
Orville would act as the deep (F)lying Centre Forward.

Suppliers

18 LOWLY CLUBS THAT SET FUTURE INTERNATIONALS ON THEIR WAY TO FAME

England players unless otherwise stated

1. *Barnsley* — Danny Blanchflower* (N.I.), Arthur Kaye, Gordon Pallister (E.F.L. Rep), Tommy Taylor.

2. *Bournemouth* — Dave Jones (Wales), Roger Jones (Eng. U.23), Kevin Reeves.

3. *Bradford City* — Sam Barkas, Derek Hawksworth (Eng. 'B'), Trevor Hockey (Wales); Laurie Scott, Derek Stokes (Eng. U.23).

4. *Bradford Park Avenue* — Billy Elliott, Albert Geldard, Jeff Hall, Kevin Hector, Derek Kevan, Len Shackleton.

5. *Chester* — Ron Davies (Wales), Paul Futcher (Eng. U.23), Ian Rush (Wales).

6. *Chesterfield* — Gordon Banks, Steve Hardwick (Eng. U.21), Kevin McHale (Eng. U.23), Ray Middleton (Eng. 'B'), Alan Stevenson (Eng. U.23).

7. *Crewe* — Frank Blunstone, Bruce Grobbelaar†, John Mahoney (Wales).

8. *Exeter* — Cliff Bastin, Maurice Setters (Eng. U. 23).

9. *Hartlepool* — Jack Howe, John McGovern (Scotland U.23).

---

* Although he had made an impression in Ireland with Glentoran, Barnsley gave Blanchflower his first chance across the water.
† Already a Rhodesian national player, Grobbelaar's first football in England was with Crewe in 1979–80. England have since enquired as to his availability.

10. *Millwall*	– Ken Green, Gordon Hill, Charlie Hurley (Eire), Kevin O'Callaghan (Eire), Alex Stepney.
11. *Port Vale*	– Ronnie Allen, Mark Chamberlain, Bill McGarry.
12. *Plymouth*	– Gordon Astall, Len Boyd, Paul Mariner, Eamon O'Keefe (Eire), Norman Piper (Eng. U.23).
13. *Reading*	– Johnny Brooks, Stan Wicks (Eng. 'B').
14. *Scunthorpe*	– Albert Emptage, Ray Clemence, Kevin Keegan.
15. *Southport*	– Jimmy Meadows, Peter Withe.
16. *Swindon*	– Don Rogers (Eng. U.23), Mike Summerbee, Rod Thomas (Wales), Ernie Hunt (Eng. U.23).
17. *Tranmere*	– Steve Coppell, Bill 'Dixie' Dean, Roy McFarland, John Wheeler.
18. *Walsall*	– Allan Clarke, Johnny Hancocks, Doug Lishman (Eng. 'B'), Phil Parkes, Mark Wallington (Eng. U.23), Bert Williams.

Supporters – Fame in the Boardroom and in the Stands

62 FAMOUS SUPPORTERS.

1. *John Alderton* – Hull City
2. *Arthur Askey* – West Ham
3. *Richard Attenborough* – Chelsea
4. *Hylda Baker* – Bolton Wanderers
5. *Tony Banks* (Current GLC Arts Chairman) – Chelsea
6. *Christopher Blake* – Arsenal
7. *Tim Brooke-Taylor* – Derby County
8. *Ian Carmichael* – Hull City
9. *Keith Castle* – Fulham
10. *Lorraine Chase* – Millwall
11. *Keith Chegwin* – Everton and Liverpool
12. *Eric Clapton* – West Brom
13. *Peter Cook* – Tottenham Hotspur

14. *Tom Courtenay* – Hull City
15. *Steve Cram* – Sunderland
16. *Michael Crawford* – Chelsea
17. *Ken Dodd* (Ex Walsall share holder) – Liverpool
18. *Michael Foot* – Plymouth Argyle
19. *Harry Fowler* – Fulham
20. *David Frost* – Norwich City and Gillingham
21. *Ian Gillan* – Reading
22. *Graham Gooch* – West Ham
23. *Roy Hattersley M.P.* – Sheffield Wednesday
24. *Lenny Henry* – West Brom
25. *James Herriot* – Sunderland
26. *Ronnie Hilton* – Leeds
27. *Chas Hodges* (of Chas and Dave) – Tottenham
28. *David 'Kid' Jensen* – Q.P.R.
29. *Eddie Large* – Manchester City
30. *Andrew Lloyd-Webber* – Orient
31. *Kenny Lynch* – West Ham
32. *E.L.O.'s Jeff Lynne* – Birmingham City
33. *Tony Mercer* – Sheffield United
34. *Warren Mitchell* – West Ham
35. *Eric Morecambe* – Luton Town
36. *Eric Morley* – Arsenal
37. *Arthur Mullard* – Arsenal
38. *Pete Murray* – Arsenal
39. *Natasha* – Tottenham Hotspur
40. *Trevor Nunn* – Ipswich Town
41. *Des O'Connor* – Northampton Town
42. *Michael Palin* – Sheffield Wednesday
43. *Michael Parkinson* – Barnsley
44. *Dave Peacock* (of Chas and Dave) Tottenham
45. *John Peel* – Liverpool
46. *Lance Percival* – Chelsea
47. *Alan Price* – Fulham
48. *James Prior M.P.* – Norwich City
49. *Ted Rogers* – Chelsea
50. *Jack Rollin* – Aldershot
51. *Terry Scott* – Chester
52. *Harry Secombe* – Swansea
53. *Jack Smethurst* – Manchester United
54. *Ed Stewart* – Everton
55. *Eric Sykes* – Oldham Athletic
56. *Jimmy Tarbuck* – Liverpool
57. *Denis Tuohy* – Q.P.R.
58. *Sir Harold Wilson* – Huddersfield
59. *Gordon Williams* – Q.P.R.
60. *Bernie Winters* – Arsenal
61. *Norman Wisdom* – Brighton A.F.C.
62. *Mike Yarwood* – Stockport County

22 CURRENT OR FORMER FAMOUS DIRECTORS

1. *Anthony Buck M.P.* – Colchester (Patron)
2. *Jasper Carrot* – Birmingham (Director)
3. *Bobby Charlton* – Wigan Athletic (Director)
4. *Sebastian Coe* – Fulham (Hon. Vice President)
5. *Colin Cowdrey* – Charlton (Director)
6. *Jim Davidson* – A.F.C. Bournemouth (Director)
7. *Jack Dunnett M.P.* – Notts County (Chairman, Chairman of Football League)
8. *Arthur English* Aldershot (Director)
9. *David Hamilton* – Fulham (Director)
10. *Sir Michael Havers* – Wimbledon (President)
11. *Lord Hesketh* – Northampton (Director)
12. *Elton John* – Watford (Chairman)
13. *Bob Mellish* – Millwall (Vice President)
14. *Viscount Montgomery* – Portsmouth (President)
15. *Brian Moore* – Gillingham (Director)
16. *Sir Desmond Morris* – Oxford United (Vice President)
17. *Don Robinson ('Dr Death' the wrestler)* – Hull City (Chairman)
18. *Sir Jack Scamp* – Coventry (Director)
19. *Peter Sellers* – Wood Green Town in the Spartan League (Hon. Vice President)
20. *Tommy Trinder* – Fulham (Life President)
21. *Mike Watterson (the snooker promoter)* – Derby County (Chairman)
22. *Charlie Williams* – Barnsley (Director)

12 DIRECTORS OF CLUBS THAT THEY FORMERLY MANAGED OR PLAYED FOR

1. *Ted Bates* – Southampton (Director)
2. *Sir Matt Busby* – Manchester United (President and Director until early 1983)
3. *Derek Dougan* – Wolves (former player, Chairman and Chief Exec.)
4. *Ted Drake* – Fulham (Life President)
5. *Tony Ingham* – Q.P.R. (Former Player, Director)
6. *Malcolm MacDonald* – Fulham (Director)

7. *Bertie Mee* – Watford (Director)
8. *Johnnie Steele* – Barnsley (Director)
9. *Alec Stock* – Bournemouth (Director)
10. *Barry Swallow* – York (Former player, Director)
11. *Ernie Tagg* – Crewe (Director)
12. *Terry Venables* – Q.P.R. (Director)

2 LEADING FOOTBALLERS WHO WERE DIRECTORS OF CLUBS FOR WHICH THEY WERE PLAYING

1. *Gianni Rivera* – Brilliant Inside Forward of the 60's and 70's. 'The golden boy of Italian football' who briefly controlled his club A.C. Milan in the mid 70's.
2. *Vivian Woodward* – A subtle and elegant Forward for England and Tottenham before the First World War. Among the greatest of amateur players, he was an architect by profession and served on the Tottenham board in his last season 1908–09.

Tongue Twisters

26 PLAYERS RESULTING IN A COMMENTATORS' NIGHTMARE

Fortunately the following players didn't all grace the Football League at the same time. Had they done so, and played for only two different sides, imagine the difficulties John Motson or Brian Moore would have experienced in commentating on *The Unpronounceables* match.
1. *Eddie Niedzwiecki** – Wrexham
2. *Eryk Kubicki* – York
3. *Manny Andruszewski** – Southampton, Tampa Bay Rowdies and Aldershot
4. *Steve Wojciechowicz* – Blackpool

* Currently playing.

5. *Mike Czuczman* – Six clubs including Grimsby and
    Scunthorpe
 6. *Jan Einer Åas†* – FC Moss, Bayern Munchen, Nottingham
    Forest and Norway
 7. *Pelham von Donop* – Royal Engineers and England
 8. *Ellanah Onyeali* –Tranmere and Newport
 9. *Bela Olah* – Northampton
10. *Emment Kapengwe* – Aston Villa and Zambian
    International
11. *Felix Staroscik* – Northampton

Subs:
12. *Adam Wasilewski* – Rochdale
13. *Fred Mwila* – Aston Villa

versus *The Unspeakables*
 1. *Albert Uytenbogaardt* – Charlton
 2. *Frank Kletzenbaoer* – Coventry and Walsall
 3. *Reginald de Courtney Welch* – Harrow Chequers,
    Wanderers and England
 4. *Peter Olinyk* – Bolton and Stockport
 5. *John Sleeuwenhoek* – Aston Villa, Birmingham, Oldham
    and England under 23.
 6. *Åge Hareide** – Molde F.K. and Manchester City and
    Norway
 7. *Dick Kryzwicki* – W.B.A., Huddersfield, Lincoln and
    Wales
 8. *Ron Oosthuizen* – Charlton and Carlisle
 9. *Leroy De Graaft Rosenior** Fulham
10. *Ralph Oelofse* – Chelsea and Watford
11. *Benny Nieuwenhuys* – Liverpool

Subs:
12. *Danny Le Roux* – Arsenal
13. *Edouard Wojtczak* – York

* Currently playing.
† Retired prematurely through injury in February, 1983.

Two-Timers

THE 3 PEOPLE TO REPRESENT ENGLAND AT BOTH FOOTBALL AND RUGBY

Football	Rugby
1. *Reginald H. Birkett* – Clapham Rovers Utility Player 1879 – 1 Cap	Clapham Rovers (4 Caps – 1871–77)
2. *Charles P. Wilson* – Hendon Casuals and Corinthians Wing Half 1884 – 2 Caps	Cambridge (1 Cap – 1881)
3. *John W. Sutcliffe* – Bolton, Millwall, Manchester United Goalkeeper 1893–1903 – 5 Caps	Heckmondwike R.U. Club (1 Cap – 1889)

THE 14 FOOTBALL AND CRICKET DOUBLE INTERNATIONALS

Football	Cricket
1. *John Arnold* – Southampton, Fulham Outside Left 1933 – 1 Cap	Oxon and Hants (1 Test – 1931)
2. *Andrew Ducat* –Woolwich Arsenal, Aston Villa, Fulham Right Half 1910–26 – 6 Caps	Surrey (1 Test – 1921)
3. *Reginald Foster* – Old Malvernians Corinthians Inside Forward 1900–1902 – 5 Caps	Worcestershire (8 Tests – 1903–07)
4. *C. B. Fry* – Southampton, Portsmouth Right Back 1901 – 1 Cap	Surrey, Sussex, Hants (26 Tests – 1899–1912)
5. *Leslie H. Gay* –Old Brightonians Corinthians Goalkeeper 1893–94 – 3 Caps	Hants, Somerset (1 Test – 1894–95)

6. *William Gunn* – Nottingham Forest, Notts County Forward 1884 – 2 Caps — Notts (9 Tests – 1888–99)

7. *Harold T. W. Hardinge* – Maidstone United, Newcastle, Sheffield United, Arsenal Inside Left 1910 – 1 Cap — Kent (1 Test – 1921)

8. *Hon. Alfred Lyttleton* – Old Etonians, Forward 1876 – 1 Cap — Worcester and Middlesex (4 Tests – 1880–84)

9. *Harry Makepiece*– Everton Left Half 1906 – 4 Caps — Lancashire (4 Tests – 1921)

10. *Arthur Milton* – Arsenal, Bristol City Right Wing 1952 – 1 Cap — Gloucester (6 Tests – 1958–59)

11. *John Sharp* – Hereford Thistle, Aston Villa, Everton Outside Right 1903–05 – 2 Caps — Herefordshire, Lancashire (3 Tests – 1902)

12. *William Watson* – Huddersfield, Sunderland, Halifax Right Half 1950–51 – 4 Caps — Yorkshire (23 Tests – 1953–58)

13. *Denis Compton* – Not a recognized International but represented England during the World War II as a Wing Half — Middlesex (78 Tests – 1937)

14. *Elias 'Patsy' Hendren* – Manchester City, Coventry, Brentford Inside Forward 1920 Victory International player — Middlesex (51 Tests – 1920's)

14 POST-WAR ENGLAND FOOTBALLERS WHO PLAYED COUNTY CRICKET

Senior Honours unless otherwise stated

Name	Clubs	County
1. *Graham Cross*	Leicester, Brighton, Preston, Lincoln and England Under 23	Leicestershire
2. *Les Compton*	Arsenal	Middlesex

3. *Jack Dyson*	Manchester City, Oldham and England Under 23	Lancashire
4. *Mike Hellawell*	Q.P.R., Birmingham, Sunderland, Huddersfield and Peterborough	Warwickshire
5. *Stuart Leary*	Charlton, Q.P.R. and England Under 23	Kent
6. *Eric Houghton*	Aston Villa and Notts County	Warwickshire
7. *Geoff Hurst*	West Ham, Stoke and W.B.A.	Essex
8. *Jackie Lee*	Leicester, Derby and Coventry	Leicestershire
9. *Tony Pawson*	England Amateur International, Pegasus and Charlton	Kent
10. *Don Roper*	Southampton, Arsenal and E.F.L.	Hampshire
11. *Phil Taylor*	Bristol Rovers and Liverpool	Gloucestershire
12. *Ron Tindall*	Chelsea, West Ham, Reading, Portsmouth and E.F.L.	Surrey
13. *Derek Ufton*	Charlton	Kent
14. *Sam Weaver*	Hull, Newcastle, Chelsea and Stockport	Somerset

7 POST-WAR ENGLAND CRICKETERS WHO PLAYED LEAGUE FOOTBALL

Name	County	Clubs
1. *Chris Balderstone*	Yorkshire and Leicestershire	Huddersfield, Carlisle and Doncaster
2. *David Bairstow*	Yorkshire	Bradford City
3. *Ian Botham*	Somerset	Scunthorpe
4. *Brian Close*	Yorkshire and Somerset	Leeds, Arsenal and Bradford City
5. *John Flavell*	Worcestershire	W.B.A. and Walsall

6. *Cyril Poole*   Nottinghamshire   Mansfield and Gillingham
7. *Alan Watkins* Glamorgan   Cardiff and Plymouth

What's in a Name?

THE 92 FOOTBALL LEAGUE CLUB NICKNAMES

Aldershot — 'The Shots'

Arsenal — 'The Gunners' formerly 'Royals' then 'Reds'

Aston Villa — 'The Villans'

Barnsley — 'The Colliers' or 'The Tykes'

Birmingham City — 'The Blues'. Formerly 'The Heathens' (when known as Small Heath)

Blackburn Rovers — 'The Blue and Whites'

Blackpool — 'The Seasiders' or 'The Tangerines'

Bolton Wanderers — 'The Trotters'

A.F.C. Bournemouth — 'The Cherries'

Bradford City — 'The Bantams' or 'The Paraders'

Brentford — 'The Bees'

Brighton and Hove Albion — 'The Seagulls'

Bristol City — 'The Robins'

Bristol Rovers — 'The Pirates'

Burnley — 'The Turfites' or more commonly 'The Clarets'

Bury — 'The Shakers'

Cambridge United — 'United'

Cardiff City — 'The Bluebirds'

Carlisle United — 'The Cumbrians'

Charlton Athletic — 'The Haddicks' (now slightly outdated), 'The Valiants' or 'The Robins'

Chelsea	– 'The Blues' formerly 'The Pensioners'
Chester	– 'The Seals'
Chesterfield	– 'The Spireites' or 'The Blues'
Colchester United	– 'The U's'
Coventry City	– 'The Sky Blues'
Crewe Alexandra	– 'The Railwaymen'
Crystal Palace	– 'The Eagles' formerly 'The Glaziers'
Darlington	– 'The Quakers'
Derby County	– 'The Rams'
Doncaster Rovers	– 'The Rovers'
Everton	– 'Toffeemen' or 'Toffees', sometimes 'The Blues'
Exeter City	– 'The Grecians'
Fulham	– 'The Cottagers'
Gillingham	– 'The Gills'
Grimsby Town	– 'The Mariners'
Halifax Town	– 'The Shaymen' or 'Town'
Hartlepool United	– 'The Pool'
Hereford United	– 'United'
Huddersfield Town	– 'The Terriers'
Hull City	– 'The Tigers'
Ipswich Town	– 'The Blues' or 'Town'
Leeds United	– 'The Peacocks'
Leicester City	– 'The Filberts' or 'The Foxes'
Lincoln City	– 'The Red Imps' or 'The Imps'
Liverpool	– 'The Reds' or 'Pool', once 'The Anfielders'
Luton Town	– 'The Hatters'
Manchester City	– 'The Citizens'
Manchester United	– 'The Red Devils' or 'The Reds'
Mansfield Town	– 'The Stags'
Middlesbrough	– 'The Boro', once 'The Ironsides' (Malcolm Allison favours a nickname of 'Cleveland Cowboys')
Millwall	– 'The Lions'
Newcastle United	– 'The Magpies'
Newport County	– 'The Ironsides'
Northampton Town	– 'The Cobblers'
Norwich City	– 'The Canaries'

Nottingham Forest	– 'The Foresters' or 'The Reds'
Notts County	– 'The Magpies' began as 'The Lambs'
Oldham Athletic	– 'The Latics'
Orient	– 'The O's'
Oxford United	– 'The U's'
Peterborough United	– 'The Posh'
Plymouth Argyle	– 'The Pilgrims'
Portsmouth	– 'Pompey'
Port Vale	– 'The Valiants'
Preston North End	– 'The Lilywhites' or 'North End'
Queens Park Rangers	– 'The R's' or 'Rangers' also 'The Superhoops'
Reading	– 'The Royals' also 'The Biscuitmen'
Rochdale	– 'The Dale'
Rotherham United	– 'The Merry Millers', or 'The Millers'
Scunthorpe United	– 'The Irons'
Sheffield United	– 'The Blades'
Sheffield Wednesday	– 'The Owls'
Shrewsbury Town	– 'The Town'
Southampton	– 'The Saints'
Southend United	– 'The Shrimpers'
Stockport County	– 'County' or 'The Hatters'
Stoke City	– 'The Potters'
Sunderland	– 'The Rokerites'
Swansea City	– 'The Swans'
Swindon Town	– 'The Robins', or among old supporters 'The Railway Men'
Torquay United	– 'The Gulls'
Tottenham Hotspur	– 'The Spurs'
Tranmere Rovers	– 'The Rovers'
Walsall	– 'The Saddlers'
Watford	– 'The Hornets'
West Bromwich Albion	– 'The Baggies', 'The Throstles' or 'Albion'
West Ham United	– 'The Hammers'
Wigan Athletic	– 'The Latics'
Wimbledon	– 'The Dons'
Wolverhampton Wanderers	– 'The Wolves'

Wrexham	– 'The Robins'
York City	– 'The Minster Men' or 'The Minster'

36 SCOTTISH LEAGUE CLUBS WITH THEIR NICKNAMES

Aberdeen	– 'The Dons'
Airdrieonians	– 'The Diamonds' occasionally 'The Waysiders'
Albion Rovers	– 'The Wee Rovers'
Alloa Athletic	– 'The Wasps'
Arbroath	– 'The Red Lichties' or 'The Lichties'
Ayr United	– 'The Honest Men'
Berwick Rangers	– 'The Borderers' or 'The Black and Gold'
Brechin City	– 'City'
Celtic	– 'The Bhoys'
Clyde	– 'The Bully Wee'
Clydebank	– 'The Bankies'
Cowdenbeath	– 'Cowden'
Dumbarton	– 'The Sons'
Dundee	– 'The Dee' or 'Dark Blues'
Dundee United	– 'The Terrors'
Dunfermline Athletic	– 'The Pars'
East Fife	– 'The Fifers'
East Stirling	– 'The Shire'
Falkirk	– 'The Bairns'
Forfar Athletic	– 'The Loons' or 'The Sky Blues'
Hamilton Academical	– 'The Accies'
Heart of Midlothian	– 'The Jam Tarts'
Hibernian	– 'The Hi-Bees'
Kilmarnock	– 'The Killies'
Meadowbank Thistle	– 'Thistle'
Montrose	– 'The Gable Endies'
Morton	– 'Ton'
Motherwell	– 'Well'
Partick Thistle	– 'The Jags'
Queen of the South	– 'The Doonhammers'
Queens Park	– 'The Spiders' or 'The Queens'
Raith Rovers	– 'Rovers'

Rangers	– 'The Blues' or 'Gers'
St. Johnstone	– 'The Saints'
St. Mirren	– 'The Buddies'
Stenhousemuir	– 'The Warriors'

50 LEADING NON-LEAGUE CLUB NICKNAMES

1.	Alvechurch	– 'The Church
2.	A. P. Leamington	– 'The Brakes'
3.	Ashford Town	– 'Nuts and Bolts'
4.	Aylesbury United	– 'The Ducks'
5.	Bedworth United	– 'Greenbacks'
6.	Belper Town	– 'The Nailers'
7.	Bognor Regis Town	– 'The Rocks'
8.	Boston	– 'Poachers'
9.	Bourne Town	– 'The Wakes'
10.	Bridlington Trinity	– 'Emerald Greens'
11.	Brigg Town	– 'The Zebras'
12.	Burton Albion	– 'The Brewers'
13.	Buxton	– 'The Bucks'
14.	Dagenham	– 'The Daggers'
15.	Darwen	– 'The Anchormen'
16.	Dorking	– 'The Chicks'
17.	Eastwood Town	– 'Badgers'
18.	Feltham	– 'Flyers'
19.	Fleetwood Town	– 'The Fishermen'
20.	Formby	– 'The Squirrels'
21.	Grantham	– 'The Gingerbreads'
22.	Gresley Rovers	– 'Moatmen'
23.	Halesowen Town	– 'Yeltz'
24.	Hayes	– The Missioners'
25.	Hednesford Town	– The Pitmen'
26.	Hornchurch	– 'Urchins'
27.	Kempston Rovers	– 'Walnut Boys'
28.	Kettering Town	– 'The Poppies'
29.	Lancaster City	– 'The Dollies'
30.	Leatherhead	– 'The Tanners'
31.	Lewes	– 'The Rooks'
32.	Macclesfield Town	– 'The Silkmen'
33.	Maidstone United	– 'The Stones'
34.	Matlock Town	– 'The Gladiators'

35. *Merthyr Tydfil*	– 'The Martyrs'
36. *Nantwich Town*	– 'The Dabbers'
37. *Northwich Victoria*	– 'The Vics'
38. *Poole Town*	– 'The Dolphins'
39. *Rhyl*	– 'The Beavers'
40. *Rothwell Town*	– 'The Bones'
41. *Rushden Town*	– 'Russians'
42. *Slough Town*	– 'The Rebels'
43. *Spalding United*	– 'The Tulips'
44. *Stourbridge*	– 'The Glassboys'
45. *Tonbridge*	– 'The Angels'
46. *Wellingborough Town*	– 'The Doughboys'
47. *Weymouth*	– 'The Terras'
48. *Wisbech Town*	– 'Fenmen'
49. *Woking*	– 'The Cardinals'
50. *Yeovil Town*	– 'The Glovers'

35 FORMER NAMES OF CURRENT LEAGUE CLUBS

There have been various attempts over the years to change the names of football clubs, some of which have been unsuccessful, for instance Herbert Chapman's wish to call Arsenal, London F.C. Below are some of the successful attempts.

Old Name	Current Name
1. *Abbey United* (1919–1949)	*Cambridge United*
2. *Ardwick F.C.* (1887–1895)	*Manchester City*
3. *Argyle Athletic Club* (1886–1903)	*Plymouth Argyle*
4. *Barnsley St. Peter's* (1887–1898)	*Barnsley*
5. *Blackburn Grammar School Old Boys*	*Blackburn Rovers*
6. *Black Arabs* (1883–1884)	*Bristol Rovers*
7. *Boscombe St. John's* (1890–1899)	*A.F.C. Bournemouth*
8. *Boscombe F.C.* (1899–1923)	*A.F.C. Bournemouth*

9.	*Bournemouth and Boscombe Athletic F.C.* (1923–1971)	A.F.C. Bournemouth
10.	*Bristol South End* (1894–1897)	*Bristol City*
11.	*Burslam Port Vale* (1911–1913)	*Port Vale*
12.	*Christchurch F.C.* (1874–1877)	*Bolton Wanderers*
13.	*Eastville Rovers* (1884–1897)	The second name of *Bristol Rovers;* the name they adopted in 1898
14.	*Fulham St. Andrews* (1879–1898)	*Fulham*
15.	*Headington United* (1896–1960)	*Oxford United*
16.	*Heaton Norris Rovers* (1883–1888) and then *Heaton Norris* (1888–1890)	*Stockport County*
17.	*Leeds City* (1904–1919)	After *City* were ejected from the F.A. *Leeds United* emerged from their ashes
18.	*Leicester Fosse* (1884–1919)	*Leicester City*
19.	*Lindsey United*	Amalgamated with *Scunthorpe* in 1910 to become *Scunthorpe United*
20.	*Millwall Rovers* (1885–1889)	*Millwall*
21.	*New Brompton* (1893–1913)	*Gillingham*
22.	*Newton Heath* (1880–1902)	*Manchester United*
23.	*Peterborough and Fletton United* (1923–1934)	*Peterborough United*
24.	*Pine Villa* (1894–1899)	*Oldham Athletic*
25.	*Riverside* (1899–1910)	*Cardiff City*

26. *Singers*   *Coventry City*
    (1883–1898)
27. *Small Heath Alliance*   *Birmingham City*
    (1875–1888) and then
    Small Heath
    (1888–1905)
28. *Southampton St. Mary's*   Became *Southampton* in 1895;
29. *South Shore*   amalgamated with *Blackpool*
                         (then 12 years old) in 1899
30. *St. Jude's*   *Queens Park Rangers*
    (1885–1887)
31. *St. Luke's Blakenhall*   Combined with the *Wanderers*
                         to become *Wolverhampton*
                         Wanderers in 1880
32. *Sunderland and District*   *Sunderland*
    Teachers' A.F.C.
    (1879–1881)
33. *Thornhill United*   Became *Rotherham County*,
    (1884–1905)   before joining with
                         Rotherham Town to become
                         Rotherham United in 1925
34. *Walsall Town Swifts*   Formed from the coupling of
    (1888–1895)   *Walsall Swifts* and *Walsall*
                         Town, *W.T.S.* was shortened
                         to *Walsall* in 1895
35. *Wimbledon Old Centrals*   *Wimbledon*
    (1899–1905)

5 FORMER NAMES OF ORIENT

1. *Glyn Cricket and Football Club* (1881–1886)
2. *Eagle Football Club* (1886–1888)
3. *Orient Football Club* (1888–1898)
4. *Clapton Orient* (1898–1946)
5. *Leyton Orient* (1946–1966)

CLASSIFICATION OF PLAYERS' NAMES

The information following the name is the club with which the player experienced most success. Where there have been several players with the same name the most famous or in some cases current players have been selected.

4 Directions
1. EAST Keith – Bournemouth 1967–69
2. NORTH Stacey – Luton
3. SOUTH Alex – Halifax 1956–64
4. WEST Gordon – Everton and England 1961–72

5 Fishy Names
1. CODD Ronnie – Bolton 1950–53
2. HADDOCK Andy – Chester 1967–68
3. ROACH Bobby – Liverpool mid 1960's
4. ROE Len – Brentford 1955–56
5. SPRATT Tommy – Bradford Park Avenue 1960–63

4 Sport Types
1. BADMINTON Roger – Brighton 1966–67
2. BALL Alan* – Everton 1966–71 and England
3. CRICKETT Norman – Carlisle 1955–56
4. HOCKEY Trevor – Birmingham 1965–70 and Wales

6 Measurements
1. ACRES Basil – Ipswich 1951–59
2. FOOTE Chris – Cambridge United 1970–73

3. FURLONG Stephen – Everton (S) 1981–
4. INCH Trevor – Portsmouth 1982–
5. MILES Terry – Port Vale 1956–67
6. YARD Ernie – Reading 1966–69

5 Players with a Wealth of Talent
1. MONEY Richard – Luton 1982–
2. PENNY Shaun – Bristol Rovers 1979–81
3. POUND Ken – Bournemouth 1966–68
4. PRICE David – Arsenal 1972–80
5. TANNER Graham – Bradford Park Avenue 1967–68

12 Who Came in All Shapes and Sizes
1. BROAD Ron – Crewe 1955–56
2. BROADFOOT Joe – Millwall 1958–63
3. LARGE Frank – (Q.V.) Northampton 1969–72
4. LEAN David – Plymouth 1969–70
5. LITTLE Roy – Manchester City 1952–58
6. LOFTY Jim – Reading 1963–64

7. LONG Terry – Crystal Palace 1955–69
8. LOW Roy – Watford 1966–68
9. SHORT John – Wolves 1948–53
10. SMALL Peter – Nottingham Forest 1954–57
11. SMALLMAN David – Wrexham 1971–74 and Wales
12. TRIM Reg – Nottingham Forest Pre-War

Dave Short, a 5'2" Wing Forward and Ray Long, a 6'3" Centre Half played together in Lincoln Reserves in the 1958–59 Season.

10 Footballing Aristocrats

1. BARON Kevin – Liverpool 1947–53
2. DUKE George – Luton 1946–48
3. EARL Stan – Leyton Orient 1953–55
4. KING Ian – Leicester City 1957–65
5. KNIGHT Alan – Portsmouth 1977–
6. LORD Frank – Plymouth 1963–65
7. NOBLE Peter – Burnley 1973–79
8. PRINCE Frank – Bristol Rovers 1967–80
9. QUEEN Gerry – Orient 1972–76
10. ROYAL Eric – Huddersfield mid 1960's.

8 Players' Attributes

1. FORWARD Fred – Portsmouth
2. GOODGAME Tony – Orient 1966–67
3. POWER Paul – Manchester City 1975–
4. SCORER Ivor – Bristol Rovers pre-war
5. SHOOTER Frank – Norwich
6. STRONG Les – Fulham 1972–
7. THROWER Dennis – Ipswich 1955–63
8. TOUGH Peter – Norwich

11 Weather Prospects

Listed as a team

1. LIGHTENING Arthur – Coventry 1958–62
2. FOGG David – Oxford 1976–
3. FLOOD Eddie – Tranmere 1972–81
4. BRIGHT Stewart – Colchester 1975–76
5. BLIZZARD Les – Leyton Orient 1950–56
6. GALE Tony – Fulham 1977–
7. TEMPEST Dale – Fulham 1980–
8. HALE Ken – Coventry 1962–66
9. SNOW Simon – Scunthorpe 1981–83
10. RAINE David – Port Vale 1956–61
11. FROST Des – Halifax 1950–53

11 'Spirited' Players

1. ABBOTT Gregory – Bradford City 1982–
2. BISHOP Sid – Leyton Orient 1953–64
3. CHURCH John – Norwich 1946–49
4. MONK Fred – Brentford 1947–53
5. NUNN Walter – Swindon 1947–48
6. PARSONS Eric – West Ham 1946–50 and England 'B'.
7. POPE Terry – Newport 1950–54
8. PRIEST Philip – Chelsea 1983–
9. PRIOR George – Millwall 1954–56
10. TEMPLE Derek – Everton 1956–67 and England
11. USHER Brian – Sunderland 1961–65 and England Under 23

5 Endearing Names

1. DARLING Malcolm – Blackburn 1964–69
2. DEAR Brian – West Ham 1960–69
3. DEVINE John – Arsenal 1976 and Eire
4. LOVE John – Nottingham Forest 1948–55
5. PRECIOUS Derek – Crewe 1955–56

19 High Fliers

Listed as a team with a flight of reserves

1. SWIFT Frank – Manchester City early 1930's to 1949 and England
2. PARTRIDGE Malcolm – Grimsby 1974–79
3. SPARROW John – Chelsea 1973–79
4. CROWE Chris – Wolves 1961–63 and England
5. SWAN Peter – Sheffield Wednesday 1953–65 and England
6. ROOKS Dickie – Middlesbrough 1965–69
7. BIRD John – Newport 1966–71
8. PEACOCK Alan – Middlesbrough 1954–64 and England
9. DRAKE Ted – Arsenal 1930's
10. HERON Brian – Oxford United 1974–77
11. FINCH Roy – Lincoln City 1948–58

Reserves

12. DOVE Henry – Millwall 1958–59
13. DUCK George – Southend 1971–73
14. EAGLES Alan – Orient 1957–60
15. GREYGOOSE Dean – Cambridge United 1981–
16. 'PARROTT' John – Scunthorpe 1955–56
17. STARLING Alan – Northampton 1971–77
18. SWALLOW Barry –

York City 1969–75

19. WREN John –
Rotherham 1960–61

Naturally, the referee for a
game involving this imaginary
team would be former
whistler, Pat Partridge.

11 Four-Legged Runners

1. BADGER Len –
Sheffield United 1962–75
and England under 23
2. BUCK Tony – Rochdale
1968–72
3. BULL Mike – Swindon
1953–55
4. BULLOCK Mike –
Orient 1968–76
5. FOX Peter – Stoke 1978–
6. HARE Tom – Luton
1967–68
7. HOGG Derek – Leicester
1952–58 and E.F.L.
8. KIDD Brian –
Manchester United
1966–74 and England
9. LAMB Alan – Preston
1970–77 and Scottish
under 23
10. MOLE Len –
Middlesbrough mid
1960's.
11. POINTER Ray – Burnley
1957–65 and England

16 Tasty Players

1. BACON Ron –
Gillingham 1958–61
2. BEAN Alf – Lincoln City
1940's
3. CHERRY Trevor –
Leeds 1972–83 and
England
4. CURRY Billy – Derby
1960–65 and England
under 23
5. FUDGE Mickey – Exeter
1967–68
6. GAMMON Steve –
Cardiff City 1958–6 and
Wales under 23
7. GRAPES Steve – Cardiff
City
8. HAM Bobby – Bradford
City 1964–67 and 1973–75
9. JELLY Horace –
Leicester City 1946–51
10. LEEK Ken – Birmingham
1961–64 and Wales
11. LEMON Paul –
Sunderland 1982–
(Apprentice)
12. OLIVE Les – Manchester
United 1952–53
13. PEACH David –
Southampton 1973–80
and England under 21
14. PEARS Jeff – York City
1947–48
15. RICE Pat – Arsenal
1966–80 and Northern
Ireland
16. VENISON Barry –
Sunderland 1981– and
England under 21

67 Forenames as Surnames

1. ALLAN Jim – Swindon
1971–
2. AMBROSE Leroy –
Charlton 1979–82
3. ANGUS John – Burnley
1955–71 and England

4. ARCHIBALD Steve – Tottenham 1980– and Scotland
5. ARTHUR Jackie – Rochdale 1946–53
6. AUSTIN Terry – Doncaster 1982–
7. BARRY Roy – Coventry City 1969–73
8. BILL Roger – Reading 1962–63
9. BRYAN Peter – Oldham Athletic 1965–66
10. CHARLES John – Leeds United 1948–56 and Wales
11. CHRISTOPHER Paul – Mansfield 1973–74
12. CLIFF Phil – Chesterfield 1970–72
13. DANIEL Ray – Sunderland 1953–57 and Wales
14. DICK John – West Ham 1953–62 and Scotland
15. DONALD Alex – Port Vale 1965–67
16. EUSTACE Peter – Sheffield Wednesday 1962–70
17. FELIX Gary – Chester 1979–80
18. FRANCIS Gerry – Queens Park Rangers 1969–79 and England
19. GABRIEL Jimmy – Everton 1955–67 and Scotland
20. GEORGE Charlie – Arsenal 1968–75 and England
21. GILBERT Billy – Crystal Palace 1976– and England under 21
22. GILES Johnny – Leeds United 1963–75 and Eire
23. GODFREY Brian – Aston Villa 1967–71 and Wales
24. GORDON Johnny – Portsmouth 1949–58 and 1961–66
25. GRAHAM George – Arsenal 1966–72 and Scotland
26. GUY Ivor – Bristol City 1946–56
27. HECTOR Kevin – Derby County 1966–77 and England
28. HENRY Ron – Tottenham 1952–65 and England
29. HERBERT Bobby – Doncaster 1950–55
30. HOWARD Pat – Newcastle United 1971–76
31. ISAAC Jim – Huddersfield Pre-War
32. JACK David – Arsenal 1928–34 and England
33. JAMES Alex – Arsenal 1929–38 and Scotland
34. JEFFREY Alick – Doncaster 1954–68 and England under 23
35. JOHN Bob – Arsenal 1930's and Wales
36. JOSEPH Leon – Tottenham 1946–47
37. JOY Bernard – Arsenal 1946–47
38. JOYCE Joe – Barnsley 1979–

39. KAY Tony – Sheffield Wednesday 1954–62 and England
40. KEITH Bobby – Newcastle 1956–74 and Northern Ireland
41. KIRK Roy – Coventry 1951–59
42. LAWRENCE Tommy – Liverpool 1957–71 and Scotland
43. LEONARD Keith – Aston Villa 1972–75
44. LESLIE Lawrie – Stoke 1963–66 and Scotland
45. LUKE George – Newcastle 1959–61
46. MARTIN Alvin – West Ham 1976–and England
47. NEAL Phil – Liverpool 1974– and England
48. NEIL Billy – Millwall 1964–71
49. NICHOL George – Aldershot 1951–52
50. NICHOLAS Peter – Crystal Palace 1976–81 and Wales
51. NORMAN Maurice – Tottenham 1955–65 and England
52. NORRIS George – Aldershot 1958–63
53. OLIVER Ken – Derby County 1949–57
54. OWEN Gary – West Bromwich Albion 1979– and England under 21
55. PAUL Roy – Manchester City 1950–56 and Wales
56. PHILIP Ian – Crystal Palace 1972–73
57. RAY John – Shrewsbury 1965–66
58. ROY Andy – Exeter 1949–50
59. RUSSELL Billy – Sheffield United 1957–63
60. SAMUEL Bobby – Lincoln 1967–68
61. SAUL Frank – Tottenham 1960–67
62. STEPHEN Jimmy – Portsmouth 1949–53 and Scotland
63. STEWART Ray – West Ham 1979– and Scotland
64. STUART Eddie – Wolves 1951–62
65. THOMAS Mickey – Manchester United 1978–82 and Wales
66. TOM Steve – Brentford 1971–73
67. VINCENT Johnny – Birmingham 1964–71

10 Countries or Mother Tongues

1. BRAZIL Alan – Ipswich 1977– and Scotland
2. ENGLAND Mike – Tottenham 1966–75 and Wales
3. ENGLISH Jack – Northampton 1946–59
4. FRANCE Tony – Darlington 1961–63
5. FRENCH Graham – Luton 1965–73
6. HOLLAND Pat – West Ham 1968–
7. IRELAND Geoff –

Shrewsbury 1959–61

8. POLAND George –
Livepool Pre-War and
Wales
9. SCOTT Laurie – Arsenal
1937–51 and England
10. WELSH Don – Charlton
1935–47 and England

26 Cities, Towns and Villages

1. BARNES Wally –
Arsenal 1946–55 and
Wales
2. BOLTON Ron –
Bournemouth 1958–65
3. BRADFORD Geoff –
Bristol Rovers 1949–63
and England
4. DUBLIN Keith – Chelsea
1982– Apprentice
5. DURHAM Dennis – Hull
City 1946–58
6. EASTWOOD Eric – Port
Vale 1946–48
7. HAMILTON Bryan –
Ipswich 1971–75 and
Northern Ireland
8. HULL Jeff – Colchester
1983–
9. LANCASTER RAY —
Rotherham 1958–64
10. NORTON Ralph –
Reading 1959–66
11. OXFORD Ken – Derby
County 1957–64
12. PAISLEY Bob –
Liverpool 1939–53
13. RICHMOND John –
Derby County 1956–62
14. SCARBOROUGH Jim –
Darlington 1951–53

15. SELBY Dennis – Chester
1946–47
16. SELKIRK Jack –
Rotherham 1944–56
17. SHEFFIELD Laurie –
Newport County 1961–65
18. SHREWSBURY Phil –
Notts County 1965–67
19. STAFFORD Andy –
Halifax 1978–81
20. STEPNEY Alex –
Manchester United
1966–78
21. STOCKTON Graham –
Ipswich 1981–82 –
Schoolboy
22. STRATFORD Paul –
Northampton 1972–78
23. SUNDERLAND Alan –
Arsenal 1977– and
England
24. WEARMOUTH Mike –
Preston 1964–67
25. WHITBY Brian – Luton
1957–58
26. YORK Alan – Bradford
City 1964–67

10 Horror Strikers

1. BLOOD John – Notts
County Pre-War
2. BODDY Charles –
Bradford City First World
War Player
3. COFFIN Geoff – Chester
1947–54
4. DEATH Steve – Reading
1968–82
5. FEAR Keith – Bristol
City 1969–78
6. GHOST – Crystal Palace
Pre-War

7. GORE Tommy – Bury 1980–
8. GRAVES Bobby – Lincoln 1959–65
9. SAVAGE Bobby – Wrexham (on loan from Liverpool) 1982–
10. SKULL John – Swindon 1957–59

18 Countryside Features

1. BANKS Gordon – Leicester 1959–67 and England
2. BROOK Harold – Sheffield United 1946–53
3. CLIFF Eddie – Burnley 1968–73
4. DALE Gordon – Portsmouth 1951–57
5. FELL Jimmy – Grimsby 1954–61
6. FIELD Tony – Sheffield United 1973–75
7. FORD Trevor – Sunderland 1950–53 and Wales
8. FORREST Gerry – Rotherham 1977–
9. HEATH Adrian – Everton 1980– and England under 21
10. HILL Freddie – Bolton 1957–69 and England under 23
11. LEA Cyril – Orient 1957–64 and Wales
12. MARSH Rodney – Queens Park Rangers 1965–72 and England
13. MEADOWS Jimmy – Manchester City 1950–54

and England
14. MOOR Tony – Darlington 1965–72
15. MOUNTAIN Bob – Huddersfield 1973–75
16. RIVERS Alan – Luton 1964–67
17. SPRING Andy – Coventry 1982– Apprentice
18. WOOD Ray – Manchester United 1949–58 and England

12 Who Talked to the Trees

1. ALLDER Doug – Millwall 1969–75
2. ALMOND Bobby – Tottenham 1967–69 and New Zealand
3. ASH Micky – Scunthorpe 1965–67
4. ASPIN Neil – Leeds United 1980–
5. BEECH Ken – Walsall 1980–
6. BIRCH Brian – Manchester United 1949–52
7. CORK Alan – Wimbledon 1977–
8. ELDER Alex – Burnley 1959–67 and Northern Ireland
9. ELMS Jimmy – Crewe 1960–61
10. HAZELL Tony – Queens Park Rangers 1964–74
11. LAUREL John – Ipswich 1959–62
12. ROWAN Barry – Millwall 1964–68

17 Grow in an English
Country Garden

1. BERRY Johnny – Manchester United 1951–58 and England
2. BUSH Terry – Bristol City 1960–70
3. FERN Rodney – Leicester 1966–72
4. FLOWERS Ron – Wolves 1951–67 and England
5. LEAF Andy – York 1979–80
6. MOSS Frank – Arsenal 1931–6
7. PARSLEY Norman – Darlington 1946–52 and England
8. PLANT Ken – Colchester 1953–59
9. POPPY Arthur – Northampton 1977–78
10. REED Billy – Ipswich 1953–58 and Wales
11. ROSE Mick – Notts County 1966–70
12. SAGE Mel – Gillingham 1981–
13. SEED Jimmy – Tottenham 1920–7 and England
14. SHRUBB Paul – Brentford 1976–82
15. STOCK Harry – Oldham 1948–50
16. TULIP Billy – Darlington 1956–58
17. VIOLLET Dennis – Manchester United 1950–61 and England

38 Piece Job Lot

1. BAKER Joe – Arsenal 1962–66 and England
2. BARBER Mike – Queens Park Rangers 1959–63
3. BUTLER Ian – Hull 1964–73
4. CARPENTER Tom – Watford 1951
5. CARTER Raich – Sunderland 1931–45 and England
6. CARTWRIGHT Ian – Wolves 1982–
7. CHANDLER Jeff– Bolton 1981–
8. COLLIER Gary – Bristol City 1972–78
9. COOK Maurice – Fulham 1958–65
10. COOPER Terry – Leeds 1962–75 and England
11. DRAPER Derek – Chester 1968–77 and Wales under 23
12. DRIVER Allenby – Ipswich 1949–52
13. DYER Paul – Colchester 1975–80
14. FALCONER Andy – Blackpool 1949–50
15. FARMER Ron – Coventry 1958–67
16. FLETCHER Paul – Burnley 1970–80
17. GLAZIER Bill – Coventry 1964–75 and England under 23
18. GOLDSMITH Martin – Cambridge United 1980–

19. GUARD Tony – Swansea City 1981–
20. HATTER Steve – Fulham 1976–83
21. HAWKER Phil – Birmingham 1980–
22. MASON Dick – Coventry 1946–54
23. MILLER PAUL — Tottenham 1977–
24. PACKER Mick – Colchester 1973–
25. PAINTER Ian – Stoke City 1982–
26. PIPER Norman – Portsmouth 1970–78
27. POTTER Ray – West Bromwich Albion 1958–67
28. PORTER Andy – Watford 1959–62
29. SADLER David – Manchester United 1963–73 and England
30. SHEARER David – Middlesbrough 1977–
31. SHEPHERD Ernie – Queens Park Rangers 1950–56
32. SHIPWRIGHT Bill – Watford 1952–59
33. SLATER Bill – Wolves 1952–63 and England
34. STEWARD Alf – Manchester United pre-war
35. TANNER John – Huddersfield 1948–49
36. TAYLOR Tommy – Manchester United 1952–58 and England
37. TILER Brian – Rotherham 1962–68
38. WEAVER Sam – Newcastle 1929–36 and England

22 Players 'Of' Quality. Listed as a team

1. Jan VAN BEVEREN – PSV Eindhoven and Holland
2. Georges VAN STRAELEN – Brest and France under 23
3. Adrie VAN KRAAJ – PSV Eindhoven and Holland
4. Rene VANDEREYCKEN – FC Bruges and Belgium
5. Gilbert VAN BINST – FC Bruges and Belgium
6. Theo VAN DUIVENBODE – Feyenoord and Holland
7. Paul VAN HIMST – Anderlecht and Belgium
8. Wilfried VAN MOER – Standard Liège and Belgium
9. Erwin VANDENBERGH – Anderlecht and Belgium
10. Gerald VANENBURG – Ajax Amsterdam and Holland
11. Wim VAN HANAGEM – Feyenoord and Belgium

Reserves

12. Hans VAN BREUKELEN – FC Utrecht and Holland
13. Pim VAN DORD – Ajax Amsterdam
14. Richard VAN DER MEER – AZ 67 Alkmaar and Holland
15. Willie VAN DER KERKHOF – Feyenoord and Holland

16. Kees VAN IERSSEL – Twente Enschede and Holland
17. Guy VANDERSMISSEN – Standard Liège and Belgium
18. Dick VAN DIJK – Ajax Amsterdam and Holland
19. Rene VAN DER GIJP – Lokeren and Holland
20. Francois VAN DER ELST – Anderlecht and Belgium
21. Kees VAN KOOTEN – Go Ahead Eagles and Holland
22. Willy VAN DER KUYLEN – PSV Eindhoven and Holland.

52 BRITISH FOOTBALL PLAYERS' NICKNAMES

1. *R. Aitken*	'Daddler'	Dumbarton and Scotland
2. *Alan Ball*	'Mr Perpetual Motion'	Everton and England
3. *Cliff Bastin*	'Boy Bastin'*	Arsenal and England
4. *Jim Baxter*	'Slim Jim'	Rangers and Scotland
5. *Colin Bell*	'Nijinsky'	Manchester City and England
6. *Peter Bonetti*	'Katsy' or 'The Cat'	Chelsea and England
7. *Liam Brady*	'Chippy'	Arsenal and Eire
8. *Trevor Brooking*	'Hadleigh'	West Ham and England
9. *Tony Brown*	'Bomber'	West Brom and England
10. *Johnny Byrne*	'Budgie'	West Ham and England
11. *J. Campbell*	'Bummer'	Kilmarnock and Scotland
12. *John Charles*	'The Gentle Giant'	Leeds, Juventus and Wales
13. *Jackie Charlton*	'Giraffe'	Leeds United and England
14. *Allan Clarke*	'Sniffer'	Leeds United and England
15. *George Cohen*	'Moisher'	Fulham and England

* He was called this for a time after his move from Exeter to Arsenal as an 18 year old.

16.	Terry Cooper	'Top Cat'	Leeds United and England
17.	Stan Cullis	'Flipper'	Wolves and England
18.	William Dean	'Dixie'	Everton and England
19.	Tom Finney	'Preston Plumber'	Preston and England
20.	Tom Forsyth	'Jaws'	Rangers and Scotland
21.	Billy Foulke	'Fatty'	Sheffield United
22.	Gordon Fraser	'Puskas'	Meadowbank Thistle
23.	Tommy Gemmell	'Big Tam'	Celtic and Scotland
24.	Ron Harris	'Chopper'	Chelsea
25.	Jimmy Hill	'Rabbi'	Brentford and Fulham
26.	Ray Hiron	'Charlie'	Portsmouth
27.	Emlyn Hughes	'Crazy Horse'	Liverpool and England
28.	Peter Lorimer	'Lash'	Leeds United and Scotland
29.	Paul Madeley	'Revie's "Rolls Royce of Football" '	Leeds United and England
30.	Stan Matthews	'The Wizard of Dribble'	Blackpool and England
31.	M. B. McKennan	'Ma Ba'	Pre-war Scottish Player
32.	Bob McPhail	'Greeting'	Airdrie and Scotland
33.	Jackie Milburn	'Wor Jackie'	Newcastle and England
34.	Alan Morton	'The Wee Blue Devil'	Rangers and Scotland
35.	C. E. Napier	'Happy Feet'	Celtic and Scotland
36.	Maurice Norman	'Big Mo'	Tottenham and England
37.	Alan O'Neil	'The Cod Liver Oil Kid'	Sunderland
38.	Jimmy Quinn	'Sunny Jim'	Celtic and Scotland

39.	Johnny Quinn	'The Mighty Quinn'†	Sheffield Wednesday
40.	Alf Ramsey	'The General'	Tottenham and England
41.	Paul Reaney	'Mr. Reliable'	Leeds and England
42.	Bryan Robson	'Pop'	Sunderland
43.	Ian St. John	'The Saint'	Liverpool and Scotland
44.	Len Shackleton	'The Clown Prince of Soccer'	Sunderland and England
45.	Jimmy Smith	'Jinky'	Newcastle and Scotland
46.	Peter Storey	'Snouty'	Arsenal and England
47.	Frederick Walden	'Fanny'	Tottenham and England
48.	Thomas Waring	'Pongo'	Aston Villa and England
49.	Billy Wedlock	'Smiler'	Bristol City and England
50.	John White	'The Ghost'	Tottenham and Scotland
51.	George Woodhall	'Spry'	West Bromwich and England
52.	George Young	'Corky'	Rangers and Scotland

† His nickname came about through the Manfred Mann hit record.

26 FOREIGN PLAYERS' NICKNAMES

1.	Jose Altafini	'Mazzola'	Palmeiras and Brazil
2.	Franz Beckenbauer	'Kaiser Franz'	Bayern München and West Germany
3.	Leonardo Cuellar	'The Caveman'	U.N.A.M. and Mexico
4.	Johannes Edvaldsson	'Shuggie'	Celtic and Iceland
5.	Francisco Gento	'Paco'	Real Madrid and Spain
6.	Gunnar Gren	'The Professor'	Milan and Sweden
7.	Gerhard Hanappi	'Engineer Hanappi'	Rapid Vienna and Austria

8. *Rudi Hiden*	'The Flying Baker' (1958 World Cup)	Wiener AC and Austria (Racing Club de Paris and France)
9. *Horst Hrubesch*	'Der Ungeheuer' (The Monster)	Hamburger S.V. and West Germany
10. *Alexi Khomich*	'Tiger'	Moscow Dynamo and Russia
11. *Sandor Kocsis*	'Golden Head'	Barcelona and Hungary
12. *Angel Labruna*	'El Viejo' – 'The Old One' or 'El Eterno'	River Plate and Argentina
13. *Leonidas da Silva*	'The Black Diamond'	Vasco da Gama and Brazil
14. *Benito Lorenzi Veleno*	'Poison'	Inter-Milan and Italy
15. *Marola*	'Frankenstein'	Santos and Brazil
16. *Luis Monti*	'The Man Who Strolls'	Boca Juniors and Argentina Juventus and Italy
17. *Carlos Morete*	'El Puma'	River Plate and Argentina
18. *Raimondo Orsi*	'Nummo'	Argentina Turin and Italy
19. *Ferenc Puskas*	'The Galloping Major'	Holland and Spain Real Madrid and Hungary
20. *Ramon Quiroga*	'El Loco'	Sporting Cristal and Peru
21. *José Martinez Sanchez*	'Pirri'	Real Madrid and Spain
22. *Manoel Francisco dos Santos*	'Garrincha' – A Species of Bird	Botafogo and Brazil
23. *Matthias Sindelar*	'The Man of Paper'	FK Austria and Austria
24. *Lennart Skoglund*	'Nacka'	Inter-Milan and Swede
25. *Socrates*	'Doctor'	Corinthians and Br?
26. *Lev Yashin*	'The Panther'	Moscow Dynamo ? Russia

6 OF THE BEST

The following players share the same surname. While one was among the World's biggest super-stars and another couple experienced some moments of adulation, the rest faded into relative obscurity, as ill befits their 'monicker'.

1. *Billy Best* – Northampton Town (twice) and Southend United, 469 appearances from 1962–77 as a more than useful utility player.

2. *Clyde Best* – Bermudan born Centre Foward with West Ham 1969–76. After 200+ First Team appearances he continued to play out his career in the North American Soccer League.

3. *Dave Best* – Goalkeeper who moved up the League from Bournemouth to First Division, Ipswich, via Oldham. He turned out on almost 200 occasions for the Suffolk Club before playing out the autumn of his career with Portsmouth and his original club, Bournemouth, in 1975.

4. *George Best* – Possibly the most naturally gifted British footballer of all time, whose reputation as a goalscoring Winger was only surpassed by his off the field notoriety. Both for Manchester United and Northern Ireland he was renowned for his jinking runs, great pace, swashbuckling play and meticulous passing. His Irish charm, good looks and naively generous personality have kept him in the headlines in the years since leaving Old Trafford, the scene of so many of his greatest feats. In 1973 he announced a premature retirement from the game but since then he has played pro football in the USA, with L A Aztecs, Fort Lauderdale Strikers, San José Earthquakes and Golden Bay, Hongkong, Scotland, with Hibernian, and England, with Stockport, Dunstable, Fulham and Bournemouth, without ever reaching his previous heights. However, such is the enduring magic of his name that he has frequently doubled the gate receipts at these less illustrious venues.

5. *John Best* – Wing Half on whom fortune failed to smile. Before his 21st birthday he had left the ranks of professionalism with just 7 League appearances for Tranmere and 3 years as a Liverpool reserve behind him.

6. *Tom Best* – Three clubs in as many years immediately after the second war gave this Inside Forward a chance to prove his latent talent, (he was 26 when he made his League debut with Chester) but unfortunately, while netting consistently for his

first club and subsequently for Cardiff and Queens Park
Rangers, his career came to a close after only 80 appearances.

THE FAMOUS 5

This forward line went down in Scottish footballing history for
their swashbuckling exploits with Hibernian from 1949–52.

1. *Gordon Smith* – Outside Right whose dribbling prowess
resulted in being labelled the Scottish Stanley Matthews.

2. *Bobby Johnstone* – Inside Right who was to win acclaim
with Manchester City.

3. *Lawrie Riley* – Centre Forward who was to become 'Hi-
Bees' most capped player.

4. *Eddie Turnbull* – Inside Left whose talent as a creative
footballer was so important and recognizable in management
with Aberdeen and Hibernian.

5. *Willie Ormond* – Left Winger who was rewarded least in
terms of national honours. But was more than adequately
compensated by leading Scotland to the 1974 World Cup Finals.

The Name's the Same

100 FOOTBALLERS WHO SHARE
THEIR NAMES WITH THE FAMOUS

Footballer's Name	Celebrity	Position and Player's Clubs
1. *Ian Bannon*	Stage, film and T.V. actor – *The Hard Word*	Centre Back – Rochdale 1976–80
2. *Chris Barnard*	South African Heart Transplant pioneer	Inside Forward – Ipswich, Southend, Torquay and Charlton 1965–71
3. *Robert Beattie*	Canadian stage, film and T.V. actor	Inside Forward – Preston 1946–53 and Scotland.
4. *Alex Bell*	Scientist and inventor (telephone)	Goalkeeper – Exeter City and Grimsby 1954–58
5. *Allan Bennett*	Playwright and satirist	Outside Left – Port Vale and Crewe 1948–57
6. *Dave Berry*	Hit singer of the 60's – 'The Crying Game'	Half Back – Blackpool and Chester 1966.
7. *Mike Berry*	Pop Singer of the 60's and 70's – 'The Sunshine of Your Smile'; T.V. actor *Worzel Gummidge* and *Are You Being Served*	Full Back – Southampton 1970's.

Footballer's Name	Celebrity	Position and Player's Clubs
8. *Anthony Booth*	Film and T.V. actor *Till Death Us Do Part*; boyfriend of Pat Phoenix	Midfielder – Charlton 1978–79
9. *Ken Booth*	Jamaican Reggae Singer 'Everything I Own'	Forward – Blackpool, Bradford P.A., Workington and Southport 1954–60
10. *Jim Bowie*	Noted for the famous Bowie knife. Died at 'The Alamo'	Inside Forward – Chelsea, Fulham, Brentford and Watford 1947–55
11. *Dougie Brown*	Comedian and T.V. actor, *The Enigma File* and *The Hard Word*	Forward – Sheffield United 1978–79
12. *Rod Cameron*	American film and T.V. actor	Full Back – Bradford City 1958
13. *Don Campbell*	Speed King of the 1950's and 1960's on land and sea in 'Blue-Bird'	Full Back – Liverpool, Crewe and Gillingham 1953–63
14. *Billy Carter*	Brother of former U.S.A. President, Jimmy Carter	Wing Half – Orient 1965–66
15. *Neville Chamberlain*	British Prime Minister 1937–40	Forward – Port Vale 1977–82 and Stoke 1982–
16. *Jeff Chandler*	Film actor, remembered best for *Cochise*	Midfielder – Blackpool, Leeds, Bolton 1977 and Eire
17. *Ray Chandler*	American novelist – his character Philip Marlowe was brought to life by Humphrey Bogart	Goalkeeper – Bristol Rovers and Swindon 1953–58

Footballer's Name	Celebrity	Position and Player's Clubs
18. *Tom Conway*	Film actor and brother of George Sanders	Forward – Port Vale 1955
19. *Peter Cook*	Comedian, T.V. and film actor and currently star of *The Three of Us*	Centre Half – Hull, Bradford P.A. and Crewe 1946–52
20. *John Craven*	T.V. personality – *News Round* and *Swapshop*	Centre Back – Blackpool, Crystal Palace, Coventry and Plymouth 1965–78
21. *Peter Davidson*	T.V. actor Davison is the current 'Dr Who'	Winger – Queens Park Rangers 1979–
22. *Cyril Davies*	Trombonist and leader of Cyril Davies 'All Stars' in the 1960's	Inside Forward – Swansea, Carlisle and Charlton 1966–78.
23. *Lyn Davies*	Welsh Olympic long jumper	Goalkeeper – Cardiff and Swansea 1965–72
24. *Fred Davis*	The Champion Snooker player and brother of Joe	Wing Half – Reading and Wrexham 1953–60
25. *Joe Davis*	World Snooker Champion from 1927 to his retirement in 1946	Full Back – Carlisle 1969–71
26. *Peter Dawson*	Great operatic singer of the 1930's–50's	Half Back – Crewe 1955–56
27. *Richard Dix*	Film actor – *Cimarron*	Forward – Bradford P.A. and Bradford City 1946–52
28. *Anthony Eden*	Conservative Prime Minister 1955–56; Foreign Minister during World War II	Half Back – Aston Villa and Walsall 1962

Footballer's Name	Celebrity	Position and Player's Clubs
29. *Barry Foster*	Film and T.V. actor – *Van der Valk, The Family Way* and *Twisted Nerve*	Full Back – Mansfield Town 1971–82
30. *William Franklin*	Film and T.V. actor – *Sch. . . You Know Who*	Goalkeeper – Charlton 1972–74
31. *Barry Gibb*	One of the Bee Gees – 'Night Fever' 'Massachusetts' etc	Wing Half – Workington 1959–60
32. *Billy Gilbert*	Film actor – *Blockheads, Destry Rides Again*	Goalkeeper – Coventry and Stockport 1951–54
33. *Billy Graham*	American evangelist	Full Back – Doncaster and Torquay 1950–58
34. *Robert Graves*	Poet and author, best known for *I, Claudius*	Goalkeeper – Lincoln City 1959–64
35. *John Gregson*	Film actor, *Whisky Galore, Genevieve* and on T.V., *Gideon's Way*	Inside Forward – Blackpool, Chester, Shrewsbury, Mansfield, Lincoln City and Cambridge 1957–70
36. *Peter Hall*	Former director of R.S.C. and now Head of the National Theatre	Forward – Port Vale, Bournemouth and Gillingham 1958–67
37. *William Hamilton*	Obsessive Royalty hater, Scottish Labour M.P.	Inside Forward – Sheffield United, Middlesbrough and Aston Villa 1956–66
38. *Albert Hammond*	Pop singer – Free Electric Band	Brentford and Exeter 1946

225

Footballer's Name	Celebrity	Position and Player's Clubs
39. *Alex Harvey*	Late singer and guitarist with his Sensational Alex Harvey Band – 'Delilah'	Centre Forward – Carlisle 1946
40. *Arthur Haynes*	T.V. actor / comedian of the 1950's and early 1960's	Aston Villa and Walsall 1946–48
41. *Jack Hedley*	Film and T.V. actor – *Colditz*	Full Back – Everton, Sunderland, Gateshead 1947–59
42. *Joe Henderson*	Pianist on radio and T.V. for more than two decades	Goalkeeper – Northampton and Accrington 1953
43. *Ian Hendry*	Film, stage and T.V. actor – *The Beauty Jungle*	Midfielder – Aston Villa, Hereford and Cambridge, late 1970's
44. *George Hepplewhite*	18th century furniture manufacturer	Centre Half – Huddersfield, Preston and Bradford City 1946–54
45. *James Herriot*	Vet and writer of many humorous semi-autobiographical books, turned into T.V. and film successes	Goalkeeper – Birmingham City and Mansfield 1965–70
46. *Charles Hill*	'Radio Doctor' and Conservative M.P. of the 1950's	Inside Forward – Cardiff, Torquay, Q.P.R. and Swindon 1946–50

Footballer's Name	Celebrity	Position and Player's Clubs
47. *William Holden*	Film actor – *The Wild Bunch, Sunset Boulevard, Bridge Over the River Kwai*	Centre Forward – Burnley, Sunderland, Stockport, Bury and Halifax 1950–62
48. *Ken Horne*	Comedian, radio, T.V. and stage actor – *The Navy Lark, Round the Horn*	Full Back – Blackpool and Brentford 1950–59
49. *Trevor Howard*	Film actor – *Brief Encounter, Ryan's Daughter, Von Ryan's Express*	Midfielder – Norwich, Bournemouth and Cambridge 1967–78
50. *Jack Howarth*	T.V. actor renowned as *Coronation Street*'s Albert Tatlock	Centre Forward – Chelsea, Swindon, Aldershot, Rochdale, Bournemouth and Southport 1964–77
51. *David Hughes*	Popular and operatic singer of the 1950's and 1960's – 'By the Fountains of Rome'	Midfielder – Aston Villa and Lincoln 1976–80
52. *David Jenkins*	Britain's best 400 and 800 metre runner of the 1970's until the emergence of Coe and Ovett	Forward – Arsenal, Tottenham, Brentford, Hereford, Newport, Shrewsbury and Workington 1967–75
53. *Brian Johnson*	British singer with 1960 Eurovision Song Contest hit 'Looking High, High, High'	Wing Forward – Plymouth 1973–82
54. *Paul Johnson*	Former editor of *The New Statesman*, political commentator	Midfielder – Stoke and Chester 1973–

Footballer's Name	Celebrity	Position and Player's Clubs
55. *Freddie Jones*	Stage, film and T.V. actor – *Otley*	Outside Left – Arsenal, Brighton, Swindon, Grimsby and Reading 1958–64
56. *Paul Jones*	Lead singer of Manfred Mann group and The Blues Band; also solo singer and actor – *Guys and Dolls*	Centre Back – Bolton Wanderers 1970–
57. *Tom Jones*	Idolized Welsh popular singer – 'It's Not Unusual', 'Green, Green Grass of Home', 'Help Yourself'	Midfielder – Chelsea (Apprentice) 1982–
58. *Chris Kelly*	T.V. Interviewer, Tyne Tees T.V.'s *Friday Live* and *Wish You Were Here*	Winger – Millwall 1974–75
59. *Bobby Kennedy*	American politician and brother of President John F. Kennedy, assassinated in 1968	Full Back – Manchester City and Grimsby and Scotland U.23 1961–70
60. *Dave King*	Comedian and actor in T.V. and films	Inside Forward – Hull 1959–62
61. *Harold Lloyd*	Silent film comedy actor who specialized in exciting and dangerous stunts	Goalkeeper – Tranmere 1946–56
62. *Brian Marshall*	Film and T.V. actor, recently emigrated to Australia	Half Back – Huddersfield and Scunthorpe 1972–74

Footballer's Name	Celebrity	Position and Player's Clubs
63. *James Mason*	Stage and film actor – *A Star is Born, Rommel, Desert Fox, Lolita*	Half Back – Accrington, Chester and Crystal Palace 1955–
64. *Peter May*	Test cricketer for England	Midfielder – Ipswich schoolboy 1980–82
65. *Roger Miller*	American pop singer – 'King of the Road' and 'England Swings'	Forward – Northampton 1956–58
66. *John Mills*	Knighted film, stage and latterly T.V. actor. Films include *In Which We Serve, Scott of the Antarctic, King Rat*	Right Half – Chester 1946–47
67. *Dave Moorcroft*	Britain's 5000 metre World Record holder	Wing Half – Tranmere 1968–71
68. *Brian Moore*	I.T.V.'s football anchorman	Outside Right – Mansfield, Notts County and Doncaster 1960–63
69. *Mike Moran*	Pop song writer and performer – 'Rock Bottom'	Winger – Port Vale and Crewe 1957–58
70. *Alf Morris*	Labour Shadow minister for the disabled	Utility Player – Accrington 1946–47
71. *Colin Morris*	T.V. interviewer	Winger – Burnley, Southend, Blackpool and Sheffield United 1974–
72. *Johnny Morris*	Radio and T.V. personality – *Animal Magic*	Inside Forward Manchester United, Derby County, Leicester 1946–57 and England

Footballer's Name	Celebrity	Position and Player's Clubs
73. *John Mortimer*	A leading Q.C. and brilliant playwright – *A Voyage Round My Father*	Defender Wrexham and New Brighton 1946–50
74. *George Murphy*	Film actor and dancer – American *Broadway Melody of 1938*	Forward – Bradford City and Hull 1946–47
75. *John Osborne*	Among the 1950's new school of playwrights – *Look Back in Anger, The Entertainer*	Goalkeeper – Chesterfield and West Bromwich Albion 1960–77
76. *Geoffrey Palmer*	Stage and television actor, *Butterflies*	Full Back – Wolves 1972 and England U.23
77. *Graham Parker*	New wave singer backed by The Rumour	Full Back – Aston Villa, Rotherham, Lincoln, Exeter and Torquay 1963–75
78. *Fred Perry*	Tennis champion of the 1940's and 1950's	Liverpool 1955–56
79. *Baden Powell*	Founder of the Boy Scout Movement	Outside Right – Darlington 1950–53
80. *Johnnie Ray*	'The Prince of Wails', American pop singer of the 1950's – 'Just Walkin in the Rain', 'Cry'	Forward – Shrewsbury 1964–66
81. *Gordon Richards*	Famous jockey – knighted	Outside Left – Wrexham and Chester 1952–60
82. *Robert Robinson*	T.V. and radio quizmaster and personality	Goalkeeper – Sunderland and Newcastle 1947–52

Footballer's Name	Celebrity	Position and Player's Clubs
83. *William Russell*	T.V. and stage actor	Inside Forward – Sheffield United, Bolton, Rochdale 1957–67
84. *Peter Scott*	Knighted painter, Director General of the World Wildlife Fund and conservationist	Defender – Everton, Southport, York and Aldershot 1971– and Northern Ireland
85. *Walter Scott*	Knighted Scottish novelist and poet – *Ivanhoe, Waverley, Rob Roy* among many others	Halifax 1954
86. *Bernard Shaw*	Irish dramatist, critic and early socialist – *Major Barbara, St. Joan, Pygmalion* and countless others	Full Back – Sheffield United, Wolves, Sheffield Wednesday 1962–75 and England U.23
87. *John Slater*	Late T.V., stage and film actor *Love on the Dole, Passport to Pimlico*	Right Half – Rochdale and Crewe 1946
88. *George Stephenson*	Inventor of the steam engine 'The Rocket'	Forward – Derby County, Shrewsbury and Rochdale 1961–66
89. *James Stewart*	American film actor – *It's a Wonderful Life, Bell, Book and Candle*	Goalkeeper – Middlesbrough 1978–81 and Scotland
90. *James Taylor*	American singer ('You've Got a Friend') married to Carly Simon	Forward – Charlton, Gillingham, Watford 1956–57
91. *Robert Taylor*	Film actor *Quo Vadis, Ivanhoe*	Forward – Millwall 1954–59

231

Footballer's Name	Celebrity	Position and Player's Clubs
92. *Danny Thomas*	American comedian and actor	Full Back – Coventry City 1978–
93. *Fred Titmuss*	England cricketer of the 1950's–60's	Left Full Back – Southampton, Plymouth and England 1919–32
94. *Ian Wallace*	Musical entertainer, T.V. and radio personality	Striker – Coventry City and Nottingham Forest 1976–
95. *George Wallace*	U.S. politician now confined to a wheelchair after an assassination attempt	Forward – Scunthorpe 1951–52
96. *Barry White*	Heavy, black soul singer	Goalkeeper – Hull and Halifax 1971–74
97. *Danny Williams*	Black singer – had massive hit with Bacharach's 'Moon River' in 1961	Wing Half – Rotherham 1946–59
98. *Carl Wilson*	Founder member of the Beach Boys – 'Good Vibrations', 'God Only Knows', etc	Forward – Newcastle, Gateshead, Doncaster and Millwall 1958–62
99. *Harold Wilson*	Labour Prime Minister on two occasions – 1964–70, 1974–76 – knighted	Full Back – Burnley, Brighton, Preston and Darlington, 1971–
100. *Henry Wood*	Knighted conductor and initiator of 'The Promenade' concerts at the Albert Hall	Half Back – Chesterfield 1953–54

In a few cases – Bannen, Boothe, Davison, Titmus – the celebrity's name is spelt slightly differently from his footballing counterpart.

. . .Z

5 MAJOR 'Z' CLUBS

1. *Dynamo Zagreb* – Yugoslavia
2. *Zeljeznicar Sarajevo* – Yugoslavia
3. *Zenit Leningrad* – Soviet Union
4. *Zurich F.C.* – Switzerland
5. *Sachsenring Zwickau* – East Germany

5 CURRENT 'Z' INTERNATIONALS

1. *Jesus Maria Zamora* – Real Sociedad and Spain
2. *Werner Zanon* – Wacker Innsbruck and Austria
3. *'Zico'* – Flamengo and Brazil
4. *Wlodzimierz Zmuda* – Verona and Poland
5. *Dino Zoff* – Juventus and Italy

10 FORMER 'Z' INTERNATIONALS

1. *Renato Zaccarelli** – Italy. Midfielder with Torino in the 1970's and early 1980's.
2. *Klaus Zaczyk* – West Germany. Midfielder, who won 1 Cap while with Karlsruher SC in 1967.
3. *Mario Zagalo* – Brazil. Left Winger whose role in the 1958 and 1962 World Cups was of major importance to Brazil.
4. *Ricardo Zamora* – Spain. Goalkeeper with Espanol and Barcelona in the 1920's and 30's.
5. *Branco Zebec* – Yugoslavia. Outside Left and later Centre Half throughout the 1950's with Partizan and then Red Star Belgrade.
6. *José Maria Ze Maria* – Brazil. Right Full Back in the 1974 World Cup.
7. *Herbert Zimmermann** – West Germany. 1. F.C. Köln Full Back since the mid 70's.
8. *Jose Elim iranda 'Zito'* – Brazil. Right Half in the 1958 and 1962 World Cup team.

9. *Tomaz Soares da Silva 'Zizinho'* – Brazil. Striker outstanding in the 1950's with Flamengo and later Bangu.
10. *'Zoco'* – Spain. Centre Back long server with Real Madrid.

* Still playing at League level.